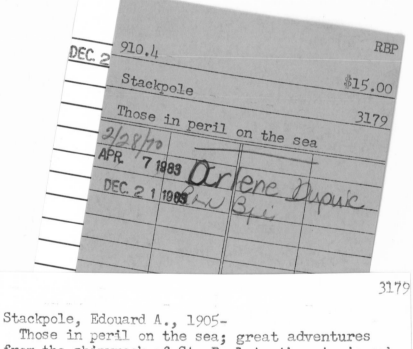

THOSE IN PERIL ON THE SEA

THOSE IN PERIL
ON THE SEA

Great Adventures: from the Shipwreck
of St. Paul to the Atomic Submarine
with a Profusion of Illustrations

EDITED BY
EDOUARD A. STACKPOLE

New York: THE DIAL PRESS *Publishers*

Typography & Arrangement by Richard Ellis

MANUFACTURED IN THE UNITED STATES OF AMERICA

DEDICATED TO

H. H. KYNETT & STARR KYNETT

FRIENDS THROUGHOUT

THE VOYAGE

Author's Foreword

THE MARINERS who write of their adventures do so for the most part without flourish. As seafarers they have ranged across the seas and oceans very much as a matter of course, and, reaching land, often view the shore as an even greater danger than the sea, at least until discovering a safe harbor. But there are those among them who have been conscious of taking part in a great adventure in a larger sense: the eternal struggle of man against the elemental forces of nature. To these chroniclers we owe much of the great literature of the sea.

Some of these narratives appear in the following pages. Here are stories the more gripping because they are true, the more inspiring because they are told by the men who lived the adventures they recount. And in the writing of these seafarers are reflected the personalities of the great seas that they have traversed. From the ancient Mediterranean to the frozen Arctic we range with them in their quests; we walk the decks with them, discover new lands, fight wars, sail among tropical islands and into ice-locked oceans. All these events are dominated by the great seas themselves, which carry in them an unalterable and inscrutable mystery—the mystery of elemental power, never to be completely conquered, never to be fully understood.

To the true mariner, the sea must be met on its own terms, and this meeting has given differing values to these mariner authors. Some show confidence in successfully facing the sea's challenge; others betray an inherent fear. But through all these accounts runs a central theme: the contest between man and nature, which may bring victory or defeat, but at least results in better understanding, of nature by man, and of man by himself.

List of Adventures

THOSE IN PERIL ON THE SEA

Eternal Father, strong to save,
Whose arm hath bound the restless wave,
Who bidd'st the mighty ocean deep
Its own appointed limits keep:
    O hear us when we cry to thee
    For those in peril on the sea.

WILLIAM WHITING, 1860

Adventure 1

The Shipwreck of St. Paul

from The Acts of the Apostles

A Greek Jew called Paul was embarked as one of a group of prisoners being sent from Palestine to Rome in the late autumn of A.D. 61, well beyond the season of safe navigation. Probably the most influential and certainly the most widely active of the early converts to Christianity, he developed a missionary fervor that frightened and angered the Jewish religious authorities and eventually led to his imprisonment at their insistence. Having been born at Tarsus in the Roman province of Cilicia gave him automatic Roman citizenship and the right to demand trial "before Caesar"—to plead his case in a court in the city of Rome. One of his companions on this journey was the physician Luke, who is generally considered to have been the author of this account.

In the charge of a Roman centurion identified only as Julius, the group transferred at the Lycian port of Myra onto a grain ship bound from Alexandria to Italy. These cumbersome vessels were the freighters of the first century—round-bottomed, high-sterned craft some eighty feet long and thirty wide. They carried a large square mainsail and triangular topsail on the single mast, with another square sail on a yard attached to the bowsprit to balance the clumsy steering oars at the stern. The usual passenger-crew capacity was around seventy-five. The "two hundred threescore and sixteen souls" of the text are more likely only threescore and sixteen, or seventy-six.

The unpredictable Mediterranean was considered with good reason a dangerous place; insofar as they could, navigators sailed only in fair winds and within sight of land. Long-distance craft were sometimes undergirded with ropes to keep the planks from springing; sometimes a heavy line was run taut from bow to stern in an attempt to keep waves from springing the hog (sag) in the keel and thus breaking the vessel's back. A ship unlucky enough to be caught in a storm nevertheless could do little more than jettison cargo and run before the wind, the crew more likely than not invoking the sea deities to keep them from swamping or being wrecked on a lee shore.

Such perils Paul faced on his journey to Rome when a northeast gale struck his ship off the coast of Crete. For his time, he was an experienced sailor. He had traveled much of the Mediterranean—he had already been shipwrecked three times. He was, too, a man of unflagging courage and enormous force of character. It is therefore not too surprising that in this time of crisis, as Luke's vivid narrative makes clear, Paul took virtual command of the ship on which he was officially a prisoner.

A seventeenth-century map of Paul's voyage.

2

"They cast four anchors out of the stern, and wished for the day"

AND when it was determined that we should sail into Italy, they delivered Paul and certain other prisoners unto one named Julius, a centurion of Augustus' band. And entering unto a ship of Adramyttium, we launched, meaning to sail by the coasts of Asia; one Aristarchus, a Macedonian of Thessalonica, being with us. And the next day we touched at Sidon. And Julius courteously entreated Paul, and gave him liberty to go unto his friends to refresh himself. And when we had launched from thence, we sailed under Cyprus, because the winds were contrary. And when we had sailed over the sea of Cilicia and Pamphylia, we came to Myra, a city of Lycia. And there the centurion found a ship of Alexandria sailing into Italy; and he put us

therein. And when we had sailed slowly many days, and scarce were come over against Cnidus, the wind not suffering us, we sailed under Crete, over against Salmone; and, hardly passing it, came unto a place which is called The fair havens; nigh whereunto was the city of Lasea. Now when much time was spent, and when sailing was now dangerous, because the fast was now already past, Paul admonished them, and said unto them, Sirs, I perceive that this voyage will be with hurt and much damage, not only of the lading and ship, but also of our lives. Nevertheless the centurion believed the master and the owner of the ship, more than those things which were spoken by Paul. And because the haven was not commodious to winter in, the more part advised to depart thence also, if

A relief on a Roman sarcophagus showing three merchant ships at the mouth of a harbor.

3

by any means they might attain to Phenice, and there to winter; which is an haven of Crete, and lieth toward the south west and north west. And when the south wind blew softly, supposing that they had obtained their purpose, loosing thence, they sailed close by Crete.

But not long after there arose against it a tempestuous wind, called Euroclydon. And when the ship was caught, and could not bear up into the wind, we let her drive. And running under a certain island which is called Clauda, we had much work to come by the boat: which when they had taken up, they used helps, undergirding the ship; and, fearing lest they should fall into the quicksands, strake sail, and so were driven. And we being exceedingly tossed with a tempest, the next day they lightened the ship; and the third day we cast out with our own hands the tackling of the ship. And when neither sun nor stars in many days appeared, and no small tempest lay on us, all hope that we should be saved was then taken away. But after long abstinence Paul stood forth in the midst of them, and said, Sirs, ye should have hearkened unto me, and not have loosed from Crete, and to have gained this harm and loss. And now I exhort you to be of good cheer: for there shall be no loss of any man's life among you, but of the ship. For there stood by me this night the angel of God, whose I am, and whom I serve, saying, Fear not, Paul; thou must be brought before Caesar: and, lo, God hath given thee all them that sail with thee. Wherefore, sirs, be of good cheer: for I believe God, that it shall be even as it was told me. Howbeit we must be cast upon a certain island.

Loading a small Roman merchant ship with grain. A fresco found at Ostia.

The Acts *of the* Apostles

But when the fourteenth night was come, as we were driven up and down in Adria, about midnight the shipmen deemed that they drew near to some country; and sounded, and found it twenty fathoms: and when they had gone a little further, they sounded again, and found it fifteen fathoms. Then fearing lest we should have fallen upon rocks, they cast four anchors out of the stern, and wished for the day. And as the shipmen were about to flee out of the ship, when they had let down the boat into the sea, under colour as though they would have cast anchors out of the foreship, Paul said to the centurion and to the soldiers, except these abide in the ship, ye cannot be saved. Then the soldiers cut off the ropes of the boat, and let her fall off.

And while the day was coming on, Paul besought them all to take meat, saying, This day is the fourteenth day that ye have tarried and continued fasting, having taken nothing. Wherefore I pray you to take some meat: for this is for your health: for there shall not an hair fall from the head of any of you.

And when he had thus spoken, he took bread, and gave thanks to God in presence of them all: and when he had broken it, he began to eat. Then were they all of good cheer, and they also took some meat. And we were in all in the ship two hundred threescore and sixteen souls. And when they had eaten enough, they lightened the ship, and cast out the wheat into the sea.

A merchant ship coming into harbor. The crew make the ship fast and prepare to take in the sails, while the master and his family offer sacrifices in thanks for a safe voyage. Engraved after a relief from Portus.

1

4

3

2

THESE *charming and ingenuous illuminations from a thirteenth-century manuscript, dramatizing several episodes from Paul's shipwreck, capture the spirit of the adventure despite anachronisms of detail.*

1. *The ship is strengthened at Clauda.*
2. *Paul tells of the angel's prophecy.*
3. *The sailors anchor the ship to wait for daylight.*
4. *Paul prevents the sailors from fleeing.*
5. *Those aboard, at Paul's urging, break their fast.*
6. *The cargo is jettisoned.*
7. *The anchor is weighed, and the sail set.*
8. *The ship runs aground.*
9. *The soldiers advise killing the prisoners.*
10. *The ship is abandoned.*

5

8

6

9

7

10

And when it was day, they knew not the land: but they discovered a certain creek with a shore, into the which they were minded, if it were possible, to thrust in the ship. And when they had taken up the anchors, they committed themselves unto the sea, and loosed the rudder bands, and hoisted up the mainsail to the wind, and made toward shore. And falling into a place where two seas met, they ran the ship aground; and the forepart stuck fast, and remained unmoveable, but the hinder part was broken with the violence of the waves. And the soldiers' counsel was to kill the prisoners, lest any of them should swim out, and escape. But the centurion, willing to save Paul, kept them from their purpose; and commanded that they which could swim should cast themselves first into the sea, and get to land: and the rest, some on boards, and some on broken pieces of the ship. And so it came to pass, that they escaped all safe to land.

St. Paul's Bay, Malta, where the wreck is believed to have occurred.

Adventure 2

The Capture of the Crusaders on the Nile

from Histoire de St. Louis, by Jean de Joinville

In the eleventh and twelfth centuries, and at intervals thereafter, Western Europe was diverted from local wars and rivalries by a rare spirit of unity, a collective impulse at once generous and intolerant, gallant and ignoble. The emotional fervor—part religious piety, part urge for adventure, part hope for spoil—that led to the Crusades is hard for the modern mind to fathom. These intermittent invasions of the Arab-ruled Levant produced some of the most heroic achievements and darkest deeds recorded in medieval history.

The Crusades were essentially a maritime and amphibious operation. The resistance of that reluctant ally, the Byzantine Empire, added to the difficulty of fighting through Turkey and Syria, made it necessary to convey the Crusaders to Egypt and Palestine by ship. Primitive ships they were, too, clumsy round craft with high wooden towers or "castles" fore and aft for men to fight from. The use of foresails and topsails had apparently been neglected after Roman times, and these craft were usually driven by a single square sail on a single mast. In some cases two masts were used, each carrying a triangular lateen sail; sometimes hatches were built into the hull below the water line, to furnish a passage for horses when the ship was pulled up on the beach. These ships were commonly hired from the Genoese or Venetians, then the best seamen of the Mediterranean; in these

campaigns they frequently behaved with all the enthusiasm customary among mercenaries.

These ships were a poor match for the faster, well-drilled Saracen galleys, heavily manned with archers whose arrows were often tipped with the dreaded incendiary material known as Greek fire. In the calm waters along the coasts and estuaries they could fairly easily outmaneuver sailing ships, ram them with sharp metal beaks, and sink them or overpower them with superior numbers.

The Seventh Crusade, led in 1248 by Louis IX of France against the Saracens in Egypt, typified the unhappy results of all. Louis, who was later sainted, was beloved by his followers, and from all accounts he emerges a truly selfless, brave, kind, idealistic man. He led his men not wisely but too well. Success crowned every venture when he first came to the Nile delta; he landed without serious resistance and threw the Saracens into near-panic by seizing their principal fortress, the town of Damietta. But before he could move much farther into Egypt, his ill-planned campaign bogged down; dysentery and "the sickness of the host" (probably the deficiency disease scurvy) decimated his forces. The Saracens counterattacked with their powerful galleys, superb cavalry, and Greek fire, and eventually defeated the Crusaders up the river at Mansourah. Louis then tried to make peace, offering the return of Damietta in exchange for control of

9

Jerusalem. During the negotiations a traitor in the Crusaders' camp spread a rumor that Louis had surrendered, causing many of his men to throw down their arms. Louis' attempt to retreat with the rest of his force turned into a rout, and he and most of his men were captured. Many of them were slaughtered as they surrendered. Eventually Louis was able to ransom himself and the remains of his army, but the defeat was total.

The best source of information on this hapless expedition is a colorful and intensely personal account by one of Louis' most devoted lieutenants,

the doughty nobleman Jean de Joinville. Joinville perhaps made too perfect a hero of his beloved king, but he had the ability to see others—and himself—plain. He recalls, for instance (even though he wrote his account many years after the event) the miseries of his dysentery, and how, when one of his men wanted them to sacrifice their lives by not surrendering to the enemy, "we heeded him not." The story of his ignominious capture from his helpless ship in a muddy stream of the Nile, and of how he saved his life by pardonable guile, is a classic both of the period and of military literature.

Battle between Crusader ships and Saracen galleys, from a fifteenth-century manuscript.

"There were Saracens standing by with naked swords, who slew those that fell"

WHEN the king saw that he could only remain there to die, he and his people, he ordered and arranged that they should strike their camp, late on Tuesday (5th April 1250), at night, after the octave of Easter, to return to Damietta. He caused the mariners who had galleys to be told that they should get together the sick, and take them thither. He also commanded Josselin of Cornaut, and his brothers, and the other engineers, to cut the ropes that held the bridge between us and the Saracens; but of this they did nothing.

We embarked on the Tuesday, after dinner, in the afternoon, I and two of my knights whom I had remaining, and the rest of my followers. When the night began to fall, I told my mariners to draw up their anchor, and let us go down the stream; but they said they dared not, because the soldan's galleys, which were between us and Damietta, would surely put us to death. The mariners had made great fires to gather the sick into their galleys, and the sick had dragged themselves to the bank of the river. While I was exhorting the mariners to let us begone, the Saracens entered into the camp, and I saw, by the light of the fires, that they were slaughtering the sick on the bank.

While my mariners were raising their anchor, the mariners appointed to take away the sick cut the ropes of their anchors and of their galleys, and came alongside our little ship, and so surrounded us on one side and the other that they well-nigh ran

us down. When we had escaped from this peril, and while we were going down with the stream, the king, who had upon him the sickness of the host and a very evil dysentery, could easily have got away on the galleys, if he had been so minded; but he said that, please God, he would never abandon his people. That night he fainted several times; and because of the sore dysentery from which he suffered, it was necessary to cut away the lower part of his drawers, so frequent were his necessities.

They cried to us, who were floating on the water, that we should wait for the king; and when we would not wait, they shot at us with crossbow bolts; wherefore it behooved us to stop until such time as they gave us leave to fare forward.

Now I will leave off speaking of this matter, and tell you how the king was taken, as he himself related it to me. He told me how he had left his own division and placed himself, he and my Lord Geoffry of Sargines, in the division that was under my Lord Gaucher of Châtillon, who commanded the rear guard.

And the king related to me that he was mounted on a little courser covered with a housing of silk; and he told me that of all his knights and sergeants there only remained behind with him my Lord Geoffry of Sargines, who brought the king to a little village, there where the king was taken; and as the king related to me, my Lord Geoffry of Sargines defended him from the Saracens as a good

*St. Louis departing for the Crusades
in one of the double-masted ships used by his expedition.*

servitor defends his lord's drinking cup from flies; for every time that the Saracens approached, he took his spear, which he had placed between himself and the bow of his saddle, and put it to his shoulder, and ran upon them, and drove them away from the king.

And thus he brought the king to the little village; and they lifted him into a house, and laid him, almost as one dead, in the lap of a burgherwoman of Paris, and thought he would not last till night. Thither came my Lord Philip of Montfort, and said to the king that he saw the emir with whom he had treated of the truce, and, if the king so willed, he would go to him and renew the negotiation for a truce in the manner that the Saracens desired. The king begged him to go, and said he was right willing. So my Lord Philip went to the Saracen; and the Saracen had taken off his turban from his head, and took off the ring from his finger in token that he would faithfully observe the truce.

Meanwhile, a very great mischance happened to our people; for a traitor sergeant, whose name was Marcel, began to cry to our people: "Yield, lord knights, for the king commands you, and do not cause the king to be slain!" All thought that the king had so commanded, and gave up their swords to the Saracens. The emir saw that the Saracens were bringing in our people prisoners, so he said to my Lord Philip that it was not fitting that he should grant a truce to our people, for he saw very well that they were already prisoners.

So it happened to my Lord Philip that whereas all our people were taken captive, yet was not he so taken, because he was an envoy. But there is an evil custom in the land of paynimry that when the king sends envoys to the soldan, or the soldan to the king, and the king dies, or the soldan, before the envoys' return, then the envoys, from whithersoever they may come, and whether Christians or Saracens, are made prisoners and slaves.

12

Jean de Joinville

WHEN this mischance befell our people, that they should be taken captive on land, so did it happen to us, to be taken captive on the water, as you shall shortly hear; for the wind blew from Damietta, and so counteracted the current of the river; and the knights, whom the king had placed in the lighter vessels to defend the sick, fled. Thus our mariners lost the current and got into a creek, and we had to turn back towards the Saracens.

We, who were going by water, came, a little before the break of dawn, to the passage where were the soldan's galleys that had prevented the coming of provisions from Damietta. Here there was great confusion and tumult; for they shot at us and at our mounted folk who were on the bank so great a quantity of darts with Greek fire, that it seemed as if the stars of heaven were falling.

When our mariners had brought us out of the creek into which they had taken us, we found the king's light boats, that the king had appointed to defend our sick, and they went flying towards Damietta. Then arose a wind, coming from Damietta, so strong that it counteracted the current of the river.

St. Louis, on his way to the Holy Land, sails between Scylla and Charybdis.

Embarking for the Crusades, from a fourteenth-century manuscript.

13

St. Louis landing before Damietta, from a fifteenth-century manuscript.

By the one bank of the stream, and by the other, were a great quantity of boats belonging to our people who could not get down the stream, and whom the Saracens had taken and stayed; and the Saracens slew our people, and cast them into the water, and were dragging the coffers and baggage out of the boats that they had taken. The mounted Saracens on the bank shot at us with darts because we would not go to them. My people had put on me a jousting hauberk, so that I might not be wounded by the darts that fell into our boat.

At this moment my people, who were at the hinder point of the boat, cried out to me: "Lord, Lord, your mariners, because the Saracens are threatening them, mean to take you to the bank!" I had myself raised by the arms, all weak as I was, and drew my sword upon them, and told them I should kill them if they took me to the bank. They

14

Jean de Joinville

answered that I must choose which I would have: whether to be taken to the bank, or anchored in mid-stream till the wind fell. I told them I liked better that they should anchor in mid-stream than that they should take me to the shore where there was nothing before us save death. So they anchored.

Very shortly after we saw four of the soldan's galleys coming to us, and in them full a thousand men. Then I called together my knights and my people, and asked them which they would rather do, either yield to the soldan's galleys or yield to those on land. We all agreed that we would rather yield to the soldan's galleys, because so we should be kept together, than yield to those on land, who would separate us, and sell us to the Bedouins.

Then one of my cellarers, who was born at Doulevant, said: "Lord, I do not agree in this decision." I asked him to what he did agree; and he said to me: "I advise that we should all suffer ourselves to be slain, for thus we shall go to paradise." But we heeded him not.

When I saw that we must be taken, I took my casket and my jewels, and threw them into the river, and my relics also. Then said one of my mariners to me: "Lord, if you do not suffer me to say you are the king's cousin, they will kill you all, and us also." And I told him I was quite willing he should say what he pleased. When the people on the first galley that came towards us to strike us amidships heard this they threw down their anchors near to our boat.

The capture of Damietta, from the manuscript of Joinville's Histoire de St. Louis. Joinville is portrayed in the center of this fierce attack. Damietta was in fact taken without resistance.

15

Then did God send me a Saracen belonging to the emperor's [Frederick II of Germany] land. He had on drawers of unbleached linen, and came swimming across the stream to our vessel, and threw his arms about my waist, and said: "Lord, if you do not take good heed, you are but lost; for it behooves you to leap from your vessel on to the beak that rises from the keel of that galley; and if you leap, these people will not mind you, for they are thinking only of the booty to be found in your vessel." They threw me a rope from the galley, and I leapt on to the beak, so as God willed. And you must know that I tottered so that if the Saracen had not leapt after me, and held me up, I should have fallen into the water.

They set me in the galley, where there were full fourteen score men of their people, and he held me always in his arms. Then they threw me to the ground, and jumped upon my body to cut my throat, for any one would have thought it an honour to kill me. But the Saracen held me constantly in his arms, and cried: "Cousin to the king!" In this manner they bore me down to the ground twice, and once upon my knees, and then I felt the knife at my throat. In this extremity God saved me by the help of the Saracen, who took me to the castle of the ship, where the Saracen knights were assembled.

When I came among them, they took off my hauberk; and for the pity they had upon me, they threw over me a scarlet coverlet lined with miniver, which my lady mother had given me erewhile; and one of them brought me a white belt, and I girt myself over the coverlet; and in the coverlet I had made a hole, donning it as a garment. And another brought me a hood which I put upon my head. And then, because of the fear in which I was, I began to tremble very much, and also because of the sickness. Then I asked for drink, and they brought me some water in a jar; and as soon as I set the water to my mouth to drink it down, it spurted out through my nostrils.

When I saw this, I sent for my people, and told them I was a dead man, seeing I had the tumour in my throat; and they asked how I knew it; and I

Medieval sea battles, as these thirteenth and fourteenth-century illuminations suggest, were mainly land engagements fought on floating wooden forts.

16

showed them; and as soon as they saw the water spurting from my throat and from my nostrils, they took to weeping. When the Saracen knights who were there saw my people weeping, they asked the Saracen who had rescued us why they were weeping; and he replied that he understood I had the tumour in the throat, so that I could not recover. Then one of the Saracen knights told him to bid us be of good comfort, for he would give me somewhat to drink whereby I should be cured within two days; and this he did.

My Lord Raoul of Wanou, who was one of my following, had been hamstrung in the great battle of Shrove Tuesday, and could not stand upon his feet; and you must know that an old Saracen knight, who was in the galley, would carry him, hanging from his neck, whenever the sick man's necessities so required.

THE chief emir of the galleys sent for me and asked me if I were cousin to the king; and I said "No," and told him how and why the mariner had said I was the king's cousin. And he said I had acted wisely, for otherwise we should all have been

A knight receiving Communion, while a Saracen sneers. A relief from Reims Cathedral.

put to death. And he asked me if I was in any manner of the lineage of the Emperor Frederick of Germany, who was then living. I replied that I thought my lady mother was the emperor's cousin-german. And he said that he loved me the more for it.

While we were at meat, he caused a citizen of Paris to be brought before us. When the citizen came in, he said to me: "Lord, what are you doing?" "Why, what am I doing?" said I. "In God's name," said he, "you are eating flesh on a Friday!" When I heard that, I put my bowl behind me. And the emir asked my Saracen why I had done so, and he told him. And the emir replied that God would not take what I had done amiss, seeing I did it unwittingly. And you must know that this same reply was given to me by the Legate after we were out of prison; and yet, notwithstanding, I did not afterwards forbear to fast on bread and water, every Friday in Lent; wherefore the Legate was very wroth with me, seeing that I was the only man of substance that had remained with the king.

Jean de Joinville

Scenes from the crusades of St. Louis, painted upon a parchment map of the Mediterranean in the fifteenth century. Included are the departure from Aigues-Mortes, the landing in Egypt and capture of Damietta, the imprisonment of St. Louis by the Saracens, and his death near Tunis, during a later crusade, in 1270. Among the many other places specifically identified are Morocco, Spain, Rome, Sicily, Athens, Constantinople, Cyprus, Armenia, Syria, Jerusalem, and Cairo (then called Babylon).

On the Sunday after, the emir caused me, and all the other prisoners taken on the water, to be landed on the bank of the river. While they were taking my Lord John, my good priest, out of the hold of the galley, he fainted, and they killed him and threw him into the river. His clerk fainted also, by reason of the sickness of the host that was upon him, and they threw a mortar on his head, so that he died, and they threw him into the river.

While the other sick people were being disembarked from the galleys in which they had been kept prisoners, there were Saracens standing by, with naked swords, who killed those that fell, and cast them all into the river. I caused them to be told, through my Saracen, that it seemed to me this was not well done; for it was against the teachings of Saladin, who said you ought never to kill a man after he had partaken of your bread and of your salt. And the emir answered that the men in question were of no account, seeing they were helpless because of the sickness they had upon them.

He caused my mariners to be brought before me, and told me they had all denied their faith; and I told him never to place confidence in them, for lightly as they had left us, so lightly, if time and opportunity occurred, would they leave their new masters. And the emir made answer that he agreed with me; for that Saladin was wont to say

19

that never did one see a bad Christian become a good Saracen, or a bad Saracen become a good Christian.

After these things he caused me to be mounted on a palfrey, and to ride by his side. And we passed over a bridge of boats and went to Mansourah, where the king and his people were prisoners; and we came to the entrance of a great pavilion, where the soldan's scribes were; and there they wrote down my name. Then my Saracen said to me: "Lord, I shall not follow you further, for I cannot; but I pray you, lord, always to keep hold of the hand of the child that you have with you, lest the Saracens should take him from you." And this child was called Bartholomew, and he was the bastard son of the Lord of Montfaucon. When my name had been written down, the emir led me into the pavilion where the barons were, and more than ten thousand persons with them. When I entered, the barons made such joy that we could not hear one another speak, and they gave thanks to our Saviour, and said they thought they had lost me.

Joinville presenting his book to Louis le Hutin, later Louis X.

Adventure 3

Discovery of the Strait of Magellan

from Primo viaggio intorno al mondo, by Antonio Pigafetta

IT is difficult to conceive the world of both mystery and menace that faced the European explorers of the fifteenth and sixteenth centuries who ventured westward across the uncharted reaches of the Atlantic. It is hard to imagine a world so totally unknown to its discoverers, who could only be guided by their conviction that land *did* lie to the west and that it *could* be reached by ship. They were not afraid of sailing off the edge of the world—few ocean sailors of the period were so unsophisticated as to think the earth was flat. But they had good reason to fear foundering in ocean storms or being wrecked on unsuspected reefs, being murdered by hostile natives or falling prey to typhus or scurvy, or, worst of all, simply sailing out upon the open sea and finding no land before reaching the end of meager provisions.

It is with this perspective we must read such accounts as that of Antonio Pigafetta, an Italian nobleman who served as secretary to Magellan on the greatest sea voyage of them all, the first circumnavigation of the world. His is a curious document, crammed not only with details of the voyage but also with hundreds of miscellaneous observations of its energetic if not always discriminating author. It captures perfectly, however, the sense of excitement and wonder at the marvels of these new lands, never before seen by Europeans and strange beyond the wildest exaggeration of travelers' legends.

The commander of this expedition, Ferdinand Magellan, was a remarkable and dedicated person,

"a man of courage," according to the contemporary historian Las Casas, "and valiant in his way of undertaking great things, although not of imposing presence, being small in stature." Magellan devoted and finally sacrificed his life to his vision of a Southwest Passage to the Orient.

Portuguese by birth, he served as seaman and soldier in the wars in India and the Malacca Straits that opened the East Indies to Portuguese trade. But when King Manuel showed no interest in his dream of reaching the Indies by sailing south of the Americas, he offered his services to Portugal's great rival, Spain. The Spanish had good reason to be interested in Magellan's theories. By the treaty of Tordesillas in 1493 Pope Alexander VI had divided the pagan world in half like an apple between Spain and Portugal, giving the latter the eastern half (including Africa, India, and the Indian Ocean), thus cutting off Spain, for all her supposed dominion over the half containing most of America, from the approaches to the Spice Islands. Emperor Charles V granted Magellan five ships and two years' provisions to pursue his dream.

Magellan took his fleet to sea from the mouth of the Guadalquivir on September 20, 1519, with a total crew list of 285 men: French, Italian, German, and Malay sailors as well as Spanish and Portuguese. As Captain-General, Magellan was endowed with "full power of rope and knife" and was warned to anticipate intrigue and possible mutiny. The voyage was plagued with misfortunes, including the predicted mutiny, plus desertion, shipwreck, hunger, and scurvy. But Magellan found his passage into the Pacific; it bears his name and is his chief memorial.

A few days short of three years after departing, one lone ship, the *Victoria*, limped back into Sanlúcar on the Guadalquivir, under the command of Sebástian del Cano. Magellan himself was not on board. He had been killed in a native war on the island of Mactan in the Philippines. All the other ships had deserted, been captured, or sunk.

There were eighteen men aboard, according to Pigafetta, and most of them were sick. But on the first ship to go around the world was a cargo from the Spice Islands of cloves, nutmeg, cinnamon, and sandalwood worth a little more than the original cost of the expedition.

At the point at which this part of Pigafetta's narrative begins, Magellan had spent several months in the port of San Julian, in what is now Argentina, before venturing further south. One of his ships had already been wrecked and lost.

In ships hardly bigger than the one in this irreverent drawing by Holbein, Magellan's expedition sailed around the world.

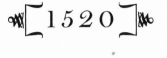

♦[1 5 2 0]♦

"We wept with joy"

S for us, we fared tolerably in this port . . . to which we gave the name of St. Julian . . . Here we planted a cross on the summit of a neighboring mountain, which we termed Monte Christo, and took possession of the country in the name of the King of Spain.

At length, we left St. Julian on August 21, 1520 [a year after departing from Spain] and keeping along the coast, in latitude 50° 40′ south, discovered a river of fresh water [named Santa Cruz] into which we entered. The whole squadron nearly experienced shipwreck here owing to the furious winds with which it was assailed, and which occasioned a very rough sea. But God and the Corpora Santa (that is to say, the lights which shone on the summits of the masts) brought us succor, and saved us from harm. We spent two months here, to stock our vessels with wood and water. We laid in provisions also, of a species of fish nearly two feet in length and covered with scales, which made tolerable eating but were not in sufficient quantity. Before we quitted this spot our captain ordered all of us to make confession, and, like good Christians, to receive Communion.

Continuing our course towards the south, on October 21st, in latitude 52°, we discovered a strait, which we named the Strait of the Eleven Thousand Virgins, and the Cape of the same name, in honor of the day. This strait, as will appear in the sequel, is one hundred and ten maritime leagues in length

[336 miles]; it is half a league in breadth, sometimes more, sometimes less, and terminates in another sea, which we called the Pacific Ocean. This strait is enclosed between lofty mountains covered with snow, and is likewise very deep, so that we were unable to anchor, except close to shore, where was from twenty-five to thirty fathoms of water.

The whole of the crew were so firmly persuaded that this strait was a *cul-de-sac* and had no western outlet, that we should not, but for the deep science of the Captain-General, have ventured on for its exploration. This man [Magellan], as skillful as he was intrepid, knew that he would have to pass by a strait very little known, but which he had seen laid down on a chart of Martin de Boheme, a most excellent cosmographer, the chart which he had seen in the treasury of the King of Portugal.

As soon as we entered on this water, then imagined to be only a bay, the Captain-General sent forward two vessels, the *San Antonio* and the *Concepción*, to examine where it terminated, or whither it led, while we in the *Trinidad* and *Victoria* awaited them in the mouth of it.

At night came on a terrible hurricane, which lasted six and thirty hours, and forced us to quit our anchors, thus leaving our vessels to the mercy of the winds and waves in the gulf [Possession Bay]. The two other vessels, equally buffeted, were unable to double a cape [Cape Possession] in order to rejoin us. By abandoning themselves to the gale, which drove them constantly towards what they conceived to be the bottom of a bay, they were fearful of being driven ashore at any moment. But, at the instant they gave themselves up for lost, they saw a small opening [First Gut] which they took for an inlet of the bay, into which they entered, and perceiving that this channel was not closed, they threaded it, and found themselves in another [Boucault Bay]. Thus, they pursued their course into another strait [Second Gut] leading into a third bay still larger than the preceding. Then, in lieu of following up their exploration they deemed it most prudent to return, and render account of what they had observed to the Captain-General.

Two days passed without the two vessels returning, sent to examine the bottom of the bay, so that we reckoned they had been swallowed up during

Constellations of the Southern Hemisphere.
The most famous, the Southern Cross, is near the Pole.

24

Antonio Pigafetta

the tempest. Seeing smoke on shore we conjectured those who had escaped had kindled those fires to inform us of their existence and distress.

While in this painful uncertainty as to their fate we saw the missing vessels advancing towards us under full sail, and their flags flying, and, when sufficiently near, heard the reports of their bombards [cannon] and their loud exclamations of joy. We returned their salute, and when we learned from them that they had seen the promulgation of the bay, or better speaking, the strait, we made towards them to continue our voyage in this course, if possible.

When we had entered the third bay, which I had never before noticed, we saw two openings, or channels, one running to the southeast, the other southwest [the former is near Cape Monmouth]. The Captain-General sent the *San Antonio* and the *Concepción* to the southeast channel [Strait Suppose of Bouganville] to examine whether or no this channel terminated in an open sea. The *San Antonio* set sail immediately, under press of canvas, not choosing to wait for the second. The pilot wished to leave behind the other, as he had an intention of availing himself of the darkness of the night to retrace his course and return to Spain by the same way we had come.

This pilot was Emanuel Gomez, who hated the Captain-General. The reason for this is as follows: When Magellan came to Spain to lay his project before the Emperor of proceeding to the Moluccas by a western passage, Gomez himself had requested, and was on the point of obtaining, some caravels for an expedition of which he would have had the command. This expedition had for its object to make new discoveries; but the arrival of Magellan prevented his request from being complied with and he could only obtain the subaltern position as pilot. What further served to increase his irritation was the reflection of his serving under a Portuguese.

In the course of the night Gomez conspired with the other Spaniards on board the ship. They put in irons the Captain, Alvaro de Meschita, the cousin of Magellan, after first wounding him, and carried

A crude chart of the Strait of Magellan, from the manuscript of Pigafetta's narrative. Pigafetta's own knowledge of geography, as the account indicates, was more sophisticated. North is at the bottom. Among the places well identified are the Atlantic Ocean (Mare oceano), the Pacific (Mare pacifico), San Julián (Sto. Juliano), and Cape Desire (Capo deseado). The strait itself is called Streto patagonico — Patagonian Strait.

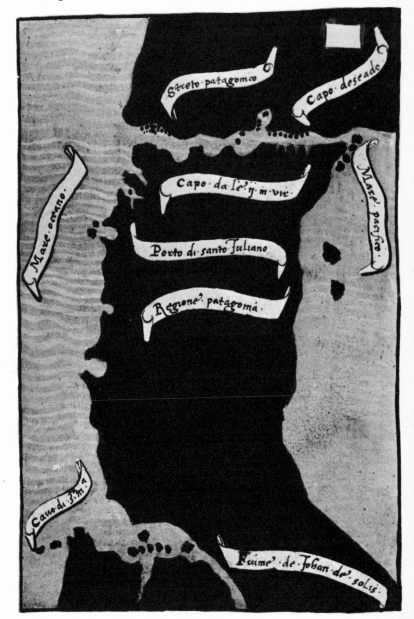

25

him thus to Spain. They reckoned likewise on transporting thither one of the two giants [Patagonians], and who was on board their ship, but we later learned he died on approaching the equinoctial line, unable to bear the heat of the tropical regions. Meanwhile, the *Concepción*, which could not keep up with the *San Antonio*, continued to cruise in the channel to await her return but of course in vain.

We, with the two remaining vessels, entered the remaining channel on the southwest. Continuing our course, we came to a river which we called Sardine River on account of the vast number of these fish we found in it. We anchored here to await the other two ships [the *Concepción* and *San Antonio*] and remained in the river four days. In the interim we sent out a boat, well manned, to reconnoiter the cape of this channel which promised to terminate in another sea. On the third day the sailors so dispatched returned and announced having come to the place where the Strait ended and found with it a great sea—that is to say the ocean. We wept with joy; this cape was called Cape Deseado [Wished-for Cape] for in truth we had long wished to see it.

We returned to join the other two vessels of the squadron, and found the *Concepción* alone. On enquiring of the pilot, Johan Serano, what had become of the *San Antonio*, we learned he believed her to be lost, as he had not once seen her since he entered the channel. The Captain-General then ordered a search for our missing ship, especially in the channel which she had penetrated. The *Victoria* was sent back to the mouth of the strait with orders that if the missing ship could not be found a standard was to be hoisted on some eminent spot. At the

foot of the standard a letter was to be placed in a small pot, pointing out the course the Captain-General would take in order to enable the *San Antonio* to follow the squadron. Two other signals were hoisted in the same manner on eminent sites in the first bay, and on a small island of the third bay [Isle of Lions], on which we saw a number of sea-wolves and birds. Magellan with the *Concepción*, awaited the return of the *Victoria* near the river of Sardines, and erected a cross on a small island, at the foot of two mountains covered with snow, where the river had its source.

Had we not discovered this strait, leading from one sea to the other, it was the intention of the Captain-General to continue his course towards the south, as high as 75°, where in summer there is no night, or very little, as in winter there is scarcely

Explorers meeting naked but otherwise very European-looking natives in this chart from the famous Collectiones Peregrinationum in Indiam Orientalem et Occidentalem *by Theodor de Bry and his sons.*

26

any day. While we were in the strait, in the month of October, there were but three hours of night.

The shore in this strait, which on the left turns to the Southeast, is low. We called it the Strait of the Patagonians. At every half league it contains a safe port, with excellent water, cedar-wood, sardines and a great abundance of shellfish. There were here also some vegetables, part of them of a bitter taste, but others fit to eat, especially a species of sweet celery, which grows on the margin of the springs and which, for the want of other, served us for food. In short, I do not think the world contains a better strait than this one.

At the very instant of our launching into the ocean we witnessed a singular chase of fish, pursued by others. There were three species, that is, dorados, albicores and bonitos, which chase the fish called colondrius, a kind of flying fish which are upwards of a foot in length and are excellent eating.

During the voyage I talked with the Patagonian giant on board our ship and, by means of a species of pantomime, enquired of him the Patagonian name of a number of objects. He had accustomed himself so perfectly to this practice that no sooner did he see me take my pen in hand than he came immediately to tell me the different things before him and of what was passing. Among other things he showed us the manner of kindling fire in this country; that is, by rubbing one piece of pointed wood against another until fire catches to a kind of pith of a tree placed between the two pieces. One day when I showed him and kissed the cross he gave me to understand through gestures that Setebos would enter my body and cause me to burn.

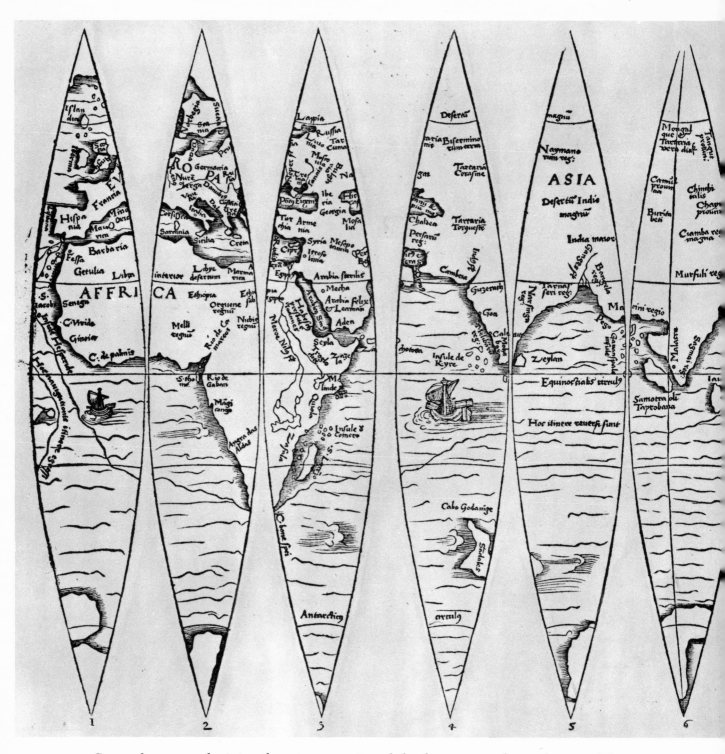

*Gores of a rare, early sixteenth-century map, intended to be cut out and pasted over a globe,
with the route of the Victoria indicated on them.*

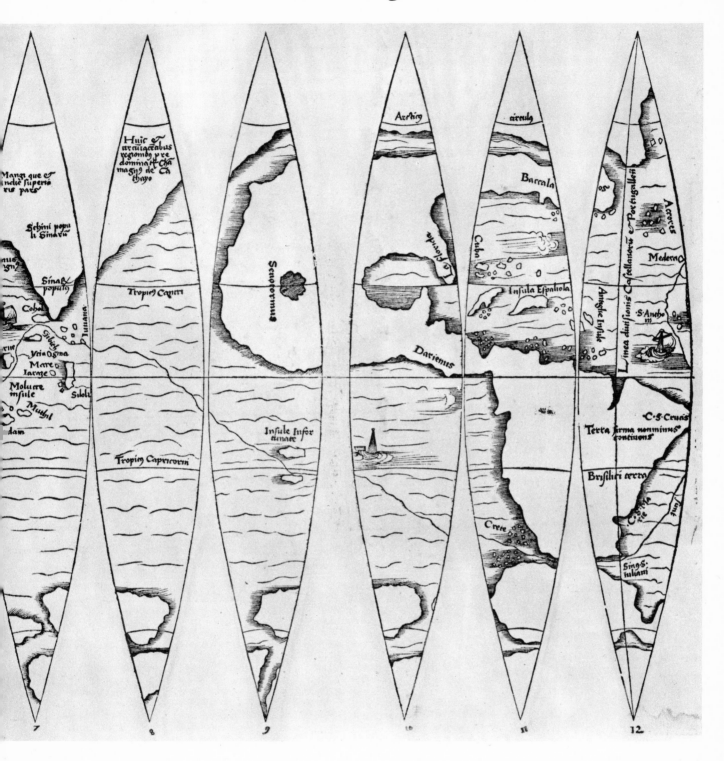

29

An allegorical commemoration by Stradanus of Magellan's voyage. On the left burn the mysterious fires that gave Tierra del Fuego its name; on the right a Patagonian giant thrusts an arrow down his throat to produce vomit. In the heavens the fabled roc carries off an elephant, while a wind god speeds the ship on its way. Apollo hovers off the port bow, since the Victoria was the first ship to follow the sun's path around the earth. The broken mast of the ship apparently symbolizes the perils Magellan endured, and possibly his death.

ON Wednesday, the 28th of November, we left the Strait, and entered the ocean to which we afterwards gave the name of Pacific, and in which we sailed for the space of three months and twenty days without taking any fresh provisions. The biscuit we were eating no longer deserved the name of bread—it was nothing but dust and worms which had consumed the substance. What is more, it smelled intolerably being impregnated with the urine of mice. The water we were obliged to drink was equally putrid and offensive.

We were even so far reduced, that we might not die of hunger, to eat pieces of the leather with

FERDINAN. MAGALA.

Antonio Pigafetta

which the main yard was covered to prevent the rope from chafing. These pieces of leather, constantly exposed to the water, sun and wind, were so hard that they required being soaked four or five days in the sea in order to render them pliable. After this we boiled them to eat. Frequently, indeed, we were obliged to subsist on saw dust, and even mice, a food so disgusting, yet these were fought over with such avidity that they sold for a ducat a piece.

Nor was this all. Our greatest misfortune was being attacked by a malady in which the gums swelled so as to hide the teeth, as well in the upper as in the lower jaw, whence those affected thus were incapable of chewing their poor food [the dreaded scurvy]. Nineteen of our number died of this complaint, among them the Patagonian giant and a Brazilian we had also brought with us. When the Patagonian was at death's door he called for the cross which he kissed; he also begged to be baptized, which was done, receiving the name of Paul. Besides those who died we had from twenty-five to thirty mariners ill, who suffered dreadful pains in their arms, legs and other parts of the body—but

Portrait of Magellan.

31

these recovered. As for myself, I cannot be too grateful to God for the continued health I enjoyed; though surrounded with sick I experienced not the slightest illness.

In the course of these three months and twenty days we traversed nearly four thousand leagues in the ocean we named Pacific, so named because during which time we experienced no tempestuous weather. We did not either throughout this whole period of time discover any land, except two desert islands which we named Las Islas Desdichados [The Unfortunate Islands] as we saw nothing but birds and trees. We found no bottom along their shores; saw no fish but sharks. The two islands are two hundred leagues apart, the first lying in latitude 15° south, the second in 9° south. From the run of our ship, estimated by the log, we traversed a space of from sixty to seventy leagues a day; and if God and His Holy Mother had not granted us a fortunate voyage we should all have perished of hunger in so vast a sea. I do not think that any one for the future will venture upon a similar voyage.

Magellan's first landing in the Pacific was a group of islands whose natives stole so much from the expedition that their home was dubbed, as on this chart from the Pigafetta manuscript, Ysole de li Ladroni, or Islands of the Thieves. Until the seventeenth century, and often thereafter, the Marianas Islands continued to be called the Ladrones.

Adventure 4

The Battle of San Juan d'Ulloa

from A True Declaration

of the Troublesome Voyadge of M. John Hawkins . . .

HE careth not to whom he speaketh, nor what he sayeth," wrote Sir William Winter about Captain John Hawkins; "blush will he not." One of Elizabeth's famous "sea dogs," Hawkins is remembered today chiefly as architect of the defeat of the Spanish Armada; he was responsible for building the English fleet of fast, low ships that decisively outmaneuvered and outgunned the towering Spanish galleons. He was also a combination—not unusual in his time—of experienced mariner, fearless soldier, and shrewd businessman, and he was by profession a fighting trader who demanded with cannon and sword the rights of free trade that the Spanish and Portuguese claimed as their rightful monopoly.

At the time of the Armada, Hawkins was already celebrated for three voyages to the New World. His trade was not a very noble one: To put it bluntly, he was, as his father had been, a slaver; he smuggled Negro captives from Africa to labor-hungry Spanish colonies in the West Indies and made, on the whole, a very good thing of it. But, in 1568, during his third voyage, his three ships— two galleons of the traditional type, the *Jesus of Lubeck* and the *Minion*, plus one smaller ship, the *Judith*—had a disastrous brush with part of the Spanish fleet.

He had collected, by warfare and kidnaping, a cargo of "400 to 500" unfortunate Negroes on the coast of Guinea, and had traded them briskly if illegally in the West Indies. He made the mistake, however, of lingering in the Caribbean too late in the summer, and his ships were so battered by the tropical storms of that season that he was forced to lay into the Mexican port of San Juan d'Ulloa for repairs. Here he was cornered by several Spanish galleons. At this time Spain and England were technically at peace, but the peace—especially at sea—was an uneasy one, and Hawkins soon had proof of the Spaniards' hostile intentions.

This skirmish had important repercussions and foreshadowed the major engagement between the English and Spanish twenty-six years later. It gave the young captain of the *Judith*—Francis Drake— an undying taste for vengeance. And two English sailors, Miles Phillips and Job Hortop, who were captured in the aftermath of this battle and later escaped, did much to inflame their countrymen against the Spanish by accounts of fearful treatment inflicted on English prisoners. Hawkins' own version of the event is probably no less partial, but he tells a dramatic story, and through it his own character emerges clearly—energetic, a bit testy, and bold as brass.

33

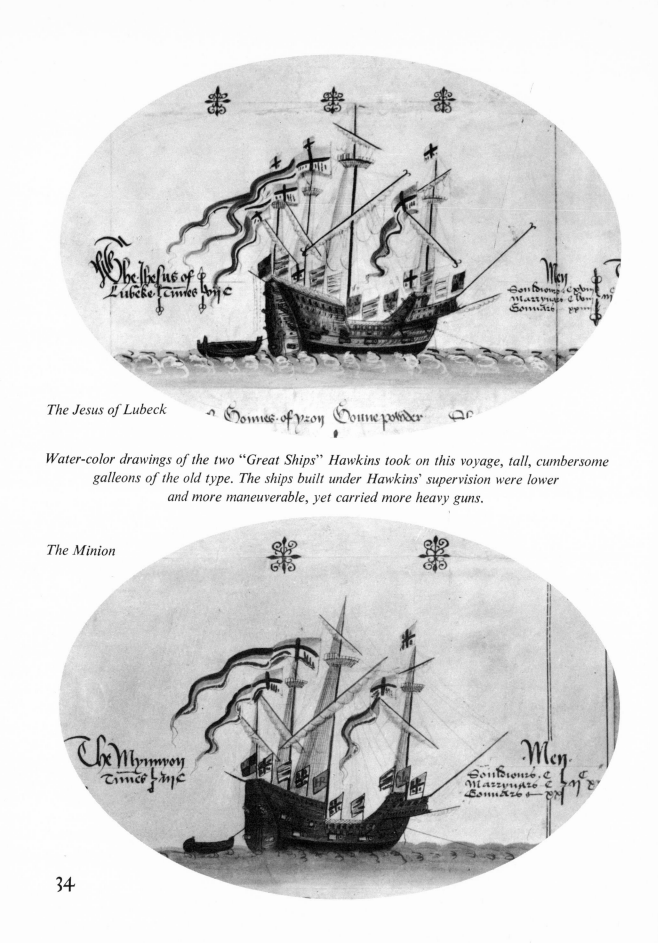

The Jesus of Lubeck

Water-color drawings of the two "Great Ships" Hawkins took on this voyage, tall, cumbersome galleons of the old type. The ships built under Hawkins' supervision were lower and more maneuverable, yet carried more heavy guns.

The Minion

34

⚔[1568]⚔

"And on all sides set upon us"

THE sixteenth of September, we entered the port of St. John de Ullua. And in our entry, the Spaniards thinking us to be the fleet of Spain, the chief officers of the country came aboard us. Which, being deceived of their expectation, [they] were greatly dismayed: but immediately when they saw our demand was nothing but victuals, were recomforted. I found also in the same port 12 ships which had in them by report £200,000 in gold and silver; all which, being in my possession, with the King's Island, as also the passengers before in my way thitherward stayed, I set at liberty, without the taking from them the weight of a groat.

Only, because I would not be delayed of my dispatch, I stayed two men of estimation and sent post immediately to Mexico, which was 200 miles from us, to the Presidents and Council there, showing them of our arrival there by the force of weather, and the necessity of the repair of our ships and victuals, which wants we required as friends to King Philip to be furnished of for our money; and that the Presidents and Council there should with all convenient speed take order, that at the arrival of the Spanish fleet, which was daily looked for, there might no cause of quarrel rise between us and them, but for the better maintenance of amity, their commandment might be had in that behalf. This message being sent away the sixteenth day of September at night, being the very day of our arrival, in the next morning, which was the seventeenth day of the same month, we saw open of the haven 13 great ships. And understanding them to

be the fleet of Spain, I sent immediately to advertise the General of the fleet of my being there; doing him to understand, that before I would suffer them to enter the port, there should some order of conditions pass between us for our safebeing there, and maintenance of peace.

Now it is to be understood that this port is made by a little island of stones not three foot above the water in the highest place, and but a bow-shoot of length any way. This island stands from the mainland two bow-shoots or more. Also it is to be understood that there is not in all this coast any other place for ships to arrive in safety, because the north wind has there such violence, that unless the ships be very safely moored with their anchors fastened upon this island, there is no remedy for these north winds but death. Also the place of the haven was so little, that of necessity the ships must ride one aboard the other, so that we could not give place to them, nor they to us. And here I began to bewail that which after followed, for, Now, said I, I am in two dangers, and forced to receive the one of them. That was, either I must have kept out the fleet from entering the port, the which with God's help I was very well able to do, or else suffer them to enter in with their accustomed treason, which they never fail to execute, where they may have opportunity to compass it by any means. If I had kept them out, then had there been present shipwreck of all the fleet, which amounted in value to six millions, which was in value of our money £1,800,000, which I considered I was not able to answer, fearing the Queen's Majesty's indignation

35

in so weighty a matter. Thus, with myself revolving the doubts, I thought rather better to abide the jut of the uncertainty than the certainty. The uncertain doubt I account was their treason, which by good policy I hoped might be prevented; and therefore, as choosing the least mischief, I proceeded to conditions.

Now was our first messenger come and returned from the fleet with report of the arrival of a Viceroy; so that he had authority, both in all this province of Mexico (otherwise called Nueva España), and on the sea. [This was Don Martin Henriquez, Viceroy of Mexico.] He sent us word that we should send our conditions, which of his part should, for the better maintenance of amity between the princes, be both favourably granted and faithfully performed; with many fair words, how, passing the coast of the Indies, he had understood of our honest behaviour towards the inhabitants where we had to do, as well elsewhere as in the same port; the which I let pass. Thus, following

Portraits of John Hawkins and Francis Drake, from a book of biographies of the greatest English heroes of the age.

our demand, we required victuals for our money, and license to sell as much ware as might furnish our wants, and that there might be of either part twelve gentlemen as hostages for the maintenance of peace: and that the island, for our better safety, might be in our own possession, during our abode there, and such ordnance as was planted in the same island, which were eleven pieces of brass: and that no Spaniard might land in the island with any kind of weapon. These conditions at the first he somewhat misliked, chiefly the guard of the island to be in our own keeping. Which if they had had, we had soon known our fare: for with the first north wind they had cut our cables and our ships had gone ashore. But in the end he concluded to our request, bringing the twelve hostages to ten, which with all speed of either part were received, with a writing from the Viceroy, signed with his

John Hawkins

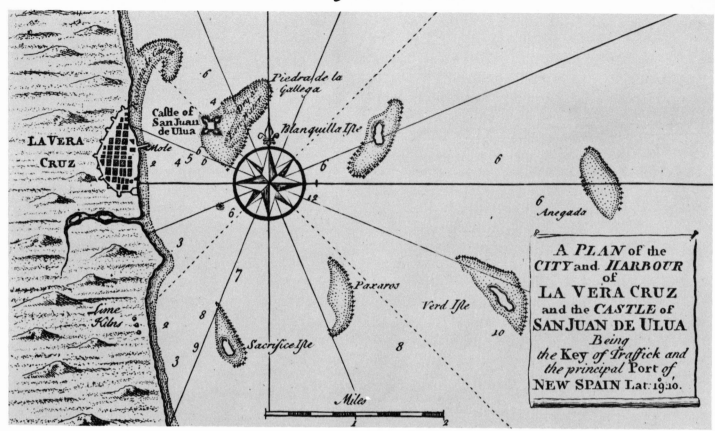

*An eighteenth-century chart of Vera Cruz, formerly Sàn Juan d'Ulloa,
showing the position of the water fort.   Below, three galleons anchored near such a fort.*

hand and sealed with his seal, of all the conditions concluded, and forthwith a trumpet blown, with commandment that none of either part should violate the peace upon pain of death: and further, it was concluded that the two generals of the fleets should meet, and give faith each to other for the performance of the promises, which was so done.

Thus at the end of three days all was concluded and the fleet entered the port, saluting one another as the manner of the sea requires. Thus, as I said before, Thursday we entered the port, Friday we saw the fleet, and on Monday at night they entered the port. Then we laboured two days placing the English ships by themselves and the Spanish by themselves, the captains of each part and inferior men of their parts promising great amity of all

sides. Which even as with all fidelity it was meant on our part, so the Spaniards meant nothing less on their parts; but from the mainland had furnished themselves with a supply of men to the number of 1,000, and meant the next Thursday, being the twenty-third of September, at dinner-time to set upon us on all sides.

The same Thursday, in the morning, the treason being at hand, some appearance showed, as shifting of weapon from ship to ship, planting and bending of ordnance from the ships to the island where our men warded, passing to and fro of companies of men more than required for their necessary business, and many other ill likelihoods, which caused us to have a vehement suspicion. And therewithal [we] sent to the Viceroy to enquire what was

meant by it; which sent immediately strict commandment to unplant all things suspicious, and also sent word that he in the faith of a Viceroy would be our defence from all villainies. Yet we being not yet satisfied with this answer, because we suspected a great number of men to be hid in a great ship of 900 tons which was moored near unto the *Minion*, sent again to the Viceroy the master of the *Jesus*, which had the Spanish tongue, and required to be satisfied if any such thing were or not.

Two engravings after Bruegel indicate the differences between English and Spanish ships of the Armada period. The English vessels built under Hawkins' direction were usually lower and often smaller than the towering Spanish galleons.

The Viceroy now seeing that the treason must be discovered, forthwith stayed our master, blew the trumpet, and on all sides set upon us. Our men which warded ashore being stricken with sudden fear, gave place, fled, and sought to recover succour of the ships. The Spaniards, being before provided for the purpose, landed in all places in multitudes from their ships, which they might easily do without boats, and slew all our men on shore without mercy; a few of them escaped aboard the *Jesus*. The great ship, which had by estimation 300 men placed in her secretly, immediately fell aboard the *Minion*. But by God's appointment, in the time of the suspicion we had, which was only one half-hour, the *Minion* was made ready to avoid, and so loosing her headfasts, and hauling away

by the sternfasts, she was gotten out: thus with God's help she defended the violence of the first brunt of these 300 men. The *Minion* being passed out, they came aboard the *Jesus*, which also with very much ado and the loss of many of our men was defended and kept out. Then were there also two other ships that assaulted the *Jesus* at the same instant, so that it was hard getting loose, but yet with some time we had cut our headfasts and gotten out by the sternfasts. Now when the *Jesus* and the *Minion* were gotten about two ships' length from the Spanish fleet, the fight began so hot on all sides that within one hour the admiral of the Spaniards was supposed to be sunk, their vice-admiral burned, and one other of their principal ships supposed to be sunk, so that the ships were little able to annoy us.

Then is it to be understood, that all the ordnance upon the island was in the Spaniards' hands; which did us so great annoyance, that it cut all the masts and yards of the *Jesus*, in such sort that there was no hope to carry her away. Also it sunk our small ships, whereupon we determined to place the *Jesus* on that side of the *Minion*, that she might abide all the battery from the land, and so be a defence for the *Minion* till night, and then to take such relief of victuals and other necessaries from the *Jesus*, as the time would suffer us, and to leave her. As we were thus determining, and had placed the *Minion* from the shot of the land, suddenly the Spaniards had fired two great ships, which were coming directly with us. And having no means to avoid the fire, it bred among our men a marvellous fear, so that some said, Let us depart with the *Minion*. Others said, Let us see whether the wind will carry the fire from us. But to be short, the *Minion's* men which had always their sails in a readiness, thought to make sure work, and so without either the consent of the captain or master cut their sail, so that very hardly I was received into the *Minion*.

The most part of the men that were left alive in the *Jesus*, made shift and followed the *Minion* in a

A battle between galleons, in this case Spanish and Dutch.

small boat. The rest which the little boat was not able to receive, were forced to abide the mercy of the Spaniards, which I [do not] doubt was very little. So with the *Minion* only and the *Judith*, a small bark of fifty ton, we escaped; which bark the same night forsook us in our great misery. We were now removed with the *Minion* from the Spanish ships two bow-shoots, and there rode all that night. The next morning we recovered an island a mile from the Spaniards, where there took us a north wind, and being left only with two anchors and

John Hawkins

at sea. So thus, with many sorrowful hearts, we wandered in an unknown sea by the space of fourteen days, till hunger enforced us to seek the land: for hides were thought very good meat, rats, cats, mice, and dogs, none escaped that might be gotten, parrots and monkeys, that were had in great price, were thought there very profitable if they served the turn one dinner.

Thus in the end, the eighth day of October, we came to the land in the bottom of the same bay of Mexico in 23 degrees and a half, where we hoped to have found inhabitants of the Spaniards, relief of victuals, and place for the repair of our ship, which was so sore beaten with shot from our enemies and bruised with shooting off our own ordnance, that our weary and weak arms were scarce able to defend and keep out water. But all things happened to the contrary; for we found neither people, victuals, nor haven of relief, but a place where having fair weather with some peril we might land a boat. Our people, being forced with hunger, desired to be set on land; whereunto I consented. And such as were willing to land, I put them apart; and such as were desirous to go homewards, I put apart; so that they were indifferently parted 100 of one side and 100 of the other side. These 100 men we set aland with all diligence, in this little place before said [the terrible sufferings of these men were later reported by survivors]; which being landed, we determined there to take in fresh water, and so with our little remain of victuals to take the sea.

The next day, having aland with me 50 of our 100 men that remained, for the speedier preparing of our water aboard, there arose an extreme storm, so that in three days we could by no means repair

two cables (for in this conflict we lost three cables and two anchors) we thought always upon death which ever was present; but God preserved us to a longer time.

The weather waxed reasonable; and the Saturday we set sail, and having a great number of men and little victuals, our hope of life waxed less and less. Some desired to yield to the Spaniards; some rather desired to obtain a place where they might give themselves to the infidels: and some had rather abide with a little pittance the mercy of God aboard our ship: the ship also was in such peril that every hour we looked for shipwreck. But yet God again had mercy on us, and sent fair weather; we had aboard our water, and departed the sixteenth day of October, after which day we had fair and prosperous weather till the sixteenth day of November, which day, God be praised, we were clear from the coast of the Indies, and out of the channel and gulf of Bahama, which is between the Cape of Florida and the islands of Lucayo. After this, drawing near to the cold country, our men being oppressed with famine, died continually, and they that were left grew into such weakness that we were scarcely able to manage our ship; and the wind being always ill for us to recover England, we determined to go into Galicia in Spain, with intent there to relieve our company and other extreme wants.

And being arrived on the last day of December in a place near unto Vigo, called Ponte Vedra, our men with excess of fresh meat grew into miserable diseases, and died a great part of them. This matter was borne out as long as it might be, but in the end although there were none of our men suffered to go aland, yet by access of the Spaniards, our feebleness was known to them. Whereupon they ceased not to seek by all means to betray us; but with all speed possible we departed to Vigo, where we had some help of certain English ships and twelve fresh men. Wherewith we repaired our wants as we might, and departing the twentieth day of January, 1569, arrived in Mount's Bay, in Cornwall, the twenty-fifth of the same month. Praised be God therefore.

If all the miseries and troublesome affairs of this sorrowful voyage should be perfectly and thoroughly written, there should need a painful man with his pen, and as great a time as he had that wrote the lives and deaths of the martyrs.

The Winter in Hudson's Bay

from Navigatio Septentrionalis, by Jens Munck

THE persistent illusion of a Northwest Passage to the Orient demonstrates the power of logic over experience. It was widely and tenaciously believed that since there was open water to the south of the American continents, there must be a navigable channel to the north as well—and for three hundred years whole generations of sailors broke their hearts, wrecked their ships, and risked (or lost) their lives trying to find it. By the time Peary finally penetrated the labyrinth of islands and ice north of Canada in 1909, it was conclusively proved that sailing the Northwest Passage was like climbing Everest: a tribute to man's ingenuity and endurance but not an achievement of practical utility.

The early explorers of the sixteenth and seventeenth centuries in their small, high-pooped, round-bottomed wooden ships were singularly ill equipped for the rigors of the Arctic. The lucky ones were those who turned back in time, before their ships were crushed by the remorseless ice or they were forced ashore on these windswept northern coasts to try to survive a winter far more severe than any Western European was used to.

The Danish expedition led by Jens Munck in 1619 was one of the unlucky ones. It was well led, by a brave and experienced seaman and warrior, and its two ships, the *Lamprenen* [*Lamprey*] and the *Enhiorningen* [*Unicorn*], were well appointed for that period. But there were two fatal lacks: there was no physician in the group, only an ignorant surgeon who did not understand the few medicines in his medicine chest, and there were no clothes adequate for the Arctic winter. And, most important, they made no useful contact with the natives.

By September, Munck had penetrated deep into Hudson Bay and, cut off by approaching ice floes, decided to winter at what is now Churchill Harbor on Churchill River. Game appeared plentiful, and for a while it seemed that the sixty-four men were well prepared for whatever onslaught nature might send. But as the winter deepened, scurvy and the cold took an appalling toll. Written in plain, blunt language by a plain, blunt man, this account of how Munck and two others survived the winter and made their way back home is a true epic of endurance in the face of overwhelming adversity.

*King Christian IV of Denmark sends Jens Munck to discover the Northwest Passage:
a fanciful woodcut from a seventeenth century Dutch version of the story.*

Two early seventeenth century ships like Munck's Enhiörningen and Lamprenen.

"Herewith, good night to all the world"

SEPTEMBER 7th. When I now had come into the harbour aforesaid, though with great difficulty, on account of wind and storm, snow, hail, and fog, I at once ordered my shallop, which was divided into six parts, to be put together; and, during the night following, we kept a watch on the land, and maintained a fire, in order that *Lamprenen*, which, during the great gale and storm, had strayed from us, might find us again. She joined us on the 9th of September, having been under the northern land, where an open passage was supposed to exist, but there was none. The crew having suffered much from the before-mentioned gale, and in other hardship and trouble, and a part in consequence being down with illness, I caused, during these days, the sick people to be brought from the ship on shore; and we gathered still some cloud-berries, gooseberries, and other berries, which in Norway are called *Tydebaer* and *Kragbaer*. I also had a good fire made on shore every day for the sick, whereby they were comforted, and in time nicely regained their health.

On the 10th and 11th of September, there was such a terrible snowstorm and gale that nothing could be done.

September 12th. In the morning early, a large white bear came down to the water near the ship, which stood and ate some Beluga flesh, off a fish so named which I had caught the day before. I shot the bear, and the men all desired the flesh for food, which I also allowed. I ordered the cook just

to boil it slightly, and then to keep it in vinegar for a night, and I myself had two or three pieces of this bear-flesh roasted for the cabin. It was of good taste and did not disagree with us.

On the 13th of September, I sent out both my shallop and the ship's boat, under the command of my second mates, Hans Brock and Jan Pettersen, with orders to proceed 8 or 9 miles along the shore, one on the western, the other on the eastern side, and to examine what accommodation the land afforded, and whether there were any better harbours there than the one we were in.

On the 16th of September, Jan Pettersen returned, who had been investigating the localities on the western side; and he reported that, where he had been, no harbours could be found; the land was low, flat, and wooded, and there was scarcely any safe harbour to protect a boat properly. On the same day, there was a terrible snowstorm from the North-East.

September 18th. As we experienced nothing but frost and snow, we deliberated together as to what measures to take. Then all the officers thought it best, and it was finally resolved, that, inasmuch as the winter was coming on us very hard and severe, increasing and getting worse day by day, we should have the ship brought in somewhere, as well as the unfavourable circumstances would allow, behind some promontory, where she might be safe from drift-ice. On the same day, the ring broke on the anchor by which we were moored.

On the 19th of September, we sailed up the

Martin Frobisher and Humphrey Gilbert were among the many explorers of the sixteenth and seventeenth centuries who tried, in vain, to find the Northwest Passage.

The durable myth of a navigable northern strait to the Pacific, indicated so clearly and falsely on this map from an account of Frobisher's voyages, deluded navigators for centuries. Other geographical myths are preserved here as well, including the Northern and Southern Continents (Terra Septentrionalis and Terra Australis), vast land masses thought to encompass both ends of the earth.

river, with the ship and the sloop, as far as we could, and stayed one night at anchor. On that night, the new drift-ice cut into both sides of the ship and of the sloop, to the depth of about two fingers'-breadths, so that I was obliged to have the ship brought nearer to the western shore by 8 cables' lengths, across a flat. It was a distance of nearly 900 fathoms across the flat, where the ship was in great danger, because the ground was covered with stones, and the ship could not well rest on it, on account of her being sharp-built. As the drift-ice got the upper hand, the ship stuck on a stone and became quite leaky, so that all the carpenters had enough to do during the ebb in order to make her tight again before the return of the flood.

September 25th. As we had now secured the ship close under the land and brought the sloop on shore by means of a high tide, I caused the ship's keel to be dug down into the ground, and branches of trees to be spread under the bilge, packed together with clay and sand, in order that the ship might rest evenly on the bilge on both sides, and thus suffer less damage.

46

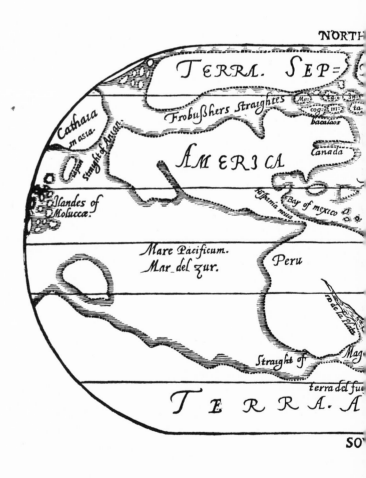

Jens Munck

On the same day, Hans Brock, the mate returned, having been to the eastward to ascertain whether better harbours could be found. He also reported that there were no harbours suitable for winter quarters in the places where he had been, but only flat, bare, and swampy land. During his exploration, he had been in great danger of losing his life amongst the quantities of new ice which floated forwards and backwards; and he lost a grapnel which they had with them, the rope having snapped on account of the bad condition of the sea bottom.

September 27th. Whilst we now thought that the ship was well protected against drift-ice and bad weather, such a tremendous drift of ice came upon us with a low ebb that, if the ship had not

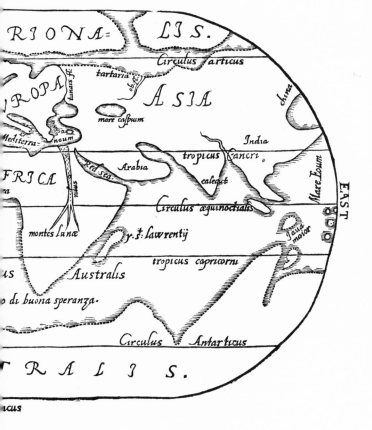

been resting so firmly on the ground, we should have been carried away by the ice. We were obliged to let go all four hawsers by which the ship was moored, and part of them went to pieces. By this breaking up of the ice, the ship also became so leaky that, at flood-time, we pumped out quite 2,000 strokes of water; the ship was, on the same occasion, moved out of the dock which we originally had made for her, and in which she was placed.

On the 28th of September, at high tide, we had the ship replaced in position and moored by 6 hawsers; and, during the lowest ebb, the leaks were looked for and made good again. Thereupon, I had a fresh dock made as before, in which the ship again was placed; and, at the same time, I ordered the carpenters and others who could ply an axe, to make five bridge-piles; the other men hauled timber and stones for these piles, which I caused to be placed before the bow of the ship, to turn off the ice so that it should not hurt us.

October 1st. Everything being now well finished, and the ship and the sloop well protected against ice and tempest, I ordered the hold to be

Munck made brief contact with the native inhabitants in Hudson Strait, but unfortunately, when he reached Hudson Bay, he found only traces of former occupancy, and met no one.

cleared out, the cannon to be placed in the hold, and a part of our goods to be brought on shore, in order that the deck might be clear and the men have more space to move about, and also that the ship should not suffer too much from the great weight resting on her deck.

On the 3rd of October, I ordered the crew of *Lamprenen* to come on board *Enhiorningen* for their meals, so that there should not be more than one galley; and I gave orders to the cook and the steward as regards the board, in accordance with the Instructions I had with me and the requirements of the time and place.

On the 4th of October, I distributed to the crew clothes, shirts, shoes, and boots, and whatever else could be of use as a protection against the cold.

On the 5th of October, I caused two large fireplaces, round each of which 20 men might easily sit, to be arranged on the deck, one before the mast, the other behind the mast, as well as a fireplace on the steerage, round which likewise 20 persons could be accommodated, in addition to that in the cook's galley, where he did his cooking; that he required to have to himself.

On the 7th of October and next following days, the carpenters were ashore with the men to cut timber and haul stones for breakwaters, which were made in order to protect the ship against damage from the ice, which sometimes drifted very much there during the rising of the tide and until the ebb was halfway out.

That same day, the weather being fine, I myself journeyed up the river to see how far I could get with a boat; but, about a mile and a half up, there were so many stones in it, that I could not advance any further, and had to return. I had brought with me all sorts of small goods, intending, if I had met any natives, to present them with some in order to become acquainted with them, but I could neither find nor perceive any. On my return journey, I came to a promontory and found there a picture on a stone, drawn with charcoal, fashioned like the half of a devil, wherefore I called the same promontory *Dieffuel's Hug* [Devil's Cape].

In many places where we came, we could quite well see where people had been and had their summer abodes. Even in the place where the ship is lying, there are certain signs and indications of people having been there. In the forest, there are,

48

likewise, in many places, great heaps of chips, where they have cut wood or timber; and the chips look as if they had been cut off with curved iron tools. As regards their food and mode of living: it would seem that they use much in a half-cooked state, because, wherever we found that they had had their meals, the bones did not seem to have been very well roasted.

On the 10th of October, I commenced to give the men rations of wine; but beer they were allowed to drink according to their want, as much as every man himself liked. At the same time, I made regulations for keeping a watch, the fetching of wood, and burning of charcoal, as well as with regard to whose duty it was to be, during the day, to melt snow into water; so that everybody knew what he was to do, and how he had to conduct himself.

October 15th. During the night, the new drift-ice had again lifted the ship out of the dock in which she was placed; but I at once ordered fresh branches to be thrown under the vessel at the next low water and the spaces to be filled up with clay and sand as before. In the same night, the ice carried one of the piers right away; in consequence of which, I was obliged at once to order another to be built in the place of it, for the protection of the ship. As soon as the ice had become quite firm, the ship suffered no further damage.

On the 22nd of October, the ice became firm for good, as it was a terribly hard frost. On the same night, we caught a black fox.

After this day, the crew commenced to go on shore in the day time in pursuit of game. A part went into the forest to set traps to catch animals, and some of these built a hut wherein to lie *for glug* [in ambush], as it is called in Norway; another part of the men betook themselves to the open country for shooting, because there was plenty of ptarmigan and hares, as well as all kinds of birds, as long as the snow was not too deep; so that, before Christmas, there was enough of pastime. At that time, all the men liked to go into the forest or

the open country for shooting, because they never went on shore when the weather was fine but that they carried home something good, which was a sufficient inducement to them to move about.

On the 30th of October, the ice everywhere covered the river, which, down to that time, could not freeze completely on account of the strong ebb and flow which prevailed. During these days, the frost was rather mild, and every day there was fine clear sunshine; wherefore I went on shore on the 7th of November with 19 men, and penetrated nearly three miles into the country, in order to ascertain whether any inhabitants were to be found. As, however, there was a sudden great fall of snow, which was too heavy for us to make our way through, we were obliged to return without effecting anything by the journey. But, if we had had snow shoes, such as are used in Norway, and men that knew how to run on them, it is not improbable that we might have got far enough to find people. Otherwise, it is impossible to get along in these countries in the winter.

Munck ran his ships aground and hauled one of them clear of the water to save them from damage by the wind-driven ice floes.

On the 10th of November, which was St. Martin's Eve, the men shot some ptarmigan, with which we had to content ourselves, instead of St. Martin's goose; and I ordered a pint of Spanish wine for each bowl to be given to the men, besides their daily allowance; wherewith the whole crew were well satisfied, even merry and joyful; and of the ship's beer there was given them as much as they liked. But, afterwards, when the frost got the upper hand, the beer froze to the bottom, so that I was afraid of letting the men drink of it before they had well melted and boiled it again; for which reason, I had every fresh barrel, as it was taken up for consumption, boiled afresh, because, in any case, it was better than snow water, which otherwise would have had to be melted for drinking or mixing with wine. However, in this matter, I let the men follow their own inclination, because the common people, after all, are so disposed that, whatever is most strongly forbidden them, they, notwithstanding, are most apt to do on the sly, without considering whether it be beneficial or hurtful to them.

November 14th. In the night, a large black dog came to the ship on the ice, when the man on the watch observed him, and not knowing but that it was a black fox, at once shot him, and, with much exultation, dragged him into the cabin, thinking that he had got a great prize. But, when, in the morning, we examined it, we found it to be a large dog, which no doubt had been trained to catch game, because he had been tied round the nose with small cords, so that the hair was rubbed off there. His right ear was cleft, and perhaps his owner was not very pleased to lose him. I should myself have been glad to have caught him alive, in which case I should have made a pedlar of him, and have let him go home to where he had come from with small goods.

November 21st. During these days, the weather was very beautiful — as fine as could be expected in Denmark at that time of the year; the sea outside us was also quite clear, and the water open as far as we could see over the sea. It is, however, to be noticed that the ice on the sea drifts mostly according to the strength of the wind. *Item:* during all these days, as long as the fine and mild weather lasted, the men were every day in the forest, although the snow was very deep. Some of them shot ptarmigan, which were of great assistance to us; whilst others visited and put in order their traps, in which they caught animals. On the same day, a sailor who had long been ill was buried.

On the 27th of November, there was a very sharp frost, by which all the glass bottles we had (which contained all kinds of precious waters) were broken to pieces; wherefore it is to be observed that whoever intends to navigate such cold seas should supply himself well with tin bottles, or others that are able to resist the frost.

On the 3rd of December, the weather being very mild, I went out into the middle of the estuary, with some of the men, in order to ascertain how thick the ice was in the middle of the channel; and we found that the ice was seven Seeland quarters [about 3 feet 7 inches] thick; and this thickness it retained until long after Christmas, whether the frost was more or less severe. But, in quiet standing water, the ice became much thicker than seven quarters. As regards much of the drift-ice which floats forwards and backwards in the sea, and exhibits very great thickness: this ice comes out of the many large rivers and bays, and owing to the great force of the wind and the current, by which it is shoved together, it attains such great thickness, and thus floats away. Amongst this ice, there occur large masses rising quite twenty fathoms above the water; and some such masses of ice, which I myself have had examined, stood firm on the sea-bottom in more than 40 fathoms, which, perhaps, may seem incredible, but, nevertheless, is so in truth.

On the 12th of December, one of my two surgeons, the one on *Lamprenen*, David Velske by name, died, and his corpse had to remain on the ship unburied for two days, because the frost was so very severe that nobody could get on shore to bury him before the 14th of December; and the cold was then so intense that many of the men got frostbites on the nose and the cheeks when they met the wind with uncovered face.

On the 20th of December, the weather was fine and mild, so that the whole crew was on shore. A part of them went shooting, so that we might have some fresh meat for the approaching Christmas Holy Days; another part occupied themselves with getting wood and burning charcoal. In the evening, the men who had been out shooting returned and brought a number of ptarmigan and hare.

On the 22nd of December, we had a sharp frost. I had a Rostock barrel filled with water; and, in the morning, when they loosened the hoops of the barrel, it was frozen quite to the bottom, and was all ice.

On the 24th of December, which was Christmas Eve, I gave the men wine and strong beer, which they had to boil afresh, for it was frozen to the bottom; so they had quite as much as they could stand, and were very jolly, but no one offended another with as much as a word.

The Holy Christmas Day we all celebrated and observed solemnly, as a Christian's duty is. We had a sermon and Mass; and, after the sermon, we gave the priest an offertory, according to ancient custom, each in proportion to his means. There was not much money among the men, but they gave what they had; some of them gave white fox-skins, so that the priest got enough wherewith to line a coat. However, sufficiently long life to wear it was not granted to him.

During all the Holy Days, the weather was rather mild; and, in order that the time might not hang on hand, the men practised all kinds of games; and whoever could imagine the most amusement was the most popular. The crew, most of whom were, at that time, in good health, consequently had all sorts of larks and pastimes; and thus we spent the Holy Days with the merriment that was got up.

Anno Domini 1620

JANUARY 1st. On New Year's Day, there was a tremendously sharp frost, and I ordered a couple of pints of wine to every bowl to be given the people, over and above their daily allowance, in order that they might keep themselves in good spirits. We had quite clear sunshine on that day; and we always had the hardest frost with a North-West wind. During these days, we had the sharpest frost that we had yet experienced during the whole winter; and at the time we suffered more severely from that terrible frost than from anything else.

On the 8th of January, and all the preceding days, the fearfully hard frost continued, with a North-West wind and clear sunshine. On that day, one of my sailors died.

On the 10th of January, the priest, Mr. Rasmus Jensen, and the surgeon, M. Casper Caspersen, took to their beds having for some time felt very unwell; and, after that time, violent sickness commenced amongst the men, which day by day prevailed more and more. The illness which then raged was very peculiar, and the sick were generally attacked by dysentery about three weeks before they died. On the same day, my head cook died.

January 18th. On all these days, the weather was as mild as it ever could be here in Denmark at that time of the year; and all the men who were still in health were in the forest, each about his business, but principally shooting, in order to get some ptarmigan for the sick.

On the 21st of January, it was fine clear weather and sunshine; and, on that date, thirteen of us were down with sickness. Then, as I had often done before, I asked the surgeon, M. Casper Caspersen aforesaid, who was also lying mortally ill, whether he knew of any good remedy that might be found in his chest and which might serve for the recovery or comfort of the crew, as well as of himself, requesting him to inform me of it. To this he answered that he had already used as many remedies as he had with him to the best of his ability and as seemed to him advisable, and that, if God would not help, he could not employ any further remedy at all that would be useful for recovery.

On the 23rd of January, died one of my two mates, Hans Brock by name, who had been ill, in and out of bed, for nearly five months. On the same day, it was fine weather and beautiful sunshine; and the priest sat up in his berth and gave the people a sermon, which sermon was the last he delivered in this world.

The harbor where Munck is thought to have spent the winter is at the mouth of Churchill River, on the southwest shore of Hudson Bay. He moored his ships on the western bank, probably in the area marked as stony flats.

On the 25th of January, when I had the body of my mate, the before-mentioned Hans Brock, buried, I ordered two falconets to be discharged, which was the last honour that I could show him at that time. But the trunnion burst off both falconets, and the man who fired them very nearly lost both his legs, so very brittle had the iron become on account of the sharp and severe frost.

On the 27th of January, died Jens Helsing, seaman. On the same day my lieutenant, the well-born Mauritz Stygge, took to his bed for good, after having been ailing some time.

Item: on the same day, the men saw the tracks of five reindeer which had been chased by a wolf, of which the footprints could also be seen; wherefore, I sent a party of the men in order to trace

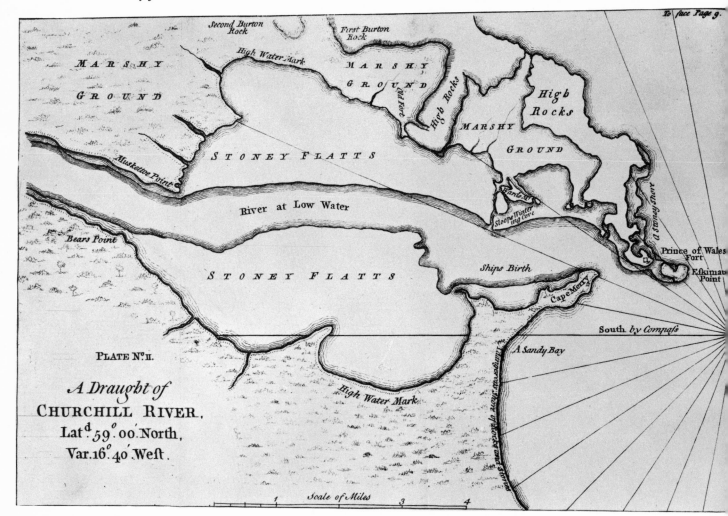

PLATE Nº. II.

A Draught of
CHURCHILL RIVER,
Lat.d 59º.oo.North,
Var.16º.40.Weſt.

Jens Munck

the said deer and wolf, hoping to obtain some of them. But, on account of a great fall of snow which overtook the men, they could not trace the said animals further, and returned without catching any.

On the 28th of January, the cold was so severe that a tin pot with some water in it, which the boy had forgotten in the cabin, had burst in the night by the frost; so that I do not know in what kind of vessels any precious waters may be preserved on voyages to such cold seas, as tin cannot stand.

On the 2nd of February, the frost was very hard. The men who were on shore obtained two ptarmigan, which were very welcome for the use of the sick.

On the 5th of February, a seaman, named Laurids Bergen, died. On the same day, I again sent to the surgeon, the before-mentioned M. Casper Caspersen, with an urgent request that, for God's sake, he would do his utmost, if he knew of any remedy or good advice; or else that, inasmuch as he was himself very ill and weak, he would let me know what medicine or remedy I could use in any way for the benefit of the crew; to which he answered, as before, that, if God would not help, he could not render any advice or assistance at all.

On the 6th of February, I went with three men to the opening by which we had entered, to see how matters stood with the ice in the sea; but, at that time, we could not see any open water, and in the evening we returned to the ship.

February 10th. During these days, the weather was rather mild, but there was much sickness and weakness amongst the crew. Two of them died on this day, after having been on their sick-bed for a very long time.

On the 12th of February, we caught two ptarmigan, which were very welcome for the use of the sick.

On the 13th of February, I ordered for each person at each meal in the day one-third of a pint of wine, and in the morning a whole measure of whisky, beyond the ordinary allowance.

February 16th. During all these days, there was nothing but sickness and weakness; and every day the number of the sick was continually increased, so that, on this day, there were only seven persons in health that could fetch wood and water, and do whatever work there was to be done on board. On the same day, died a seaman who had been ill the whole voyage; and one may truly say he was as dirty in his habits as an untrained beast.

On the 17th of February, one of my men, Rasmus Kiöbenhauffn, died; and, of the crew, there had then already died twenty persons. On that day, we got a hare, which was very welcome.

On the 20th of February, in the evening, died the priest, Mr. Rasmus Jensen aforesaid, who had been ill and had kept his bed a long time.

February 25th. During all these days, nothing particular has happened, except that the lieutenant's servant, Claus by name, who had been ill, died. In this last night, the frost has broken the bottom of a kettle which was used for melting snow in the daytime, a little water having been forgotten in it the evening before.

On the 29th of February, the frost was so severe that nobody could get on shore to fetch water or wood; and that day the cook was obliged to take for fuel whatever he could find. Towards evening, however, I got a man on shore to fetch wood. On that same day, I was obliged to mind the cabin myself: otherwise we should have got nothing to eat all day, because my servant had then also fallen ill and taken to his bed altogether.

On the 1st of March, died Jens Borringholm and Hans Skudenes; and, the sickness having now prevailed so far that nearly all of the crew lay sick, we had great difficulty in getting the dead buried.

On the 4th of March, the weather was mild, and we caught five ptarmigan in the open country, which were very welcome to us. I ordered broth to be made of them, and had that distributed amongst the sick; but, of the meat, they could eat nothing, because of their mouths being badly affected inside with scurvy.

53

On the 8th of March, died Oluf Boye, who had been ill nearly nine weeks, and his body was at once buried.

On the 9th of March, died Anders, the cooper, who had lain sick since Christmas, and his body was at once buried.

On the 11th of March, the sun entered Aries; it was then the Spring Equinox, night and day being equally long. In those quarters, the sun rose in the East-South-East, and set in the West-North-West at 7 o'clock in the evening; but it was not really more than six o'clock on account of the variation. On the same day, the weather was fine and mild, and I had all the snow thrown off the deck of the ship and had it nicely cleaned. At that time, I had but few to choose between that could do any work.

March 21st. During all these days, the weather was changeable. Sometimes it was fine and clear; at other times, sharp and severe, so that nothing particular can be recorded on that score. But, as regards the crew, the most part of them were, alas, down with illness, and it was very miserable and melancholy either to hear or see them. On that same day, died the surgeon, M. Casper, before-mentioned, and Povel Pedersen, who had both been ill almost since Christmas. Now and afterwards, the sickness raged more violently every day, so that we who were still left suffered great trouble before we could get the dead buried.

March 24th. All these days the weather was fine and mild, without frost; and we hoped now that, after this day, the weather would become favourable. One of the men, who got on shore and climbed a high rock, saw open water outside the inlet, which filled us with confident expectations.

On the 25th of March, died the skipper, Jan Ollufsen, who had been ill in bed for 19 weeks. That same day, the weather was fine, and I was ashore myself and collected *Tydebaer* (as they are called in Norway) where the snow had melted off. They were as fresh in such places as if it had been in the autumn; but one had to be careful to gather them at once: because otherwise they withered speedily.

On the 26th of March, it was also fine weather. I was on shore and gathered a quantity of berries, which I distributed amongst the men. They were very welcome, and did not disagree with them.

On the 27th of March, I looked over the surgeon's chest and examined its contents in detail, because, having no longer any surgeon, I had now to do the best I could myself. But it was a great neglect and mistake that there was not some little list, supplied by the physicians, indicating what those various medicaments were good for, and how they were to be used. I am also certain, and would venture to stake my life on it, that there were many kinds of medicaments in that surgeon's chest which the surgeon I had did not know: much less did he know for what purpose, and in what way, they were to be employed; because all the names were written in Latin, of which he had not forgotten much in his lifetime; but, whenever he was going to examine any bottle or box, the priest had to read the description out for him.

March 29th. All these days, the weather was rather mild. On the same day, died Ismael Abrahamsen and Christen Gregersen, whose dead bodies also were buried on the same day, according to our opportunity and ability at that time.

On the 30th of March, there was a sharp frost. On that day, died Suend Arffuedsen, carpenter; and at this time commenced my greatest sorrow and misery, and I was then like a wild and lonely bird. I was now obliged myself to run about in the ship, to give drink to the sick, to boil drink for them, and get for them what I thought might be good for them, to which I was not accustomed, and of which I had but little knowledge.

On the 31st of March, died my second mate, Johan Petterson, who had been ill in bed a long time.

On the 1st of April, died my late nephew, Erich Munck, and his and Johan Petterson's dead bodies were placed together in one grave.

Jens Munck

On the 3rd of April, it was a fearfully sharp frost, so that none of us could uncover himself for cold. Nor had I now anybody to command, for they were all lying under the hand of God, so that there was great misery and sorrow. On the same day, died Iffuer Alsing.

On the 4th of April, the weather was so cold and severe that it was entirely impossible for anyone to get on shore and dig a grave wherein to bury the dead bodies which were in the ship.

On the 5th of April, died Christoffer Opslöe and Rasmus Clemendsen, my chief gunner and his mate. On the same day, towards evening, died my boatswain, Lauritz Hansen by name; and the number of men in health was now so small that we were scarcely able to bury the bodies of the dead.

On the 8th of April, died Villom Gordon, my chief mate, who had long been ill, in and out of bed. On the same day, towards evening, died Anders Sodens, and his dead body and that of the above-mentioned Villom Gordon were buried together in one grave, which we who then were alive could only manage with great difficulty, on account of the miserable weakness that was upon us, in consequence of which, not one of us was well or strong enough to go into the forest to fetch wood and fuel; and we were obliged, during those days, to collect everything that was in the ship and would serve for fuel; when that was consumed, we were obliged to take our shallop for fuel.

On April the 10th, died the honourable and well-born gentleman Mauritz Stygge, my lieutenant, who had long been ill in bed; and I took some of my own linen, wherein to wrap his body as well as I could. It was with great difficulty that I got a coffin made for him.

On the 12th of April, we had fine sunshine and some rain, which had not fallen in that locality for seven months. On the same day, we carried the lieutenant's body on shore, and buried it properly, according to our ability at that time.

On the 13th of April, I took a bath in a wine-cask, which I had caused to be prepared for the purpose; and I utilized for this purpose all the kinds of herbs which we found in the surgeon's chest and thought serviceable. After that, my men likewise had a bath, as many of them as could move about and were not too weak; which bath (thanks be to God) did us much good, myself in particular.

On the 14th of April, there was a sharp frost. On that day, only four, besides myself, had strength enough to sit up in the berth and listen to the homily for Good Friday.

The 16th of April was Easter Day. Then died Anders Oroust and Jens, the cooper, who had been ill and in bed a long time; and, as the weather was fairly mild, I got their bodies buried. On the same day, I promoted my captain of the hold to be skipper, although he was ill, in order that he might assist me somewhat, as far as his strength allowed, because I was myself then quite miserable and abandoned by all the world, as everybody may imagine.

In the night following, died Hans Bendtsen.

On the 17th of April, died my servant, Olluff Andersen, who, during seven years, had served me faithfully and well.

On the 19th of April, died Peder Amundsen, who had been long ill and was quite wasted away.

On the 20th of April, we had fine sunshine, with an easterly wind. On this day, we got three ptarmigan, of which we were very glad.

On the 21st of April, the sunshine was beautiful; wherefore some of the sick crawled forth from their berths in order to warm themselves by the sun. But as they were so very weak, some of them swooned, so that it did not do them any good; and I had enough to do before I got them back again, each to his berth. On the same day, towards evening, we obtained two *Birckhöns*, of which we stood in great need in order to get something fresh for our comfort; which was due to God's special providence, because the sick could not eat any of the salted meat, but only broth of such fresh meat as we obtained.

On the 22nd of April, in the afternoon, I had a bath prepared in which we all, as many as were strong enough to move, bathed, and it did us good.

On the 24th of April, died Olluff Sundmoer, who was mate to the captain of the hold.

On the 25th of April, the wild geese began to arrive: at which we were delighted, hoping that the summer would now soon come; but, in this expectation, we were disappointed, for the cold lasted on much longer.

On the 27th of April, there was a sharp frost at night and a southerly wind. We felt the cold weather of these days more acutely than any other, and it caused us much hurt and weakness. On the same day, died Halffword Brönnie, who had lain ill more than two months; and it was with great difficulty that I got his body buried.

On the 28th of April, died Morten Nielsen, butler, and Thoer Thönsberg; and it was with great trouble that we four persons who were still able to move about a little managed to bury them.

May 3rd and 4th. During all these days, not a man left his berth save myself and the undercook, who still could do a little. On the last of the days mentioned, died Anders Marstrand and Morten Marstrand, boatswain's mate, who had both long been ill.

On the 6th of May, Johan Watzen, the English mate, who was the fourth mate I had, died. The bodies of the last-mentioned dead were left some days, because the cold was so sharp and severe that none of us three poor men who still had a little strength left, could get them buried.

On the 7th of May, the weather became milder, and we managed to bury the dead; but, on account of our extreme weakness, it was so difficult for us that we could not carry the dead bodies to their burial in any other way than by dragging them on a little sledge which had been used in the winter for the transport of wood.

May 10th. These foregoing days, we had very severe cold and frost, which greatly weakened and hindered us; but, on this day, the weather was fine and mild, and great numbers of geese arrived; we got one of them, which sufficed us for two meals. We were, at that time, eleven persons alive, counting the sick.

On the 11th of May, it was very cold, so that we all remained quietly in our berths that day; because, in our extreme weakness, we could not stand any cold, our limbs being paralyzed and, as it were, crushed by the cold.

On the 12th of May, died Jens Jorgensen, carpenter, and Suend Marstrand; and God knows what misery we suffered before we got their bodies buried. These were the last that were buried in the ground.

On the 16th day of May, it was very cold indeed. Then died the skipper, Jens Hendrichsen; and his body had to remain unburied.

On the 19th of May, died Erich Hansen Li, who, throughout the voyage, had been very industrious and willing, and had neither offended anyone nor deserved any punishment. He had dug many graves for others, but now there was nobody that could dig his, and his body had to remain unburied.

On the 20th of May, the weather was fine and mild and the wind southerly. It was a great grief to us that, whilst God gave such abundance of various kinds of birds, none of us was strong enough to go into the country and shoot some of them.

On the 21st of May, we had beautiful clear sunshine; and I and three others, though with great difficulty, went on shore, where we made a fire, and anointed our joints with bear's grease. In the evening, I and one other went on board again.

On the 22nd of May, the sunshine was as fine and warm as anyone could wish from God; and, by Divine Providence, a goose, which, three or four days before, had had a leg shot off, came near to the ship. We caught and cooked it, and we had food for two days off it.

May 28th. During these days, there was nothing particular to write about, except that we seven

Jens Munck

miserable persons, who were still lying there alive, looked mournfully at each other, hoping every day that the snow would thaw and the ice drift away.

As regards the symptoms and peculiarities of the illness which had fallen upon us: it was a rare and extraordinary one. Because all the limbs and joints were so miserably drawn together, with great pains in the loins, as if a thousand knives were thrust through them. The body at the same time was blue and brown, as when one gets a black eye, and the whole body was quite powerless. The mouth, also, was in a very bad and miserable

A woodcut from Munck's account, illustrating several scenes of his winter in Hudson Bay. At the lower left, crew members cut wood; at the upper right, they shoot a Polar bear. At the center, a body is buried, while beyond the moored ships the few survivors are warming themselves around a fire.

condition, as all the teeth were loose, so that we could not eat any victuals.

During these days, when we were lying in bed so altogether bad, there died Peder Nyborg, carpenter, Knud Lauritzsen Skudenes, and Jörgen, the cook's boy, all of whom remained on the steerage; for there was then nobody that could bury their bodies or throw them overboard.

On the 4th of June, which was Whit-Sunday, there remained alive only three besides myself, all lying down, unable to help one another. The stomach was ready enough and had appetite for food, but the teeth would not allow it; and not one of us had the requisite strength for going into the hold to fetch us a drink of wine. The cook's boy lay dead by my berth, and three men on the steerage; two men were on shore, and would gladly have been back on the ship, but it was impossible for them to get there, as they had not sufficient strength in their limbs to help themselves on board, so that both they and I were lying quite exhausted, as we had now for four entire days had nothing for the sustenance of the body. Accordingly, I did not now hope for anything but that God would put an end to this my misery and take me to Himself and His Kingdom; and, thinking that it would have been the last I wrote in this world, I penned a writing as follows:—

Inasmuch as I have now no more hope of life in this world, I request, for the sake of God, if any Christian men should happen to come here, that they will bury in the earth my poor body, together with the others which are found here, expecting their reward from God in Heaven: and furthermore, that this my journal may be forwarded to my most gracious Lord and King (for every word that is found herein is altogether truthful) in order that my poor wife and children may obtain some benefit from my great distress and miserable death. Herewith, good night to all the world; and my soul into the hand of God, etc.

Jens Munck

June the 8th. As I could not now any more stand the bad smell and stench from the dead bodies, which had remained in the ship for some time, I managed, as best I could, to get out of the berth (which no doubt was due to God's fatherly Providence, He being willing still to spare my life), considering that it would not matter where, or among what surroundings, I died—whether outside, amongst the others that were lying dead, or remaining in the berth. When, by the assistance of God, I had come out of the cabin, I spent that night on the deck, using the clothes of the dead. But, next day, when the two men who were on shore saw me and perceived that I was still alive—I, on my part, had thought that they were dead long ago—they came out on the ice to the ship, and assisted me in getting down from the ship to the land, together with the clothes which I threw to them; for the ship was not farther from the shore than about twelve or fourteen fathoms. For some time, we had our dwelling on shore under a bush, and there we made a fire in the daytime. Later on, we crawled about everywhere near, wherever we saw the least green growing out of the ground, which we dug up and sucked the main root thereof. This benefited us, and, as the warmth now commenced to increase nicely, we began to recover.

While we thus continued on shore, the sailmaker, who before had been extremely weak, died in the ship.

June 18th. When the ice drifted away from the ship, we got a net for catching flounders out of the sloop; and, when the ebb had run out one quarter, we went out dryshod and set it. When the flood returned, God gave us six large trout, which I cooked myself, while the two others went on board *Lamprenen* to fetch wine, which we had not tasted for a long time, none of us having had an appetite for it.

As we now thus every day got fresh fish which was well cooked, it comforted us much, although we could not eat any of the fish, but only the broth, with which we drank wine, so that by degrees we

Jens Munck

recovered somewhat. At last, we got a gun on shore and shot birds, from which we obtained much refreshment; so that, day by day, we got stronger and fairly well in health.

June 26th. In the name of Jesus, and after prayer and supplication to God for good fortune and counsel, we now set to work to bring *Lamprenen* alongside *Enhiörningen*, and worked as diligently

A rough map from Munck's book, showing the extent of his explorations. North is at the bottom. Among the identifiable places are Cape Farewell at the southern tip of Greenland, Davis Strait (Fretum Reij), Hudson Strait (Fretum Cristiano), and Hudson Bay (Novum Mare Cristian).

The winter haven is at the upper right.

as we could in getting sails ready for use. But herein we encountered a great difficulty and much anxiety, because *Lamprenen* stood high on the shore, having been carried up by the winter's flood. We were consequently obliged first to unload all that was in her, and then to look out for a high spring tide in order to haul her out. In this we succeeded, and brought her alongside *Enhiörningen*. When we got on board *Enhiörningen*, we were obliged first of all to throw overboard the dead bodies, which were then quite decomposed, as we could not move about or do anything there for bad smell and stench, and yet were under the necessity of taking out of *Enhiörningen* and placing on board *Lamprenen* victuals and other necessaries for our use in crossing the sea, as far as we three persons could manage.

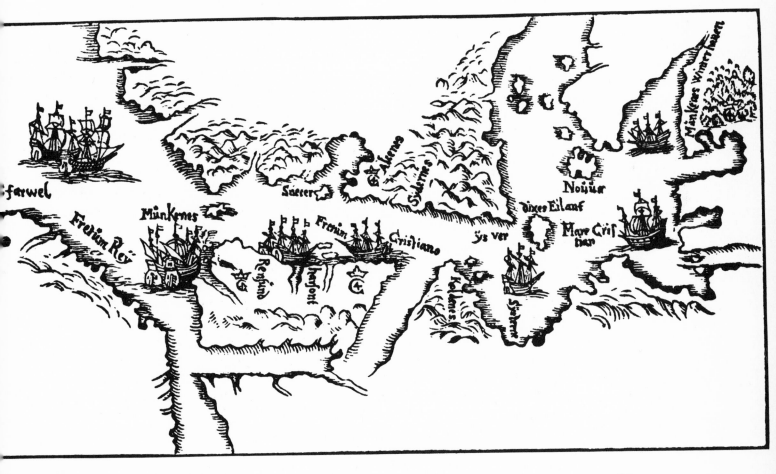

ON the 16th day of July, which was Sunday, in the afternoon, we set sail from there in the name of God. At that time, it was as warm in that country as it might have been in Denmark, and the cloud-berries were in bud. There was such a quantity of gnats that in calm weather they were unbearable. A quantity of rain also fell every day at this time of the year. Before setting out from there, I drilled two or three holes in *Enhiorningen*, in order that the water which might be in the ship might remain while the ebb was half out, so that the ship should always remain firm on the ground, whatever ice might come. And I have called the same harbour after myself, Jens Munckes Bay.

On the 17th of July, towards evening, I met much ice, and I stood off and on in front of the ice; but, in the course of the night, the weather being calm and misty, we stuck firm in the ice. I then let go the boat of *Enhiorningen*, which I had taken in tow for the purpose of having it for use if I should come near to land anywhere.

On the 20th of July, we were altogether drifting with the ice, when a large white bear came close to the ship. When he saw us, he took to flight across the ice and through the water, followed by a large dog I had with me, which strayed from the vessel in consequence, and never returned, though a couple of days after we could still hear him howl. I guessed that we were then about 40 miles from land.

On the 22nd of July, there was a severe gale, so that the ship drifted with great speed; and, each time it struck against the ice, it was as if it had struck against a rock; at that time, the ice broke my rudder; and, if I had not succeeded in throwing a grapnel on to a large mass of ice, by which I could turn the ship, so as to prevent her from drifting too fast, both the ship and we would have been lost that day.

On the 24th and the 25th of July, we continued drifting in the ice, made fast to an iceberg in order that the ship should not drift so fast and suffer too much damage.

On the 26th of July, we got clear of the ice. I then tried an easterly direction, between the ice and the southern land, and found sandy bottom in 38 fathoms, and then kept beating to and fro; but I did not succeed in getting through that way.

On the 27th of July, in the afternoon, I again fell in with the boat of *Enhiorningen*, which I was obliged to let go ten days before, when first I was caught in the ice.

On the 28th of July, I kept tacking between the ice and the land, from 10 and 15 fathoms back to the ice again in 45, 46, and 48 fathoms; and then I came to the conclusion that it was vain to hope to get past the ice on the southern side.

On the 30th of July, I became again fixed in the ice, the fog being so thick that it was difficult to exercise sufficient vigilance.

On the 1st of August, I got free of the ice again and sailed North-West; and, in the course of the day, the wind became so high that I took in the foresail and let her drift with one sail.

On the 5th of August, the ice came against me so strongly in the night that I was obliged to come into 12 fathoms before I could double that strip of ice; and it is to be noted that the ice drifts, following the direction of the shore, principally towards the South.

On the 6th of August, I came again into deep water in 45 fathoms, and then steered East-North-East, without observing any ice.

On the 13th of August, in the morning early, I arrived off the North-East point of *Digses Eyland*, where much ice was encountered near the land. Towards the South, this land is low and flat, and the Eastern point is in 63 degrees. For a night and a day, we stood off and on, on account of much ice meeting us, which we could not get through.

On the 15th of August, I found already much

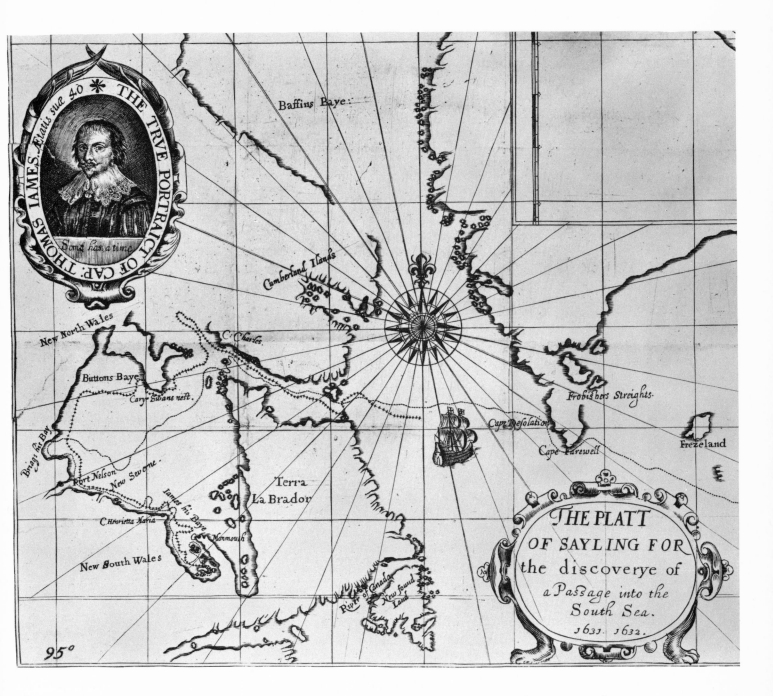

The chart of Thomas James, who explored Hudson Bay about a decade after Munck,
indicates more clearly than Munck's map the extent of geographical knowledge during this period.
Churchill River flows into Hudson Bay not far east of Longitude 95°, north of Port Nelson.

ice in that channel between the lands, though scattered, so that it was nothing but "luff on" and "hold firm the grapnel." Much snow fell, and the wild geese commenced briskly to fly south again.

August 16th. I found myself under the northern coast of *Fretum Christian*, or Huttsom Strait, and then shaped my course East by South, which was South-East-by-East according to a true course.

On the 23rd of August, our latitude was 58 degrees and 44 minutes. On the same day, towards evening, the wind fell off, fortunately enough, because I was obliged to take up and woold my pump, which did not work properly.

On the 29th of August, we got a good North-West wind again, and our course was East-by-North; but the wind shifted to North with a gale, so that we had to take in all our sails, and the pump did not forget us.

On the 31st of August, we set sail again, but only the small mainsail; and we had nothing but tempest and bad weather.

September 1st. Before a wind which could move men.

September 2nd and 3rd. Again storm and tempest from the South-East. Towards evening, we were obliged to take in the sails altogether and to lie-to, working the pump.

On the 4th of September, we had tremendous rain and wind, amounting to a gale, and we could not at all leave the pump. Towards the evening, the wind commenced to be more favourable; and, as we were quite exhausted with pumping, we drifted the whole night without sails, in order to get some rest, as far as the pump would allow of it.

On the 9th, 10th, and 11th of September, we had all kinds of wind and foggy weather; but, in the evening, towards night, a gale sprang up, and our foresail was torn from the bolt-rope, so that we three men had plenty to do to get it in, and then the ship was half full of water.

September 12th. In the course of the night, the wind shifted to the West and blew hard; our topsail-sheet was blown to pieces, the topmast-stay broken asunder, and the great parrel too; so that it was very anxious work for us three.

On the 13th of September, I conjectured ourselves to be in the longitude of Hethland; and we then descried a ship, to which at last we approached so near that we could speak to the people on board; and I requested them to assist me; but, though I got alongside him twice, he could not help me, because the wind was too high.

On the 20th of September, we saw Norway.

On the 21st of September, we came to harbour South of Allen in a flying gale, not knowing the locality. When I had come inside the rocky islands into a large fjord, I could find no anchorage, and was obliged all day to beat to and fro inside the rocks, because I had only half an anchor. Towards evening, when I saw that nobody came out, I steered into a bay, where I dropped that half of an anchor, and thus remained, without being moored, as I had no boat wherewith to carry a hawser on shore. Late in the evening, a peasant came there by accident; and I was obliged to threaten him with a gun to make him come and assist me in getting a hawser on shore. In the morning, I at once proceeded in the same boat to His Majesty's bailiff in Sundfiord, and requested him to procure fresh victuals and men to run the ship into Bergen.

As I now had seen the ship safe, and had returned into a Christian country, we poor men could not hold our tears for great joy, and thanked God that He had graciously granted us this happiness.

Adventure 6

The Voyage of the Mayflower

from Of Plimoth Plantation, by William Bradford

On September 17, 1620, a small English merchantman "of burden about 9 score," or 180 tons, and barely ninety feet long, set off across the Atlantic to the New World—so unremarkable and plebeian a vessel that no special record remains of her. She carried a crew of twenty-five and one hundred two passengers, together with all the household effects of the latter and enough provisions to last crew and passengers until the following spring. Their departure had been delayed by two false starts of a second ship that was to have accompanied the first; many of the original "goodly company" decided not to bear "the brunt of this hard adventure" and stayed behind. It was past the safe sailing season, and the Atlantic was already rough from autumn storms, but Captain Christopher Jones was an experienced sailor, and while he knew that the crossing would be difficult, and that the ship was old and somewhat leaky, he had no doubt of her ability to survive.

The ship was, of course, the *Mayflower*, and the passengers the Protestant "Separatists" known as Pilgrims. What we know of the *Mayflower* and her voyage we learn chiefly from William Bradford, a Yorkshireman, thirty years old at the time, who later was the second governor of the Pilgrims' settlement and its chief chronicler, in his immortal book *Of Plimoth Plantation*.

Most of the information available about this little ship has been gathered by such experts as R. C. Anderson and William A. Baker, through whose researches the famous replica, now at Plymouth, was built. It is generally supposed that she was a three-masted cargo ship with two and a half decks, in the style of the day, "sufficient to yield shelter and lodging for men and mariners," as Walter Raleigh put it, "and one low cabin for the captain." The half-deck took up most of the area from the mainmast to the stern, and the afterdeck was raised to provide more headroom in the cabin. On this voyage the captain apparently gave up his quarters to some of his numerous passengers and bunked with the other officers. There was also a square forecastle forward, which housed most of the crew. The passengers slung their hammocks in every available space of the 'tween-decks, and the close, uncomfortable confines during a three-month voyage can better be imagined than described. Long gratings over the main hatch let in some light and air, but also a good deal of rain and sea water in heavy weather.

With her high superstructure and odd beaked bow, the *Mayflower* in the open sea would have been very unwieldy by modern standards. Yet her rugged oak hull and heavy masts and yards made her a staunch craft. We must remember that ships of this kind could and did navigate in virtually every ocean of the world.

After three months on the ocean the Pilgrims expected to land in Northern Virginia, as they called it — a loose term by which they meant the area around the Hudson River. Instead they made a landfall at Cape Cod, and were appalled by the desolation of the New England coast in winter. They ordered Captain Jones to sail further south, but the grim aspect of the Nantucket shoals forced them back, and finally they settled upon a haven in Cape Cod Bay, which they called "New Plimouth."

Writing "with singular regard to the simple truth in all things," Bradford did more than record the experiences of this small religious community. He commemorated, as well, the courage, fortitude, and the endurance of the many settlers of these times who gave up their homes to make their hard, often dangerous way to a new land.

The rocky coast of New England.

"So they committed themselves to the will of God, and resolved to proceed"

EPT 6. These troubles being blown over, and now all being together in one ship, they put to sea again with a fair wind, which continued several days together, which was some encouragement to them. Yet, according to the usual manner, many were afflicted with sea-sickness. And I may not omit here a special work of God's providence. There was a proud and very profane young man, one of the seamen, of a lusty, able body, which made him the more haughty; who would always be condemning the poor people in their sickness, and cursing them daily with grievous execrations. He did not forget to tell them that he hoped to help to cast half of them overboard before they came to their journey's end, and to make merry with what they had; and if he were by any gently reproved, he would curse and swear most bitterly. But before they had crossed the ocean halfway it pleased God to smite this young man with a grievous disease, of which he died in a desperate manner, and so was himself the first that was thrown overboard. Thus, his curses came to light on his own head; and it was an astonishment to all his fellows, for they noted it to be the just hand of God upon him.

After they had enjoyed fair winds and weather for a season, they encountered cross winds many times, and met with many fierce storms, with which the ship was sorely shaken, and her upper works made very leaky. One of the main beams in the midship portion was bowed and cracked, which put them in some fear that the ship could not be able to perform the voyage. So some of the leaders of the company, perceiving the mariners to fear the continuing strength of the ship (as appeared by their mutterings), they entered into serious consultation with the master and other officers of the ship, to consider the danger while in time, and whether to return to England; rather to return than to cast themselves into a desperate and inevitable peril. And truly there was great distraction and difference of opinion amongst the mariners themselves. Gladly would they do what could be done for their wages' sake (being now halfway across the ocean). Yet, and on the other hand, they were loath to hazard their lives too desperately. But in examining of all opinions, the master and others affirmed they knew the ship to be strong and firm below the water line. As for the buckling of the main beam, there was a great iron screw the passengers had brought out of Holland, which would raise the beam into its place; which being done, the carpenter and master affirmed that with a post put under it, set firm in the lower deck, and otherwise bound, he would make it sufficient. And as for the decks and upper works, they would caulk them as well as they could, and though with the working of the ship they would not long keep tight, yet there would otherwise be no great danger, if they did not overpress her with sails. So they committed themselves to the will of God, and resolved to proceed.

In sundry of these storms the winds were so fierce, and the seas so high, as they could not bear a knot of sail, but were forced to heave the ship to

65

for several days together. And in one of them, as they thus lay to, in a mighty storm, a lusty young man (called John Howland) coming upon some occasion above the gratings, was, with a heeling of the ship thrown into the sea; but it pleased God that he caught hold of the topsail halyards, which hung overboard, and ran out at length; yet he held his hold (though he was several fathoms under water) till he was hauled up by the same rope to the top of the water, and then with a boathook and other means got into the ship again, and his life saved. Though he was something ill with it, yet he lived many years after, and became a profitable member both in church and commonwealth. In all this voyage there died but one of the passengers, which was William Butten, a youth, servant to Samuel Fuller, when they drew near the coast.

But to omit other things (that I may be brief), after long beating at sea they fell with that land which is called Cape Cod; the which being made and certainly known to be it, they were not a little joyful. After some deliberation, held amongst themselves and with the master of the ship, they tacked about and resolved to stand for the southward (the wind and weather being fair) to find some place about Hudson's river for their habitation. But after they had sailed that course about half the day, they fell amongst dangerous shoals and roaring breakers, and they were so much entangled therewith that they conceived themselves in great danger; and the wind dropping away from them withal, they resolved to bear up again for the Cape, and thought themselves happy to get out of those dangers before night overtook them, as by God's good providence they did. And the next day they got into the Cape harbor where they rode in safety. A word or two by the way of this cape; it was thus first named by Captain Gosnold and his company, Anno 1602, and after by Captain Smith was called Cape James; but it retains the former name amongst

A small ship very like the Mayflower, in an early seventeenth century engraving.

The famous replica Mayflower II.

NEW ENGLAND

The most remarqueable parts thus named.
by the high and mighty Prince CHARLES,
Prince of great Britaine

Captain John Smith's famous map of New England may have given Plymouth its name. There were no settlements but Indian villages when he surveyed the coast in 1614, and it is said that the genteel English names on this 1616 map were provided by the Prince of Wales, later Charles I. Plymouth is clearly shown, four years before the Pilgrims' landing, and it may have been this, as well as the fact that Plymouth, England, was their port of departure, that led them to adopt the name.

William Bradford

seamen. Also that point which first showed those dangerous shoals unto them, they called Point Care, and Tucker's Terror; but the French and Dutch to this day call it Malabar, by reason of those perilous shoals, and the losses they have suffered there.

Being thus arrived in a good harbor and brought safe to land, they fell upon their knees and blessed the God of heaven, who had brought them over the vast and furious ocean, and delivered them from all the perils and miseries thereof, again to set their feet on the firm and stable earth, their proper element. And no marvel if they were thus joyful, seeing wise Seneca was so affected with sailing a few miles on the coast of his own Italy; as he affirmed, that he had rather remain twenty years on his way by land, than pass by sea to any place in a short time; so tedious and dreadful was the same unto him.

Ships like the Mayflower weren't very big, and were a little ungainly, but they could sail in almost every wind and weather over most oceans of the world.

But here I cannot but stay and make a pause, and stand half amazed at this poor people's present condition; and so I think will the reader, too, when he well considers the same. Being thus passed the vast ocean, and a sea of troubles before in their preparation (as may be remembered by that which went before), they had now no friends to welcome them, nor inns to entertain or refresh their weather-beaten bodies, no houses or much less towns to repair to, to seek for succor. It is recorded in Scripture as a mercy to the Apostle and his shipwrecked company, that the barbarians showed them no small kindness in refreshing them, but these savage barbarians, when they met with them (as after will appear) were readier to fill their sides full of arrows than otherwise.

And for the season, it was winter, and they that know the winters of that country know them to be sharp and violent, and subject to cruel and fierce storms, dangerous to travel to known places, much more to explore an unknown coast. Besides, what could they see but a hideous and desolate wilder-

ness, full of wild beasts and wild men? And what multitudes there might be of them they knew not. Neither could they, as it were, go up to the top of Pisgah, to view from this wilderness a more goodly country to feed their hopes; for which way they turned their eyes (save upward to the heavens) they could have little solace or content in respect of any outward objects. For summer being done, all things stand upon them with a weatherbeaten face; and the whole country, full of woods and thickets, represented a wild and savage view. If they looked behind them, there was the mighty ocean which they had passed, and was now as a main barrier and gulf to separate them from all the civil parts of the world.

If it be said they had a ship to succor them, it is true; but what heard they daily from the master and company? They were told that with speed they should search for a place with their shallop, where they would be at some near distance; for the season was such as he [Captain Jones] would not stir from thence with the ship until a safe harbor was discovered by them where he might go without danger; and that victuals took up space, but he must and would keep sufficient for themselves and their return. Yea, it was muttered by some, that if they got not a place in time, they would turn them and their goods ashore and leave them. Let it also be considered what weak hopes of supply and succor they left behind them, that might bear up their minds in this sad condition and trials they were under; and they could not but be very small. It is true, indeed, the affections and love of their brethren at Leyden was cordial and entire towards them, but they had little power to help them, or themselves; and how the case stood between them and the merchants at their coming away, hath already been declared.

What could now sustain them but the spirit of God and His grace? May not and ought not the children of these fathers rightly say: Our fathers were Englishmen which came over this great ocean, and were ready to perish in this wilderness, but they cried unto the Lord, and he heard their voice, and looked on their adversity, etc. Let them therefore praise the Lord, because he is good, and his mercies endure forever. Yea, let them which have been redeemed of the Lord, show how he hath delivered them from the hand of the oppressor. When they wandered in the desert and wilderness out of the way, and found no city to dwell in, both hungry, and thirsty, their soul was overwhelmed in them. Let them confess before the Lord his loving kindness, and his wonderful works before the sons of men.

The heauens declare the glory of God, and the firmament sheweth his handy worke, *Pfal.* 19.

Adventure 7

A Pirate Voyage in the Pacific

by William Dick, from Bucaniers of America

by Alexandre-Olivier Exquemelin

IN 1679 there appeared a book by an obscure author, writing in Dutch, that made its subjects famous and began a long literary tradition. Translated into English five years later under the title *Bucaniers of America*, and the name of its author transliterated from Exquemelin to Esquemeling, it was an immediate success, presenting in gory detail the exploits of the hardened cutthroats—known euphemistically as the Brethren of the Coast—then terrorizing the sea and coasts of the Spanish Main. This collection of narratives, partly written by Exquemelin and partly compiled from the work of other adventurers, is not only famous in itself but also has the distinction of having established that durable literary figure, the Romantic Pirate.

On sober reflection it is perhaps difficult to see what is romantic about the pirates. Brave they must have been, although foolhardy seems more the apt word; their more typical traits included a powerful taste for blood, ruthless cruelty, and insatiable greed. They owed their existence to the civilized anarchy of Europe, at a time when squabbling nations tacitly connived at the depredations of "privateers" against their enemies. Henry Morgan, for instance, one of the most famous of the buccaneers and certainly one of the most successful, performed frightful barbarities upon the Spanish settlements in Central America. His customary strategy was to seize a town by impetuous attack,

demoralize the populace by indiscriminate slaughter and rape, and, after sacking whatever property was in reach, gather up the surviving inhabitants and torture from them the hiding places of their remaining valuables. Morgan was in quiet partnership with the governor of Jamaica, was knighted for his services to his country, and in his later years was himself lieutenant governor of Jamaica.

There were of course pirates and pirates, and the account that follows, from the English edition of *Bucaniers of America*, presents them in a rather different light. Not that these buccaneers were any better than the average: the author is an evident rogue and so are his companions. But there is a certain charm to these particular rascals simply in their bumbling ineptitude, for—if this author is to be believed—this was about the clumsiest and most ill-starred pack of thieves that ever put to sea. Here is a chronicle of self-generated disaster; of ships colliding or lost in the night, of ignominious routs at the hands of aroused colonials, of short rations, meager prizes, and chronic mutiny. This bland and candid narration of an almost unbroken succession of blunders and mishaps is all the more persuasive because its revelations seem entirely unintentional.

The voyage was in fact a famous one, mainly for two achievements. One was the capture of a so-called wagoner, a complete book of charts of the Pacific coasts of the Americas, containing closely guarded Spanish navigation secrets that proved of immense value to their English rivals. This prize is said to have been instrumental in getting Dick and his comrades acquitted when they were tried for piracy on their return to England. The other achievement was a feat of seamanship: these were the first English sailors to sail around Cape Horn from west to east. But even in these exploits our brave navigators ran true to type. They went around the Horn only because they completely missed the entrance to the Straits of Magellan and Le Maire Strait. And when they captured the wagoner—of the worth of which this author at least seems to have had only an inkling—they let slip by in the same ship a rich cargo of silver, thinking it was tin.

That these adventurers survived to return home at all was largely due to the hero of these pages, Captain Bartholomew Sharp, captain of one of the ships and finally of the whole expedition. It was apparently his cool courage and comparative good sense that brought the *Trinidad* safely through her remarkable ten-thousand-mile voyage around the Horn, and often in this account his is the voice of reason crying in a wilderness of fools.

At the point where this selection begins, the buccaneers had just arrived on the Pacific coast of Panama. Having been repulsed in their attack on Porto Bello, which Morgan had sacked a decade or so before, they had combined forces with some local Indians, abandoned their ships, and struck out across land, intending to besiege Morgan's other great prize, the city of Panama. They managed to take a couple of small towns on the way, including one called Santa Maria, where they established a sort of headquarters. Here they brooded upon past failures and dreamed of future victories.

"Such vast expectations"

OUR stay at Santa Maria was but short, not above the space of two days, our resolutions being to seek revenge for the huge loss, or rather disappointment, we had sustained of our vast expectations. Whereupon we all unanimously agreed to visit the South Sea, unto which we were already very near, in those canoes we had with us, which were sufficient for our number, concluding either to attack Panama and ransack it anew, as Sir Henry Morgan had done before us, or at least that we should meet with some considerable prize in that sea, where ships do navigate so quietly, and but few pirates were ever seen.

Thus, having taken in what provisions we thought necessary, we fell down the river in our canoes, taking the opportunity of the tide, and arrived the next day at the mouth of the river, in sight of the South Sea. We were a pretty considerable fleet of fisher-boats or canoes: each canoe had six, eight, or ten men on board; yea, some had fourteen and more. At Plantin Isle, which lies between the mouth of the river we came out at and Panama, we seized a Spanish bark, which had a considerable number of men aboard her—I believe above 100—but nothing else that was worth our acceptance. This vessel we took in hopes of a good prize and withal to mend ourselves in shipping, for this was now the biggest bottom we had.

By this time those at Panama had received advice of our adventures at Santa Maria, as also of our coming into the South Sea, either in quest of that city or of some other hazardous attempt. They were therefore infinitely alarmed at these news, and in great haste had thrust out to sea three or four small vessels or barks, though withal pretty well manned, which they called *la Armadilla*, or the Little Fleet, out of design to guard their coasts and oppose our attempts. Thus, the very next day one of these barks belonging to the *Armadilla* came up with us and very briskly fired at our fleet, as if they would fight us all, but soon tacked about and bid us adieu, having killed us one man and wounded six or seven more. Two days after, we met with three more of these barks of the *Armadilla* of Panama, whereof one had on board, as well as I can remember, ninety men, another had fourscore, and the third threescore and five. These small men-of-war met with us at a great disadvantage, for that morning we had sent away the Spanish bark which we had taken at Plantin Isle to seek for fresh water; and to the intent she might go the safer and peradventure bring us some good purchase by the way, we had put on board her above one hundred of our best men. So what bottoms we had left were only canoes, and in them not above two hundred good fighting men (for of the Indians we made no great account, as wanting both our arms and experience to manage them).

The *Armadilla* came up with full sail unto us, and engaged us very stoutly, thinking to take or destroy every canoe in our fleet; but we, knowing

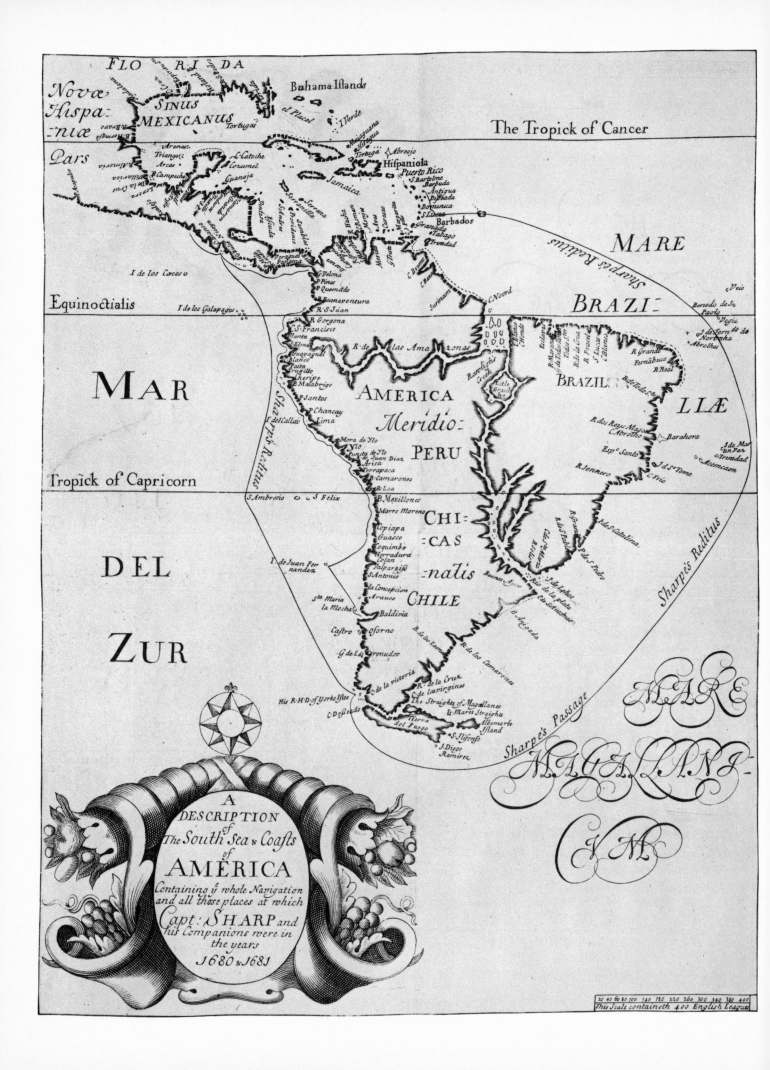

FLORIDA
Novæ Hispaniæ Pars
Bahama Islands
SINUS MEXICANUS
The Tropick of Cancer

Hispaniola
Puerto Rico
Jamaica
Barbados
Trinidad

MARE Sharpe's Reditus

Equinoctialis
I de los Cocos
I de los Galapagos
BRAZI-

MAR
R. de las Amazonas
AMERICA Meridio-
PERU
BRAZILLÆ

Tropick of Capricorn

DEL
I. de Juan Fernandez
CHI-CAS
nalis
CHILE
Sharpe's Reditus

ZUR
His R.H.D. of Yorks Isles
The Straights of Magallanes
Tierra del Fuego
Sharpe's Passage

MARE MAGALLANI-CVM

A DESCRIPTION of The South Sea & Coasts of AMERICA Containing y whole Navigation and all those places at which Capt: SHARP and his Companions were in the years 1680 & 1681

20 40 60 80 100 140 180 220 260 300 340 380 400
This Scale containeth 400 English Leagues

scarce any quarter could be expected at their hands, especially in those seas, were resolved never to surrender, and to do the utmost of our endeavor to destroy them or make them fly. Thus, after the first volleys of shot we presently encompassed one of these little men-of-war with our canoes and as desperately ran him aboard with sword and pistol in hand, causing him suddenly to surrender. Being in possession of him, we took another of their small number and forced the third to fly away towards the town of Panama with all the sail he could make. This rencounter, or engagement, though but short yet was very bloody, especially on the Spaniards' side, and sharp: for in it we had a dozen of our men killed outright and almost forty who were desperately wounded. How many the Spaniards lost or had wounded among them we could not learn, especially in the third vessel, which fought us all along very briskly and stood close to it for a good while, even after the other two were taken. We could not do otherwise than commend the courage of those Spaniards.

The *Armadilla* being destroyed, we proceeded to the road of Panama, the which we instantly blocked up with our canoes and other vessels. Here in the harbor and at the mouth thereof we took five or six vessels more—or rather ships, between great and small, but no great booty in them. Only amongst these was one, called *la Trinidad*, or the *Blessed Trinity*, which was a ship of four hundred tons, and in which we found about threescore thousand pieces of eight that were sent to pay the garrison of the town or for some other effect: the dividend of this prize amounted unto above 240 pieces of eight to each man. Yet had we good fortune in not being disappointed of this purchase, as we had been oftentimes before in other adventures; for though we had blocked up the mouth of the road and lay, as I have said, before Panama, yet this ship gave us the slip and got into the harbor in the dark of the night, both unseen and unknown to us. However, we having intelligence thereof entered the harbor when they thought themselves in

safety and had the good luck to seize and make a prize of her, though not without some small loss of men.

Both in this and other skirmishes we lost in all before Panama forty men and had about fifty more wounded, so that now our small number was almost, if not quite, reduced unto two third parts thereof. The wounded we put all into one vessel, which we appointed to be the hospital of our fleet, and the other vessels we manned as well as our number would afford to do it. After having stayed some days before Panama and blocked up the road, we weighed anchor and went unto a little island named Taboga, there to provide ourselves with several necessaries, which were at that time something scarce with us. As for the town of Panama itself, we dared not attempt it with so small a number of men, they being well provided to give us a hot reception. Only once we landed one hundred and fifty men, which were as many as we could well spare from manning and defending our fleet of canoes and ships, but found we could do no good against the town, being repulsed with some damage.

Being almost ready to raise the blockade of Panama, Captain John Croxen, or Coxen, began to vary in his resolutions, and at last openly to mutiny against the rest of the company. The effect thereof was that he departed from us and returned back with all the Indians and canoes, carrying also with him fifty of our English company and the best surgeon of the fleet, who belonged unto him, and who would not go without his instruments to work with, that is to say, the medicaments, the which we very much wanted for our wounded men. What medicines he left behind were not considerable in comparison of what he carried away, but this point we knew not until afterwards, or we should have torn in pieces the said surgeon and his master rather than have parted with those things of which we had so much necessity.

But our constant resolutions were not to go back nor return homeward until such time as we

A chart of the voyages described in this narrative,
from Bucaniers of America.

had made a diligent search into those Southern Seas and freighted, if possible, our vessels with gold, or at least as much silver as they could carry. Such vast expectations had we framed now unto ourselves in the vain ideas of our minds. Captain Croxen, who commanded in chief, being separated or departed from us, we chose in his place Captain Sawkins and Captain Sharp to lead us, and were reduced unto two hundred men, whereof many, as was said before, lay dangerously wounded in the hospital vessel.

Having therefore refitted ourselves at the island of Taboga, we sailed from thence about the middle of May, 1680, in quest of some other purchase or

A ship not unlike the Trinidad, in which Sharp cruised the whole coast of South America and sailed around Cape Horn. Principal innovations of the later seventeenth century include the topgallant sails and the third afterdeck.

William Dick

design, coasting the shore toward the northern parts of America, commonly called California. We persisted in our course the space of eight or ten days, in all which time nothing remarkable happened unto us, till at the end thereof we arrived at the isles of Quiblo, where there is a town called by the Spaniards Puebla Nova.

Here we landed to seek provisions, and by the by to plunder what we could get, but the country being alarmed since our blocking up the road of Panama, they had put themselves into an indifferent good posture of defense, and hereupon watched for our coming and were resolved to entertain us as warm as they could. Captain Sawkins, therefore, landing before the rest, as being a man of undaunted courage, and running up with a small party to some breastworks they had made before the town, was here unfortunately killed, more through his own temerity and the rashness of his conduct than any other cause. Those who followed could not possibly rescue him, as being not yet quite landed. Besides him two or three more were killed, and five or six wounded, which caused the residue of those he had led up to retreat unto the waterside as fast as they could. Thus we were beaten off from that place and got nothing but blows for our pains.

This disaster occasioned a second mutiny amongst our men: our commanders were not thought to be leaders fit enough for such great and hard enterprises. Now Captain Sharp was left in chief, and he was censured by many; the contest grew so hot and came to that degree that we divided again into parties, and about threescore and ten more of our men fell off from us, separated, and returned back overland, as Croxen and the others had done before. Others, who commanded vessels, threw up their commissions, in whose room others were placed to command their ships. Thus all things were in great distraction, and our company decreased daily, yet others held constant to their resolutions and were still determined to be buried in those seas rather than return home with-

Pirates of the seventeenth century infested the West Indies, using the islands as convenient bases for their raids on the Spanish Main. These pirates are "at home" on Santo Domingo.

out the gold they had sought for so long and through so many dangers. Our number was only of one hundred and thirty, or not quite one hundred and forty.

We sailed from Puebla Nova and steered our course for the islands called *de los Galapagos*, or in English, Tortoise Islands, from the huge number of tortoises which there are to be found. There we intended to careen our vessels and seek more provisions, but the winds proving contrary for a long while, we could not reach them and were constrained to take up for the same purpose with another little island, called Gorgona. It was towards the latter end of July before we departed from thence. Three or four days after we set out

77

we lost Captain Sharp in the dark of the night, and with him the best vessel we had, which was the *Trinity*. This loss occasioned sundry distractions in our minds, not knowing what would become of us after so many misfortunes. He was gone from us a whole fortnight or thereabouts; neither had we any hopes of finding him any more, till at last, we happening to put in at Drake's Isle to seek for provisions, he happily arrived there three days after, which caused in us infinite joy, he having the best vessel and stoutest men on board him. Yea, we had missed of him this time likewise, and perhaps forever, had we not by a misfortune of sinking our

Pirates sacking a town: like many of these illustrations from that lurid seventeenth-century bestseller, Bucaniers of America.

canoe, which was sent ashore, tarried there one day longer than we determined.

Towards the latter end of October we descried the land of Arica, having sustained beforehand for many days infinite hunger and thirst. For provisions at length grew so scarce with us that we were allowed only five ounces of meal and one pint of water to each man, the Captain himself having no more allowance than the rest. Yea, at last some were found among us who gave thirty pieces of eight for a pint of water, and very glad they were to get it, so near starving we were when we came to Arica. Here we could land no men, the sea was so big, which made us go to a port close by called He lo hè.

At this port we landed and found some provisions, especially at a sugarworks not far distant from thence. Here we refreshed and feasted ourselves pretty well for three or four days. The Spaniards came unto us with a flag of truce and promised to bring us in good store of beefs and hogs, as many as we demanded, provided we would spare their *Ingenio de azucar*, or sugarworks, and not pull it down, which we promised so to do. But two days after, these treacherous Spaniards sent 300 horsemen against us instead of bringing the cattle, with full intent to destroy us if possibly they could. We drew out our men into a plain, and at the first volley killed several of them, which made them wheel about and instantly retire, though at first they came very fierce against us. With this we retired to our vessels, knowing no more good was to be done there at that time, nor at Arica, for by this body of horse we perceived all the country was alarmed against us.

From He lo hè that day month we arrived at Coquimbo, upon which place we resolved to revenge our former affronts at Arica. Here we met with a body of 150 horse just at our landing, which always watch the bay, who instantly set upon us with great fury and made a circle about the first party of our men that were landed, thinking to make sure of our destruction and cut us all in pieces. But we stood to our arms very courageously, killed and wounded several of them, and routed them soon, having only one man wounded on our side. We followed them close at their heels into the town, which we instantly took with no loss at all. This action was performed with only fourscore men, a few more or less, and the first party that fought the horse were under forty.

When we came into the town we found it was of a considerable bigness and had no less than eight or nine churches, which made us fear there were more inhabitants than we could master, as being so few in number that it were impossible to fight our way among them should they come to a head and make any resistance. As, therefore, we met the inhabitants, we told them they must repair to the church, or churches, or else expect no quarter from them that were following us, who were many hundreds in number, for we were only the forerunners of a greater body of pirates that were at our heels. Having so done, and got several churches full of the inhabitants, we placed at each door a barrel of gunpowder with a train to it, and a man standing with a lighted match, who told them that if they offered to stir out he would presently give fire; but none offered to attempt it. So that by this means, while the inhabitants remained in that confinement, we plundered the town at our leisure.

Here another piece of treachery was put upon us by the governor of the town. After a flag of truce, and some compliments sent to and fro between us, he came to an amicable parley with our Captain and only one or two more, one on each side, where they drank very friendly together upon a hill close by the town, he keeping the fields with his horsemen and all those that were fled out of the town. There he promised to ransom the town from fire for ninety-five thousand pieces of eight, which should be sent us within a day or two. But that night or the next they contrived to fire our ship, an Indian swimming aboard under the stern with a ball of combustible matter, which he fixed there unseen to our men, so that had it not been discovered by

the stink before it burst out into a flame, we had all, both on shore and land, inevitably perished. The next day they half drowned the town by letting in many sluices of water upon us, by which acts of hostility and treachery we perceived no faith nor money more than what we had already got was to be expected from them. Thus we set fire to the town, staying as long as we could till it was all in a flame, locked up the doors of the churches, and marched out, fighting our way down to our boats, which we easily did, for they made no great opposition after the first volleys of our shot, which killed some few of them.

Most ungentle persuasion was often used to locate the hidden treasures of hapless victims. Here Henry Morgan is persuading the natives of Maracaibo.

From Coquimbo we sailed to the isles of Juan Fernandez, where we kept our Christmas, that year 1680, finding there good plenty of provisions and as much dissension among our men, who would not return home that year, as our Captain would have them do, but make a further search for gold, or golden prizes, into those seas. But the true occasion of their grudge was that Captain Sharp had got by these adventures, as it was said, almost a thousand pound, whereas many of our men were scarce worth a groat. And good reason there was for their poverty, for at the Isle of Plate, called by us Drake's Isle, and other places, they had lost all their money to their fellow buccaneers at dice, so that some had a good deal and others just nothing. Those who were thrifty men sided with Captain Sharp and were for returning home, but the others chose another commander, by name John Watling, and turned Sharp out of his commission, pretending they could do it, as being a free election. And so they might do, for they were the greatest number by far, and power may pretend to anything. This contest had like to have come to blows among us, but some prudent men moderated the matter and persuaded Captain Sharp's party to have patience for a while, at least seeing they were the fewest, and had moneys to lose, which the other party had not.

By order of our new commander, Watling, we set sail presently after the beginning of the new year 1681 from the isles of Juan Fernandez and were resolved to go and plunder Arica, both to find employment for our discontented party as being a vastly rich place, and to remember them for the shame put upon us at He lo he, or Ylo. Just as we were ready to sail, three men-of-war came upon us, one of eight, one of twelve, and the third of sixteen guns. We had not so much as one gun, for all our vessel was of four hundred ton or more. Neither had we now more than one ship, we having sunk the other upon the coast of Guayaquil, by reason we had broken her bowsprit with the stern of the *Trinity*, which had her in a tow, and could not fit her with another. These ships now being three against one, and we not able to divide them, as we endeavored to do, by running on board their admiral before the rest could come up, we thought it best to run for it. So we did, bidding them adieu in the night, and steering directly, as I have mentioned, for Arica.

We landed at Arica and fought the town with ninety-three men, which number was all we could conveniently spare. We got into the town and took several of their breastworks, yet were repulsed from the castle and afterwards beaten out of the town by the country people, who poured in upon us in huge

William Dick

The remote islands of Juan Fernandez, well off the coast of Chile, became a popular haven for buccaneers after Sharp's visit there. One later became famous as the place where Alexander Selkirk was marooned by his pirate companions to spend more than four entirely solitary years, an experience that inspired Daniel Defoe's great novel of self-reliance, Robinson Crusoe. Selkirk was rescued in 1709 by the freebooter Woodes Rogers, whose pilot was the noted buccaneer-explorer William Dampier, a former member of the Sharp expedition!

numbers, so that we were forced to retreat unto our boats, fighting our way through above one thousand men who were gathered against us. This was the hardest shock we had in all the South Sea. Captain Watling, our commander-in-chief, was here killed, through whose ill conduct, as it was thought, this misfortune happened unto us. For had he assaulted the fort in time, before the people and soldiers that ran out of the town were got into it, we had undoubtedly carried all before us. But he trifled away his time in giving quarter and taking prisoners upon the breastworks, till at last we had more prisoners than we could command. We placed some of these prisoners before the front of our men when we assaulted the castle, just as Sir Henry Morgan did the nuns and friars at Porto Bello, but the Spaniards fired as well at them as at us. In a word, we lost here forty men, nine of which were taken prisoners, being our surgeons and others while they were dressing the wounded at the hospital, which loss of our surgeons increased our damage very much. Only forty-two or forty-three were left serviceable to fight our way through so many hundred of foot and horse unto our boats, we not losing one man by the way, though several were wounded. So much did we awe them with our fuzees, and so afraid were they to break in upon us, though we were almost three miles from our boats.

Sir Henry Morgan was one of the most successful of all pirates, achieving knighthood, becoming lieutenant governor of Jamaica, and dying in bed.

Other famous buccaneers include Edward Teach, or Blackbeard, and the ferocious women pirates Anne Bonney and Mary Read.

Now Captain Sharp was chosen again, his conduct being thought safer than any other man's, and they having had trial of another leader. Our surgeons we left behind had quarter from the enemy, they being able to do good service in that country, but our wounded men were all knocked on the head, as we understood afterwards.

Having set sail from Arica, we cruised to and fro for the space of six weeks but could meet with nothing that was for our purpose. By this time provisions grew scarce again, and our men began to mutiny anew, some being for going home and others for staying longer till they had got more money. About the middle of April, 1681, our dissensions grew so high among us that above forty

more of our men deserted us to go home overland through the province of Darien, as their companions had done before. Their chief grudge was against Captain Sharp, whom they envied and would not obey; neither would we be brought to choose another commander, knowing that neither by that means we should ever be able to keep them quiet. Thus we parted with them, allowing them what was necessary for their voyage, or rather they taking it away with them. But we would not quarrel about it. Now our company and forces were extremely weakened, but our hearts as yet were good, and though we had met with many disappointments in several places, yet we hoped that at last, by some means or other, we should attain the ends of our desires, which were to enrich ourselves.

We came up with a sail at Cape Passao [Cabo Pasado], which proved to be one of the greatest adventures of this whole voyage, if not the greatest

of all, had we but known our own happy fortune and how to make good use of it. This was a ship called *el Santo Rosario*, or the *Holy Rosary*, of an indifferent big burthen, and loaded with brandy and oil, wine, and fruit, besides good store of other provisions. They fired at us first, but we came up board-to-board with them and gave them such volleys of small shot that they were soon forced to surrender, having several of their men wounded, their captain killed, and only one man more. In this ship, besides the lading abovementioned we found also almost 700 pigs of plate, but we took them to be some other metal, especially tin; and under this mistake they were slighted by us all, especially the Captain and seamen, who by no persuasions used by some few, who were for having them rummaged, could be induced to take them into our ship, as we did most of the other things. Thus we left them on board the *Rosario*, and not

knowing what to do with the bottom in that scarcity of men we were under we turned her away loose unto the sea, being very glad we had got such good belly-timber out of her and thinking little what quantity of rich metal we left behind.

One only pig of plate, out of the whole number of almost seven hundred, we took into our ship, thinking to make bullets out of it, and to this effect or what else our seamen were pleased the greatest part of it was melted or squandered away. Afterward, when we arrived at Antigua we gave the remaining part of it, which was yet about one third thereof, unto a Bristol man, who knew perfectly what it was (though he dissembled with us), brought it for England, and sold it there for seventy-five pound sterling, as he confessed himself afterward to some of our men. Thus we parted with the richest booty we had gotten in the whole voyage through our own ignorance and laziness.

Ann Bonny *and* Mary Read *convicted of Piracy Nov.ʳ 28ᵗʰ 1720 at a Court of Vice Admiralty held at* Sᵗ Jago de la Vega *in ÿ Island of Jamaica.*

In this ship the *Rosario* we took also a great book full of sea charts and maps, containing a very accurate and exact description of all the ports, soundings, creeks, rivers, capes, and coasts belonging to the South Sea, and all the navigations usually performed by the Spaniards in that ocean. This book, it seems, serves them for an entire and complete wagoner in those parts and for its novelty and curiosity was presented unto His Majesty after our return into England. It hath been since translated into English, as I hear, by His Majesty's order, but withal the printing thereof is severely prohibited, lest other nations should get into those seas and make use thereof, which is wished may be reserved only for England against its due time. We parted with the *Rosario*, and with her plate, the last day of July, 1681.

Here it was, at Cape Passao, immediately after our turning away to sea the *Rosario*, and on the first or second day of August, 1681, that we set up our resolutions to seek no farther into those seas but to come away for England round about the Strait of Magellan or by Strait Le Maire. Our chief motives for this sudden departure for England were the huge scarcity of men we had at that present, for now our whole number was reduced unto sixty-four men, whereof many were not fit to bear arms. This number, we feared, by any farther encounters might be so far lessened as scarce to be able to man our ship, at least to convey us home in safety; whereby, should we weaken it more, we might come to lose all we had got. And now we had purchased in the *Rosario* good store of provisions, especially of wine and brandy, sufficient to last, as we hoped, for such a voyage, which should we diminish upon farther adventures we knew not when we should be so well provided again. The last motive was that most of our men had gotten pretty well by this voyage and were afraid to lose by farther adventures what they had already purchased. For though some of our men had made away, or lost all their money at play, yet others were so much the richer by their losses.

Sailing east in the perpetual storms around Cape Horn

In October we had very hard weather, so that we had much ado to keep the seas. This was, if I well remember, about 50 degrees and an half of Southern Latitude. Here in this stress of winter we spied an high land, unto which we made, and came to an anchor in a good harbor, where we moved our ship to the land. Here we stayed all the remaining part of the month, which was about three weeks. Unto this place we gave the name of the Duke of York's Island, more by guess than anything else, for whether it was an island or continent we could not tell.

About the beginning of November we set forth from hence, seeking for the straits either of Magellan or Le Maire, but could find neither of them; the hardness of the weather was such that we missed of them both and were driven many degrees beyond them. Neither could we make any land but came round about such a way as peradventure never any mortals came before us; yet nothing remarkable did we see or meet withal, except hard

weather, and here and there some floats of ice of two or three leagues long. We were very nigh 60 degrees of Southern Latitude; this is all I can remember, having not any journal nor the particular observations by me, that were taken when the weather permitted.

Thus we arrived, by God's infinite mercy, in safety at the island of Barbados just at the latter end of January, 1682. Here a boat came off to us that belonged to the *Richmond* frigate. We were afraid of the said frigate, lest she should seize us for pirateering and strip us of all we had got in the whole voyage. Whereupon we stood away for the isle of Antigua but could not get leave to come into the harbor, though to obtain it we sent a present of jewels unto the governor's lady. But he would not grant it, and our jewels were returned us very civilly. Hence we resolved everyone to shift for ourselves. The ship in which we came home, which was the *Trinity*, we gave away to seven or eight of our men who had played away all their money.

Thus we all dispersed, some of our company coming for England, others going to Jamaica, Barbados, New England, Virginia, and other places.

Captain Sharp our commander, myself, and several others came for England soon after the performance of this voyage. Here several of us were put into prison and tried for our lives, at the suit of Don Pedro de Ronquillo, the Spanish ambassador, for committing piracy and robberies in the South Sea. But we were acquitted by a jury after a fair trial, they wanting witnesses to prove what they intended. Neither had they any at all against us, were it not for two or three villains of our own company who turned cat in the pan and had a spleen against Captain Sharp and others that had profited more by the voyage than they had done. One chief article against us was the taking of the *Rosario* and killing the captain thereof and another man. But it was proved the Spaniards fired at us first, and thus it was judged we ought to defend ourselves.

During the space of our imprisonment and trial several others of our company were forced to abscond and keep themselves concealed very close for fear of being taken and brought under the same indictment. Also, at Jamaica three of our company who arrived there were taken and cast into prison, and one of them was hanged, who was wheedled into an open confession of his crime. The other two stood it out and escaped, as I suppose, for want of witnesses to prove the fact against them.

Thus far I have given you an account of our adventures in the South Sea. But here you inquire of me what is become of Captain Sharp, since the time of his trial? I must tell you I could wish I had a better account to give of him than what I have at present. He wasted all his money here in good fellowship in a short while after he was set at liberty; much he spent also while he was under confinement, so that he was soon reduced low, as most of the buccaneers used to be after their voyages.

Having spent all his money he resolved to go seek for more, and that by the same means he had used formerly. Yet an order there was, either from the Privy Council or the Court of Admiralty, that no commander should carry him into those parts of the West Indies again, fearing lest he should do more mischief unto the Spaniards. As for merchant ships, they refused to carry him, fearing he would tempt the men to revolt against the masters and by this means run away with the ship to privateering, as he had done before.

Not finding, therefore, any means to get out of England, he got together a little money, and with this he bought an old boat which, as I am told, used to lie above London Bridge, for the sum of 20 pounds sterling. Into this boat he put a small quantity of butter and cheese, and a dozen or two pieces of beef. These were his provisions; his crew were only sixteen men. With this equipage he sailed down the river and came into the Downs. Hereabouts, as 'tis said, he met with a French vessel, the which he clapped aboard, seized, and made himself master thereof. Presently after, he sunk his own boat, the which he intended to carry no farther than until he could provide himself with a better bottom. Upon Romney Marsh he espied some cattle and thereupon sent some men ashore to provide what they thought fit for the present victualing of their vessel. Thus he is gone out of England, but whither, upon what design, or what adventures he has met withal since, I cannot tell you.

In the eighteenth century, more effort was made to curb piracy, and more and more buccaneers came to a bad end.

Adventure 8

The Galley Slave

from Les Memoires d'un Protestant Condamné aux Galères de France pour Cause de Religion by Jean Marteilhe

LIFE at sea can at times be hard and cruel, but the ingenuity of man can make it harder and more cruel than anything nature alone is able to inflict. As recently as the eighteenth century, it was not unusual in France and certain other Mediterranean countries to use convicted criminals in the galleys of their navies. More accurately, these poor wretches were not so much used as used up in this dreadful servitude which, by its nature, depended on the exercise of absolutely ruthless severity on its victims. Rowing such ships approached so close to the limits of human endurance that it could only be performed by slaves, under the added impetus of iron discipline and sadistic beatings. It was work that no free man would—or could—do.

Actually, by the eighteenth century galleys were nearing the end of their usefulness. With their low freeboard and shallow hulls they were strictly fair-weather ships. Furthermore, sailing ships had reached a state in which they could easily outmaneuver galleys except in a near-calm. They could only be used, in fact, in comparatively sheltered waters such as portions of the Mediterranean, or, as in this account, in the Channel and North Sea.

The slaves in the galleys of Louis XIV were a mixed crew. Some were ordinary criminals; some were bought slaves from Asia Minor and the Levant, loosely called Turks. But a sentence to the galleys was also a popular punishment for political and religious prisoners of the state. We owe what is undoubtedly the finest account of life aboard these ships to one of these religious prisoners, a French Huguenot named Jean Marteilhe. Following the revocation of the Edict of Nantes, which had given at least partial recognition and civil protection to this Protestant minority, many fled the country to escape the rising tide of persecution. Any who were caught trying to escape, however, were punished severely. Jean Marteilhe, attempting to get across the Dutch border in 1700, was captured and after a travesty trial and several months' incarceration in hideous dungeons was sentenced to lifetime servitude in the galleys. He served more than ten years—a tribute to what must have been a remarkably strong constitution—and was finally released, with other Huguenot prisoners, as a result of negotiations with the Allies following the Peace of Utrecht. After gaining his freedom, Marteilhe wrote an astonishingly detailed book about his experiences: *Memoires d'un Protestant Condamné aux Galères de France pour cause de Religion.* When he was released he was twenty-eight; when he had been put in the chain of prisoners heading toward Dunkirk, he had been only seventeen.

A chain of slaves being led aboard a galley.

88

"*Judging me to be dead, they unchained me to throw me into the sea*"

AS there may be some people who are unacquainted with the galleys, I feel it my duty to satisfy their curiosity by describing one: An ordinary galley is one hundred and fifty feet long on the keel and forty feet in beam. Her deck covers the hold, which is six feet deep at the sides and seven at the centre, for the deck is rounded and runs from one end of the vessel to the other with a foot of slope on each side from the centre to the rail. A loaded galley is very low in the water, and frequently awash, the water draining from the deck because of the camber of the planks. A *coursier*, or gangway, runs along the centre of the vessel above the highest part of the deck, forming a long box of massive planking, stopping the water which would otherwise flood the hold through the openings necessary for stepping the masts. The hatches into the hold are raised by thick coaming to the same height as the *coursier*. It may perhaps be thought that the rowers on their benches, and the rest of the crew, always have their feet in the water; but this is not so because for each bench there is what is called a *banquette*, which is removable boarding raised about a foot so that the water washing over the deck runs under it.

For the soldiers and petty officers a sort of gallery called the *bande* stretches the length of the galley on both sides. It is about two feet wide, raised to the level of the *coursier*, and runs across the outer ends of the benches. The soldiers and petty officers live here and are not able to lie down, but sit very uncomfortably on their kit-bags. The officers are not much more at their ease when the galley is at sea for, as the hold is filled with provisions or tackle, no one has room to lie down.

The hold is divided into six parts or rooms, as follows. First, the *gavon*, which is a little room under the poop, containing only a small bed for the captain. Second, the *escandolat*, where all the captain's provisions are kept, as well as his linen, money, cooking utensils, etc. Third, the *compagne*, for the liquid stores of the crew, such as beer, wine, oil, vinegar, and fresh water. Bacon, salt meat, stockfish, and cheese, etc., are also kept here, but never butter. Fourth, the *paillot* for the dry provisions of the crew, such as biscuits, pease, beans, rice, etc. Fifth, the *taverne*, a room amidships containing wine which the *comite* may sell by the pot or pint for his own profit, and which is also used to store the sails and officers' sleeping-tents. The powder magazine, which the master gunner looks after and of which only he has the key, leads off this room. Sixth, the *chambre de proue* [forepeak], for the anchor cables and other cordage, as well as for the surgeon's chest. When at sea, the sick are also lodged here, lying very uncomfortably on coils of rope; in winter, when the galley is laid up, they are accommodated in hospital on shore.

A galley has fifty rowing-benches, twenty-five on each side. They are ten feet long and are really beams half a foot thick set four feet from one another, and it is this interval which makes the bench-space. These beams are on legs which raise them to the height of rowing-thwarts, and reach from the *bandes* to the *coursier*. They are padded with flock-wool, or old sacking, in the form of little cushions covered with leather. The benches are also provided with ox hides which hang down to the *banquettes* and make the bench-spaces not unlike large boxes or coffins in which the six galley slaves are chained.

To the right and left of the vessel, outside the *bandes*, run great beams a foot thick, forming the two rails of the galley and called the *aposti*. The oars pivot on these, the blade-ends outside, and inside are the looms, which reach to the *coursier*. These oars are fifty feet long and have about thirteen feet inboard, forming very large and heavy ends to balance the thirty-seven feet outboard, for otherwise it would be impossible to row. To these large inner ends, which are too bulky to grasp, wooden handles or rings are riveted, so that each of the six rowers has his own handles.

The *coursier* is made of two thick strong walls of oak built upwards from the deck in the centre of the vessel and extending from the poop to the bow. These walls are two and a half feet apart and form an enclosure where the awning and kit-bags of the slaves are stowed. This *coursier* is covered with cross-planking, and each bench has to keep its own portion clean. When covered, the *coursier* forms a gangway down the centre line of the galley, with the rowers to right and left, and it is possible to go from the stern to the bow only by this means, though two men can scarcely walk abreast upon it without the risk of falling into the bench-spaces.

Of the two masts, the main mast, which is stepped amidships, is sixty feet long and has no topmast, shrouds, nor rope ladders by which to climb it, and the Provençal sailors go up with a simple loose rope so fast that cats could hardly equal them. This mast is quite bare, having only the halyard to attach the yard (which is twice the length of the mast) to it. The fore mast is stepped near the bow and is forty feet long and similar to the main mast, its yard being of eighty feet. While I was at Dunkirk a third mast was introduced, the mizzen, to be set up when needed at the stern of the galley, near the poop cabin, which is occupied by the senior officers. This mast is twenty feet long with a forty-foot yard, and its only purpose is to help in turning the galley. Now it is rarely used, for they later invented at Dunkirk a rudder to be hung at the bow when required; for in battle it may be necessary to turn quickly and retire—a manœuvre which a galley's great length makes difficult, especially as it enables the enemy to kill many of her crew while she is broadside or during the process of turning, which may take more than half an hour. By means of this bow-rudder and rowing astern, it is possible to retire from a fight without having to turn, and during this retreat the bow, where the guns are mounted, can be kept always towards the enemy. This manœuvre and the change

Elegant, although rather prettified engravings by Rigau

Jean Marteilhe

to rowing astern is accomplished in the blink of an eye by an order sounded on the boatswain's pipe.

Each mast has only one sail, but there are several sizes, used according to the strength of the wind. The shape of the main and fore sails is identical. When sail is to be made, the yard is lowered to the benches and the slaves bend the canvas to it; then, if the wind is not too strong, the yard is hoisted to the mast-head, the sail when set taking the shape of a pigeon's wing, for all galley sails are triangular or *lateen*. In a strong wind it would be dangerous to hoist the yard with the sail filled and, to avoid this, after it is bent to the yard it is bound round with little cords and, when hoisted, the sheet is tugged sharply so that the little cords break and the sail is instantly spread. The sailors never mount the yard to bend or unbend the sail; it is lowered every time. In battle the yards are secured by several ropes, and even by iron chains, for if a cannon shot should sever the halyard (a rope six inches thick) the yard would fall into the galley and, being large and heavy, might sink her, or would at the least injure many people.

A galley carries five pieces of bronze cannon, all at the bow. The principal one is called the *coursier-gun*, owing to the position in which it is mounted, for the *coursier* encloses it as if in a box. This gun fires a 36-pound ball and rests on a slide of strong timbers. When it is to be fired, it is loaded in its box under the *coursier* and then run forward

the construction and loading of galleys.

by side-tackles to its port-hole. On firing, it recoils as far as the fore mast, and is then in its box ready for reloading. This gun is a culverin with a long range and can do great execution upon the enemy. On each side of the *coursier* there are two other guns, a 24- and an 18-pounder. These four guns are mounted under the *rambade*, which is a deck at the bow of the galley raised about six feet above the beakhead. It is ten feet long, its width is that of the galley, about forty feet, and from it the sailors and petty officers handle the foresail. When the galley is going to board the *rambade* is the post of honour, from which the boarders leap across into the enemy ship. It is always the senior officer who commands the grenadiers and others detailed for this. These four cannon are mounted on good carriages riveted to the deck, and therefore they do not recoil when fired, as does the culverin. This artillery is always very well manned by skilled gunners.

The method of working a galley is as follows: The *premier comite* [the officer in command of the galley slaves] always remains in front of the poop, near the captain to receive his orders, and the two *sous-comites* stay on the *coursier*, one amidships and one forward. Each carries a whip which he uses with the full strength of his arm on the bare bodies of the slaves. The *premier comite*, on receiving the captain's instructions, winds a certain note or call upon a silver boatswain's pipe which hangs from

his neck by a chain of the same metal. The *sous-comites* repeat this on their pipes, and then the rowers, waiting oar in hand, move in time with so even a stroke that their fifty oars fall and enter the water all together, as if they were one. They continue this until there is occasion for a further order to be passed to them by another call on the pipe, bidding them to cease rowing. They must all row in time, for if an oar rises or falls too soon or too late, the rowers in front of the oar that has missed knock their heads on its loom when throwing themselves back on their bench, and the rowers who missed the stroke knock their heads against the oar behind them. Nor is the matter ended by contusions of the head, for the *comite* lashes them all with heavy blows, so it is in their own interest to keep time.

There is good reason for the proverb in which it is said of some onerous task, "I toil like a galley slave!" for this is indeed the most gruelling activity it is possible to imagine. Picture six chained men seated naked on their bench grasping the oar, with one foot on the *pédagne* (a heavy bar of wood fixed to the *banquette*) and the other foot braced against the bench in front of them, their bodies stretched out, arms stiff, to thrust the oar out over the bodies of those before them. Having thus thrust forward the oar, they stand up and the blade strikes the water, and they throw — or rather fling — themselves backwards to fall seated on their bench which, to lessen the jar, is covered with the piece of cushion I mentioned earlier.

How these unhappy rowers are able to endure such terrible labour has to be seen to be believed, and no one who has not seen the work of a galley slave can possibly imagine it; nor, when seeing it for the first time, believe that these unfortunates are able to keep it up for half an hour — it proves that by force and cruelty men can be made to perform the impossible. And it is very true that a galley can be worked only in this way, and that the rowers must be slaves upon whom the *comites* can exercise the most savage authority to force them to

row, not just for an hour or two, but as much as ten or twelve hours without a moment's rest. I have myself rowed full force for twenty-four hours without a moment's rest. On these occasions the *comites* and other petty officers put into our mouths, without our taking hands from the oars, a piece of biscuit steeped in wine to prevent us from fainting. Then are heard the screams of the slaves and blood flows under the whips as they crack on the backs of these wretches; then are heard the most awful insults and blasphemies from the *comites*, who become near mad and foam with fury when their galley fails to hold her station and goes less quickly than another. The captain and senior officers shout to the *comites*, who are wearied out with flogging, to redouble their blows; and when one of the hapless slaves faints at the oar, as often happens, he is flogged as long as he shows any sign of life, and when he no longer breathes he is thrown into the sea like carrion, without being shown the least pity.

Jean Marteilhe

A galley being launched by slaves.

The occasions when the slaves are thus driven are not very frequent, for if they were, all of them would soon break down. When the whole strength of the rowing-force is not required, it spared—as a carter spares his horses—for future needs. For example, when at sea with a favourable wind, sail is made and the slaves rest, for the sails are handled by sailors and free men. Similarly, when the distance from port to port is twenty-four hours or more, watches [*quartiers*] are arranged. That is, half row for one and a half hours while the other half rests, and then they change over. The half which rows is divided between the two sides of the galley, twelve oars a side from the stern to amidships, making twenty-four oars for the after-watch, and thirteen on each side from the midships to the bow, making twenty-six oars for the forward-watch. At a single call on the pipe the two watches relieve one another in an instant; no command to handle sail or oar is made by the voice—everything is done by the boatswain's pipe, which the crew and the slaves understand perfectly. The *comites* pass on every order in this fashion after having received the captain's instructions. Each manœuvre, and each particular task, is directed by a different call. Even individuals, indicated by their duties, are addressed by them; and those who hear these calls without understanding them think they hear nightingales singing. I remember that our *comite* once had a skylark in a cage. This creature learned to sing the different calls so well that it sometimes made us do things which had never been ordered, and the captain had to tell the *comite* to get rid of the bird, for it allowed us no rest.

It is not surprising to see the *comites* so cruel and merciless towards the slaves, for it is their trade; they have been trained to it from youth, and they know of no other way of working their galley; but to see the captains and senior officers, who are all well-bred men of good family, inciting them to cruelty and continually ordering the *comites* to flog without pity—that is what I cannot understand.

When a galley is at sea the officers, like the rest of the crew, never lie down to sleep; for whether under oars or sail, there is nowhere not required for the working of the vessel where anyone is able to rest. Even the hold is filled with stores, sails, ropes, and other equipment, and only the *mousses* [apprentice officers] live there. The soldiers sit on their kit-bags on the *bandes*, the sailors, petty officers, and junior officers sit where they can on the *rambade*, and the rest in places equally uncomfortable. The senior officers sit on chairs in the poop cabin. When the galley is at anchor or in port they set up the awning, which is made of a strong cotton and yarn cloth, striped blue and white. This awning covers the galley from end to end and is raised on strong bars of wood set up at certain intervals and of different lengths to make a sloping roof-edge. It is about eight feet high at the after end, twenty feet amidships, and six feet at the bow end. The bottom comes down to the rail on both sides. This awning covers all the galley and its shape and method of setting up are such that no rain, however heavy, can penetrate it.

Having thus raised the awning, all can relax and during the day can either take a meal or sew, or knit the cotton stockings which all galley slaves know how to make. Then the sailors and petty officers often amuse themselves by dancing to the sound of the tabor, at which the Provencal sailors excel. One man has the tabor hung from his neck; it is like a war-drum but longer. With one hand he beats out the rhythm with a drum-stick while playing upon a little flute held in the other hand; and it is a real pleasure to see the Provencals dancing and leaping to the sound of these instruments.

When night comes, after supper, the slaves set up tables six feet long and three feet broad, over those benches chosen by the officers. These tables rest on cross-bars and are raised about three feet above the bench. The officers have good mattresses of wool and horse-hair which are stowed in the hold by day, and these mattresses are placed on the tables, and on them a cushion or bolster held in position by a wooden head-board, then the sheets and blankets of the bed. The whole is covered by a tent of strong cotton, the head of which is attached to the top of the awning by a rope and pulley intended for this purpose. The tent thus erected, which is very spacious, covers the bed, and all these

A galley in harbor, with its tent-like canopy erected.

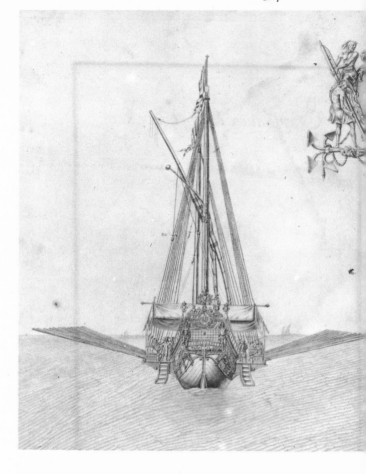

blue and white striped tents on both sides of the *coursier* make it resemble a street and provide a very pleasing vista from one end of the galley to the other. It is always well lighted by many lanterns hanging from the awning, from poop to bow.

All this preparation of beds is done in an instant, after which the slaves are ordered to lie down by a call on the pipe—but the officers and crew retire only when they wish. From the time the slaves have been ordered to lie down, not one is allowed to raise himself up, to speak, nor to make the least movement; and if one of the slaves requires to go to the rail for a natural purpose, he must call out to the *bande* and he can only go when the *argousin* [chief guard] or halberdier told off to guard the slaves gives him permission by a cry of, 'Go!' Thus profound silence reigns over the galley by night, as if there were no one on board.

Jean Marteilhe

Galleys viewed fore and aft. The window in the stern is that of the captain's cabin, and extending to either side may be seen the bande. The bow contains virtually all the armament of the galley: platforms for cannon and boarders, and the reinforced prow for ramming. Around the cartouche are shown slaves with their oars, plus comites in their customary pose.

The petty officers set up tents on each side of the *rambade*, outside the awning, and they all lie under these to shelter from the rain and from the night chills. The soldiers crouch as best they can on the *bandes*, and the slaves in their bench-spaces sit on the *pédagne*, their heads propped against their bench. Thus, when the galley is in commission, each has his place to sleep.

In April of the year 1707 we fitted out, but during the whole campaign we merely cruised about the English coast, trying only to alarm the enemy sufficiently to make him keep his troops on the alert. As soon as any large patrol-ship appeared, we escaped as quickly as possible to the French coast. This lasted till the 5th of September, a day which I shall never forget by reason of the event which then occurred, when I received the three great wounds whose scars I still bear.

At the beginning of the summer, Queen Anne of England among a large number of men-of-war which she sent to sea to cruise along the coasts possessed one of seventy guns which was commanded by a concealed Papist, whose intentions towards his country were very hostile, as experience afterwards proved. This captain was named Smith. Not belonging to any squadron, but being alone and at liberty to execute his treason, he sailed to Gothenburg in Sweden. There he sold the ship, whether to the King of Sweden or to private individuals I know not; however that may be, he sold her and received money for her, and having dismissed the crew, went in person to the Court of France to offer his services to the king against England. [This story of Smith's was untrue; he was a cashiered naval officer of no importance.] The king gave him a warm reception, and promised him the first vacant captaincy, advising him, however, to go to Dunkirk and wait for it, serving meanwhile as a volunteer in Monsieur de Langeron's galley, where he would give orders that he should be treated with honour and respect. Captain Smith saw that this *advice* was really His Majesty's *command*. He obeyed, and was received very politely by the Chevalier de Langeron, and entertained at his expense.

I have never seen anyone who hated the English as much as this infamous traitor. As soon as any Dunkirk corsair took a prize from the English — often immediately she was brought in — this irreconcilable enemy of his own countrymen always went to the prisons where the crews of the prizes were held. There he reviled them and would have torn out their eyes, had he been allowed. He even gave money to the gaoler and to the sentries who guarded these poor prisoners, so that they would prevent them from receiving the charity of kindly souls. And if we five Protestants who were also in the Chevalier de Langeron's galley had not been befriended by the chevalier, not a day would have passed without our being flogged, for he was always urging the commodore to do this as we were of the religion of his English enemies.

This traitor was so relentless against his country that he formed project upon project to injure England, and as he was perfectly acquainted with the coastline, and had knowledge and experience of war, these projects were very pleasing to the good Frenchmen, who, however, thought nothing of the man himself.

Captain Smith took part in all the expeditions which we made to the English coast. He wished very much to make a landing there, so that he might distinguish himself by burning a few villages, but it was a dangerous thing to attempt, for there were military posts all along the shore, and at short intervals bodies of troops, which our sailors feared like fire. Among other schemes which Captain Smith sent to the Court was one to burn and pillage the little town of Harwich, situated near the mouth of the Thames, provided that the six galleys at Dunkirk were placed under his command. The king approved this project and gave orders to Monsieur de Langeron to follow Captain Smith's orders, instructing the Comptroller of the Navy to provide him with everything that he might require. Monsieur de Langeron, though reluctant to submit to the orders of a foreigner, obeyed with apparent good grace, and Smith took on board all that was needed in the way of combustible materials, and everything necessary for the sack of Harwich, together with a division of soldiers.

Then one fine morning, the 5th of September, when all was ready, we put to sea with the best

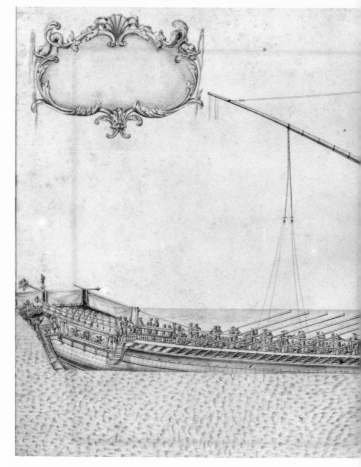

The slaves forward rowing while the slaves aft rest. While cruising, the rowers were worked in shifts to husband their strength over long distances.

weather possible for galleys. A soft breeze from the north-east favoured us so well that with very little sail and without rowing at all we arrived at the mouth of the Thames about five o'clock in the evening. But Smith, thinking that it was too early and that we might be discovered from the shore to the ruin of everything, ordered us to retire farther out to sea and to wait for night before attempting the landing.

We had not been lying-to more than a quarter of an hour when the lookout on watch at our main mast-head hailed the deck, "Sail hoa—a fleet!" "Where away?" they asked. "Northward." "Whither bound?" "Westaway," said he. "What

do you make of them?" "Thirty-five sail of merchantmen and a frigate of about thirty-six guns as escort," replied the lookout man. It was, in truth, a merchant convoy from the Texel bound for the Thames.

Our commodore at once called a council of war, at which it was decided that, instead of undertaking the Harwich expedition, we should try and make ourselves masters of this convoy, which would be more to the king's interest than burning Harwich; for the opportunity of seizing so rich a booty did not present itself every day, while the expedition to Harwich could be undertaken at any time. The commodore put all these reasons to Captain Smith, who protested against the conclusions of the council of war, asserting that he must follow the orders of the king and not turn aside to any other enterprise. But the coun-

cil of war kept firm to their resolution and were secretly glad, on account of their jealousy at having to obey the orders of Smith, that they had the opportunity to bring about the failure of the Harwich expedition.

After the decision of the council, when each captain received the commodore's orders to attack the convoy, we made sail and rowed with all our might to meet it. As it was coming towards us, we were very soon near each other.

Our commodore's orders were that four galleys should attack and, if possible, take possession of the merchant ships, knowing that most of them would be defenceless, while our galley, which was the flag-galley of the squadron, was to join with that of the Chevalier de Mauviliers in attacking and overcoming the frigate which served as an escort.

Following these directions, the four galleys proceeded to assail the merchant vessels and cut them off from the mouth of the Thames, and we with our consort made straight for the frigate. Seeing our manœuvre, she perceived that her convoy—or at all events the greater part of it—was in imminent danger. She was an English frigate and the captain in command was one of the bravest and most skilful of the age, as indeed he proved himself to be on this occasion. Having given orders to the merchantmen to crowd on all sail, and to avoid falling into the hands of the French by gaining the mouth of the Thames as quickly as possible, he added that, for himself, he reckoned on giving so much work to the six galleys that he hoped to save them all. In a word, that he was going to sacrifice himself for them. He thereupon made all sail and turned towards our two galleys which were about to attack, as if he were coming to attack them himself.

Night was approaching and, as it was feared we should not reach her in time, forced rowing was ordered. Our lieutenant told the *comite* to lash harder and the *comite* replied that, although he was doing his best, he did not see how we could take the frigate with night coming on. The lieutenant replied that if he did not see the frigate in our power, he would himself promptly hang the *comite* from the yard of the galley. "Increase your blows, executioner," said he, "to quicken up and terrify those dogs!" speaking of the slaves. "Do as I have often seen done in the galleys of Malta—cut off the arm of one of the dogs to serve as a rod to beat the others!" The barbarous lieutenant wished to compel the *comite* to carry out this cruelty; but the *comite*, more humane than he was, refused.

The galley which was to serve as our consort was above a league astern; either she did not go so fast, or her captain designed that we should bear the first brunt of the attack. But our commodore was not much disturbed by the approach of the frigate, as he thought his galley strong enough to master her; however, it will be seen that he was wrong in his conjectures.

We were soon within range of the frigate and fired at her, but she did not reply by a single shot. Our commodore said jokingly that the captain of this frigate was evidently tired of being an Englishman, and was going to surrender to us without fighting; but he soon changed his tone. We advanced so rapidly towards each other that our galley was soon within musket shot, and our musketeers had already begun to play upon the frigate, when all of a sudden she went about as if she were going to flee from us.

The flight of an enemy generally increases courage, and our crew began to cry out to the men on board the frigate that they were cowards in trying to avoid the battle, that it was now too late and, if they did not strike their flag and surrender at once, we would sink the ship. The Englishmen took no notice of this for they were preparing to enact a bloody tragedy.

The frigate, feigning flight, had turned her stern towards us, and now gave us a chance of boarding her, for the manœuvre of a galley which

A moored galley with its canopy shown erected along one side.

is about to attack and board a ship is to bring her bows to bear on the stern, the weakest part of the ship. The whole strength of a galley is in her bows, and here she has the greater part of her artillery; she therefore endeavours to force her beak into the enemy's stern, firing her five guns, and her crew then storm on board.

The commodore at once ordered the attack, bidding the *timoneer* to steer straight at the frigate. All the soldiers and sailors detailed as boarders were standing ready with naked cutlasses and axes in their hands, when the frigate, anticipating our manœuvre and just as our beak was about to strike her stern, evaded us by a clever stroke of the helm, and we suddenly found ourselves under her broadside, against which we shaved so closely that our oars were broken to pieces. The coolness and courage of the English captain were admirable; he had foreseen what would occur and was all ready with his grappling-irons, by means of which he seized our galley and secured her alongside. Then

he gave us a taste of his artillery. All his guns were charged with grape-shot, and the first discharge fired at us killed the cruel lieutenant on the *coursier*. Every man on board the galley was as exposed as if he were on an open bridge or raft. So close were the frigate's guns to us that not a single shot was without effect, and a frightful carnage ensued. Moreover, the English captain had placed aloft a number of his men with barrels full of hand-grenades which they rained down on us like hail, with such good aim that all our crew were not only unable to attack, but even to make any defence; those who were neither killed or wounded lay flat down to pretend that they were so; and the terror was as great among the officers as among the crew. The enemy perceiving this, added to our discomfiture by sending forty or fifty men on board our galley, cutlass in hand, who cut to pieces any of the crew they could lay their hands upon, only sparing the slaves, who made no attempt at defence. After they had hacked about like butchers, they returned

A galley under sail.

to their frigate and continued to pelt us with their guns and grenades.

Our bench, on which were five slaves and a Turk, happened to be just opposite to one of the guns of the frigate, which I perceived to be loaded. Our broadsides were touching and this gun was so near to us that by raising myself a little I could have reached it with my hand. This unpleasant neighbour made us all tremble and my companions lay down quite flat, thinking thus to escape its fire. On examining this cannon, I saw, from the manner in which it was pointed, that its discharge would bear directly upon our bench, and that lying down we must receive it upon our bodies. Having made this observation, I determined to stand straight up on my bench. I could not get away, I was chained to it; what else could I do? I must resign myself to pass through the cannon discharge.

As I was attentive to all that was passing on board the frigate, I saw the gunner, with his lighted slow-match in his hand, touch off the gun at the bows and then go from gun to gun as he worked his way towards the one which pointed at our bench; I then lifted up my heart to God and uttered a short but fervent prayer. I could not take my eyes off this gunner, who kept gradually approaching our gun, as he applied his match in succession to the others. Now he came to the fatal gun and, still standing straight up and commending my soul to my Saviour, I had the courage to watch him apply the linstock. The cannon fired; I was stunned and thrown prostrate, not on the bench, but in the centre of the galley, as far away as my chain could extend.

Stretched across the body of the dead lieutenant, I lay unconscious for I know not how long, but I imagine it must have been a considerable time. At last, however, I regained my senses. Raising myself from the lieutenant's body, I returned to my bench. It was night and, because of the darkness, I could see neither the blood nor the carnage. At first I thought that my comrades were still lying down for fear of the cannon. Feeling no pain, I did not know that I was wounded and said to my comrades, "Get up, lads, the danger is over." But I received no answer.

My good Turk on the bench, who had been a janissary, and who boasted that he was never afraid, remained prostrate like the others, and I said, jokingly, "What, Isouf, this is the first time you have been afraid; come, get up," and at the same time I took him by the arm to help him. I shudder still when I think of it — his arm separated from his body and remained in my hand! In terror I let it fall and perceived that he, as well as the four others, had literally been hewn in pieces, for all the shot had fallen upon them. I sat down upon the bench.

I had not been long in that attitude when I felt something cold and damp streaming down my naked body. I put my hand to it and felt directly that it was wet, but could not in the darkness distinguish if it was blood. But I soon found that it was, and that it was streaming from a large wound through my left shoulder. I felt another on my left leg, below the knee, as deep as the one in my shoulder, and a third, nearly a foot long and four inches broad, in my stomach. I was losing an immense quantity of blood and all around me, both on my bench and on the two adjoining ones, being dead, I was unable to get any assistance. Of the eighteen men who were in those three benches, I alone had escaped with my three wounds; and all this slaughter had been caused by one cannon! This can be easily understood when I mention that these guns were charged up to the muzzle, first with cartridge-powder, then a long tin box, varying in size according to the calibre of the gun, filled with large musket-balls and pieces of old iron. When they fired these guns the box broke, and the balls and langridge-shot spread haphazardly causing a fearful carnage. I was obliged to wait for assistance till the combat was over and order could be restored, for everything on board the galley was in a frightful state of chaos. No one knew who was dead, wounded, or alive and we could hear only

100

the piercing cries of the wounded, of whom there were a large number.

The *coursier* was so encumbered with dead bodies that no one could pass along it. The rowers' benches were for the most part equally full of bodies, not only of slaves, but of sailors, soldiers, and officers, either dead or wounded, so that the living and unhurt could scarcely move, either to throw the dead into the sea, or to help the wounded. Add to this the darkness and the fact that we dared not light either torches or lanterns.

Monsieur de Langeron seeing himself reduced to this condition, and that not a person on board except himself seemed able to stand, hoisted with his own hands the signal of distress, which called all the galleys of the squadron to our aid.

Our consort was soon with us, and the four galleys which had already attacked and forced the greater number of the merchantmen to strike their sails, seeing this signal and the peril of their commodore, quitted their prizes to come to his assistance. In doing so they turned away from the

Galleys were fair-weather craft that had a hard time of it in a heavy sea.

Thames, enabling the convoy to make sail again and to escape up the river. All the galleys now rowed with such speed that in less than a quarter of an hour all six surrounded the frigate, which was soon no longer in a condition to fire either cannon or musket-shot, and not a man of her crew appeared upon the deck. Twenty-five grenadiers out of each galley were ordered to board her. They had little trouble in mounting as there was no one to dispute their way, but once on the deck it was a different matter. The officers were entrenched under the poop and poured such a murderous fire on these grenadiers that they soon discovered that the

enemy had not yet surrendered. But worst of all the deck was (in the nautical term) "grated," which means a grille of iron bars was let into the planking, and most of the crew were between decks, under this grating, through the apertures of which they struck at the legs of the grenadiers with pikes and swords, so that they soon obliged them to jump back into their galleys.

Another detachment was now ordered to board, but they too came down much quicker than they had gone up. This grating had to be broken through with crowbars and other strong instruments and the crew had to be forced from between decks.

Battle between galleys.

Notwithstanding the heavy fire from the officers, and the blows of the pikes, which killed and wounded very many, this was finally done and by force of numbers the crew were made prisoners. But the officers were still entrenched under the poop, and poured forth their shot unceasingly. They, too, had to be overcome, and this was not accomplished without loss.

The whole crew of the frigate had now surrendered, with the exception of the captain, who had shut himself up in his cabin under the poop, firing the different guns and pistols which he had with him, and swearing that he would not surrender so long as a breath of life remained in him. The officers, who had already descended into our commodore's galley as prisoners of war, gave a terrible report of their captain, who, they said, made everyone tremble. He was, they said, determined to set fire to his ship rather than surrender; this was a danger more terrible than any yet, for at any moment we expected to be blown up with the frigate. The captain was master of the

stern-cabin in which was the entrance to the powder-magazine which he could, consequently, set fire to in a twinkling, destroying the frigate and the six galleys with her. There were more than three thousand men in the six galleys and so great was our danger that all were shuddering for fear of instant death. In this extremity it was resolved to call civilly and politely on the captain to surrender, promising him the best treatment possible; his reply was to open fire again.

An extreme remedy was now resorted to, in order to take him dead or alive. A sergeant and twelve grenadiers were ordered to go with fixed bayonets and force him to surrender. The sergeant at the head of his detachment soon broke through the cabin door, but the captain was waiting for him pistol in hand and at once blew out his brains. The twelve grenadiers, seeing this, and fearing the same fate, fled, and it was not possible for the officers to make any other soldiers advance, for they said in their defence that only being able to enter one by one into the cabin, the captain would kill them all one after the other. Gentle means must, then, again be employed to take him. However, the captain, who had only resisted as long as this so as to give his convoy time to enter the Thames, and who perceived by their lights that they had all now reached it, no longer turned a deaf ear to the summons to surrender. But to give still more time to a few laggards in the convoy, and to ensure that night completely hid them from the pursuit of the French, he still feigned a delay, saying that he would only surrender his sword into the hands of the commodore of the galleys, who must come on board the frigate to take it. A truce was arranged, while this message was taken to the commodore, who sent his second-in-command to the English captain, representing to him that it was not the duty of a commodore to quit his post.

The captain, who had nothing more to do for the safety of the convoy, now gave up his sword.

They brought him down into the galley to our commodore, who was surprised to see a very little man, quite deformed and hunch-backed. Our commodore complimented him, telling him that it was the fortune of war, and that he might console himself for the loss of his ship by the kind treatment which he would show him. "I have no regret," replied he, "for the loss of my ship, since I have succeeded in my design, which was to save the convoy entrusted to my care. Moreover, I had resolved from the moment I saw you to sacrifice my ship and my own person for the preservation of the property which I had undertaken to defend. You

will still find," added he, speaking to the commander, "a small quantity of lead and powder, which I had neither time nor opportunity to give you; it is the most valuable thing you will find in the ship. As for myself, if you treat me as a man of honour, I, or some other of my nation, may some day have the opportunity of acting in the same way towards you."

This noble independence quite pleased Monsieur de Langeron, who, returning him his sword, said very civilly, "Take back this sword, sir, you well deserve to wear it, and you are my prisoner only in name." Soon after our commodore had occasion to repent that he had returned his sword to him, for when the captain was introduced into the cabin of the galley he saw there the renegade Smith, on whose head the price of £1,000 sterling was set in England, and whom he immediately recognized. "Traitor," said he, "you shall receive death from my hand, since the executioners in London cannot give it you." Sword in hand he rushed upon him, and would have thrust it through his body if the commodore had not seized him by the arm and prevented him, to the great regret of the captain, who protested that he would rather have taken Smith than the six galleys.

Captain Smith, who was greatly offended at this occurrence, represented that the captain and himself ought not to be in the same galley, and begged the commodore to place his prisoner in another vessel; but the commodore replied that this captain being his prisoner, Captain Smith must

Fighting among the survivors of sinking galleys.

go to another galley, and his prisoner remain with him. This was done and we then manned our prize, which was called the *Nightingale*, but the name of her brave captain has escaped me. [It was Captain Seth Jermy.]

The combat ended with the surrender of the frigate, but our galley remained in a terrible state of chaos and confusion far into the night. The other five galleys, which had not endured nearly so much loss and injury as we had done, worked diligently, but as silently as possible and without lights, to put us into order, replacing our dead and wounded, as well as the oars and fittings which we had lost.

We saw lights proceeding from the Thames and heard several signal guns which we thought came from ships of war seeking us. Therefore we at once left the mouth of the Thames with our prize, but we had to go out of our way and profit as much as possible from the darkness of the night to evade four men-of-war which gave us chase, but failed to overtake us.

The first thing to be done on board our galley was to throw the dead into the sea, and to carry the wounded into the hold. But God knows how many wretches were thrown into the sea as dead who were not really so, for in this darkness and confusion they took for dead those who, either through fear or loss of blood, had only fainted. I myself was in this extremity, for when the *argousins* came to my bench to unchain the dead and wounded, I had fallen down in a fainting-fit, and lay motionless and unconscious among the others, bathed in their blood and my own. These *argousins* at once concluded that all belonging to this bench were dead. Without further examination they unchained them and threw them into the sea; it was quite enough if they did not hear them cry out or speak. These obsequies were so hastily performed that a bench was emptied in a moment. All my comrades who were slain were frightfully mangled. Buried and prostrate in this carnage, and making no movement or sound, I was the only one who

104

was whole. Judging me to be dead, they unchained me to throw me into the sea. Now it must be remembered that I was chained by the left leg, and that it was there that I was wounded. One *argousin* seized me by this leg, to drag me up, while another was unfastening the bolt of the iron ring which held my chain. The latter, happily for me, put his hand upon my wound, which caused me so great pain that I raised a great cry, and I heard the *argousin* say, "This man is not dead," and realizing at once that they were going to throw me into the sea, I exclaimed (for this pain had brought back my consciousness), "No, no; I am not dead." They took me down to the bottom of the hold among the other wounded, and threw me down upon a cable. What a place of repose for a wounded man, agonized with pain!

We who were wounded were all cast pell-mell into the hold, sailors, soldiers, officers, and slaves, without any distinction. Laid down upon the hard boards, we received no help or relief, for there were so many wounded that the surgeons could only attend to a few of them. As for myself, I was three days in this terrible place without having my wounds dressed, a little camphored brandy being applied to stop the bleeding, and a poor makeshift bandage. The wounded died like flies in this horrible hold, where the heat was so stifling and the stench so dreadful that gangrene set in on most of our wounds.

THREE days after the battle we arrived in the roadstead of Dunkirk. The wounded were at once landed and carried to the naval hospital. We were hauled up out of the hold with blocks and tackle, like cattle, and taken there more dead than alive. The galley slaves were separated from the free men and placed in two large wards containing forty beds each, and we were all chained to the feet of our beds. At one o'clock in the afternoon the head surgeon of the hospital came to examine and dress our wounds, accompanied by all the surgeons of the ships and galleys which were in the harbour

Jean Marteilhe

Galleys returning to port, a romantic view by Rigaud.

I had just been strongly recommended to the head surgeon, and this is how it came about.

It so happened that, having heard our galley had lost many men in the capture of the English frigate, Monsieur Piecourt, the banker [a Huguenot sympathizer who befriended Marteilhe], ran at once to the harbour to inquire about me. He learned that I was severely wounded and had already been taken to the hospital. He went immediately to the head surgeon, who was his friend, and commended me to his care as warmly as if I had been his own son. I can indeed say that, after God, I owe my life to this surgeon, who undertook, contrary to his usual custom (for he never did anything but give orders), to dress my wounds himself.

At the first visit which he made to our ward, he took his notebook from his pocket, and asked who was called Jean Marteilhe. I replied that it was I. He approached my bed, and asked me if I knew Monsieur Piecourt. I said that I did, and that he had had the kindness to procure me all the indulgence possible during the six or seven years that I had been in the galleys. "The manner," said he, "in which he has commended you to my care proves the truth of what you say. I shall with pleasure attend to his request. Let me see your wounds." The worst was that in the shoulder, very dangerous on account of its situation. He at once took off the bandage applied by the surgeon of the galley, whose negligence had caused my wounds to gangrene. He summoned this surgeon, and reproached him for being such a butcher as to have treated me thus, saying that if I died, as he feared I should do, he would be my murderer.

The galley surgeon made the best excuse that he could, and begged the head surgeon to allow him to dress me. This he refused, and declared to all the others that I was his patient, and that he would not allow anyone to dress me except himself. He took, indeed, so great care of me, and used so many remedies, that humanly speaking, I may say he saved my life. Quite three-fourths of our wounded died though the majority of them were not wounded as dangerously as I was. The large number of men who died at the hospital, both of the crews of the galleys and of the slaves, made some think that the English frigate used poisoned balls. But I believe, with all reasonable people, that it was a calumny caused by the hatred which the French bore this nation. The opinion of the head surgeon, who was the most skilful in all France, was that the great mortality arose from dirty and rusty shot tearing the wounds they made, together with carelessness of the galley surgeons in their manner of dressing the wounds.

In less than two months my wounds were healed, but the surgeon made me remain a month longer in the hospital to regain my strength; and as the director of the hospital, to whom I was also recommended, ordered the brethren of the order of St. Francis, who served this hospital, to give me anything I asked for which was not injurious to my health and to the healing of my wounds, I was fed and cared for like a prince.

At the end of three months I was sleek and fat as a monk, and the head surgeon having written out and given me a certificate that, owing to my wounds, I was rendered incapable of rowing or of doing other hard work in the galleys, I was sent back to the galley—to my usual bench!

Galley slaves disembarking from a small boat under the supervision of comites.

Adventure 9

The Discovery of Tahiti

from the Log and Journal of George Robertson

THIS account belongs to the brave and glittering age of South Seas exploration, when Anson and Byron, Bougainville and La Perouse, Carteret and Cook were bringing to the eighteenth-century world the exciting narratives of their adventures in the exotic islands of the remote South Seas. It is also of the most famous Pacific island of them all—Tahiti, the sparkling jewel of the Society group. Few realize that the uncovering of this jewel was not by one of the illustrious navigators but by a rough-and-ready British mariner named Captain Samuel Wallis, a Cornishman, then thirty-eight years old. Wallis had served under Byron on a previous South Seas voyage. It was in fact on His Majesty's ship *Dolphin* of 32 guns, the same vessel in which he had first entered the Pacific, that in 1767 he came upon Tahiti.

Surely Tahiti is one of the most naturally blessed of any land on earth, with its gentle climate, its dramatic volcanic contours, its tropical verdure, its handsome, good-natured people. Indeed, in 1769, when its European discoverers brought back enthusiastic accounts of the generous charms of the country and its natives (and in particular its girls), many believed that here was the living manifestation of the idyllic State of Nature recently celebrated by Rousseau.

The master of the *Dolphin*, George Robertson, whose delightful diary of the discovery of the island is at once the most entertaining and the most dependable of all accounts of the event, was not misled by any such romantic fancies. Robertson was a plain bluff sailor, not a naval officer appointed by the Admiralty, but a "warrant" appointed by the Navy Board and responsible for the safety and navigation of the ship. This distinction set him somewhat apart from the rest of the crew. He was also blessed with a keen eye and a sardonic sense of humor that could find equal wry amusement in the petty tyrannies of the First Lieutenant and the energetic efforts of the crew to improve cultural relations with the Tahitian girls. Robertson was as deeply impressed by the beauty of Tahiti, yet he did not consider the natives savages, noble or otherwise, but found in them the crotchets and foibles of people everywhere.

The adventure that Robertson chronicles so briskly began in violence but turned into a legendary idyl. The *Dolphin* had had a hard voyage to the South Seas; the ship had been one of two on an expedition—partly exploratory, partly scientific—sent into the Pacific to try to find the supposed "Terra Australis," a large continent presumed to extend from the tropics to the South Pole. Indeed, Tahiti was thought by its discoverers to be the northern extremity of the Southern Continent until Captain James Cook later established the separate outlines of Tahiti, New Zealand, and Australia.

The *Dolphin* was a stout vessel. Her experimental sheathing of copper, which she was the first Royal Navy vessel to carry into the Pacific, proved gratifyingly effective against the worms and barnacles that riddled the hulls of most ships of the period. But in severe storms in the Straits of Magellan she became separated from her companion ship, the *Swallow*, and in the long voyage across the Pacific scurvy and dysentery reduced her crew to a sorry state.

Consequently the landfall of Tahiti seemed an answer to prayer. The island was first sighted June 19, 1767 (old calendar), and for the next two days they sailed along the northern coast of the dumb-bell shaped island, seeking a suitable place to land for food and water. Most of the crew, including the captain, were sick, yet the dubious welcome they received from the natives whenever they tried to put a boat ashore made many believe that they must turn away and head for the known haven of Tinian, several thousand miles away. Then, on June 21, they reached the noble harbor of Matavai Bay and the haven they so desperately needed.

Note: The "days" in Robertson's journal follow the style of a ship's log; that is, instead of running from midnight to midnight, they run from noon of any given date to noon of the next.

The pleasant prospect of Tahiti, as it appeared in the period of its discovery.

"*They never saw more handsome women in their lives*"

WHEN daylight appeared, the barge and cutter was hoisted out and both boats manned and armed. Captain Wallis ordered me to go and sound the coast for anchoring ground. This I complied with and set out immediately—I went in the barge and Mr. Gore in the cutter. The instant we set out from the ship, we saw great numbers of canoes set out from the shore, steering towards us. When I saw this, in order to prevent accidents, I ordered Mr. Gore to keep sounding, and I lay close by him with the barge to prevent natives from interrupting him from sounding.

When we got in amongst the canoes they all waved us off and seemed greatly enraged when we stood in for the shore. When we found no regular soundings and all fine black sandy ground, we made the signal to the ship, that we had found good anchoring ground. This they observed and stood in to seventeen fathom, where the ship anchored in fine black sandy ground, about two miles off the shore.

When the ship anchored, I returned on board and acquainted the Captain what sort of sounding we found betwixt the ship and the shore. By this time several of the canoes came alongside with cocoanuts and several other sort of fruits, a few fowls and some fine fat young pigs, and our people and them had begun to trade, but all the country people behaved very insolently. None of them would trust any of our men with any of their things until they got nails or toys from them; then several

of them would push off and keep all, and others carried their insolence so high that they struck several of our men. This our seamen was very unwilling to put up with, but the Captain having given strict orders that no man should hurt or molest them until we tried their tempers, this made our men put up with their ill behavior for a short time.

Soon after I returned to the ship the Captain ordered me to go and sound along shore, and to look out for a proper watering place. By this time there was several thousand of the natives assembled on the shore side, upward of a hundred canoes alongside, and near twice that number between us and the shore. Several of the large double canoes with long prows had eight, twelve and sixteen men in each. All these large canoes carried sail but the small ones all paddled. The very instant that we set out in the barge and cutter, all the large sailing canoes set out after us, and hooted and made a great noise which with their insolent behavior on board made me suspect they had some design on us. I therefore told Mr. Gore in the cutter to keep on his guard, that I should keep close by him as we sailed best in the barge. In a few minutes the sailing canoes came up with us, and kept so near us that we both found it impossible to sound. We therefore made all the sail we could and left off sounding in order to look for a convenient watering place, but several of the large canoes still came up with us, and some of them attempted to board our boats. We avoided them and kept clear for some time, still making all the friendly signs we could think of and frequently waving to them to keep off, but they supposed we were afraid of them and still behaved with more insolence.

Indeed I must own we had some reason to be a little afraid, for by the time we got close to the shore there were above two hundred great and small canoes round us, and near fifteen hundred men in them. As to the numbers that was on the shore, of men, women and children, it was impossible to form any idea of them. The whole coast was lined with them as far as we could see. When we got close to the shore we saw the entry of a fine river, but no water for a boat to go into it, and the surf ran so high all along shore, that no man could land with his arms dry. We ran a little way along shore in hopes of being able to sound, but they crowded so thick about us that we found it impossible. While we sailed along shore, the natives waved to us to come ashore, but being so numerous and those in the canoes so insolent I thought it more prudent to return on board.

The instant we tacked and stood off, all the people ashore set up a loud cry. Those in the canoes began to hoot us and several of them attempted to board us, and seemed greatly enraged at us when they found we would not land. When we got within a mile and half of the ship one of the large canoes rammed the cutter, and carried away her bumphen and tore the mizzen, but we soon got clear of her by using the picks and bayonets. At the same time another attempted to board us but we soon got clear of him.

A few minutes after, three of the largest attempted to board us all at once. I then ordered the Marines to point the muskets at them, but they laughed at us. One struck his prow right into our boat stern, and four of the stoutest fellows immediately jumped on the prow of the canoe, as if

they meant to board us, with their paddles and clubs in their hands. When I found them so very resolute, I ordered one of the Marines to fire his musket right across their canoe, in hopes of frightening them, without doing them any more hurt. This did not have the desired effect—it only startled them a little. When they found none was hurt they

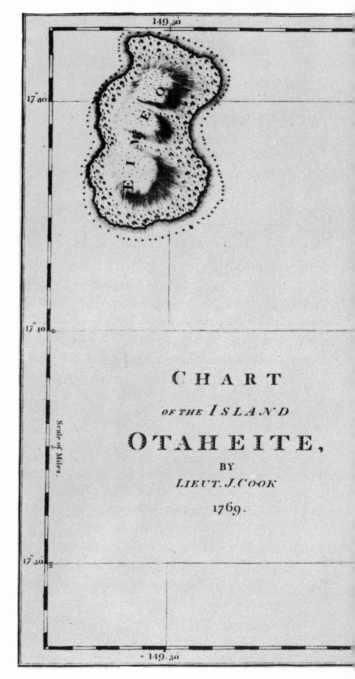

CHART

OF THE *ISLAND*

OTAHEITE,

BY

LIEUT. J. COOK

1769.

Cook's chart of Tahiti, made after his visit there, two years following its discovery.

George Robertson

all gave a shout and run directly for our boat's stern again. The other two came right for the middle of our boat, fully resolved to board us, which if they had, their prows would have certainly sunk our boat and all of us must have inevitably perished. At the same time they were attempting to board the cutter. I then found it was too late to treat them with tenderness, especially as the ship took no manner of notice of us, although they saw the whole transaction very plain. Had there been a nine-pound shot fired over their heads perhaps it may have frightened them from hurting us. But that not being done I thought myself under a necessity of using violent means.

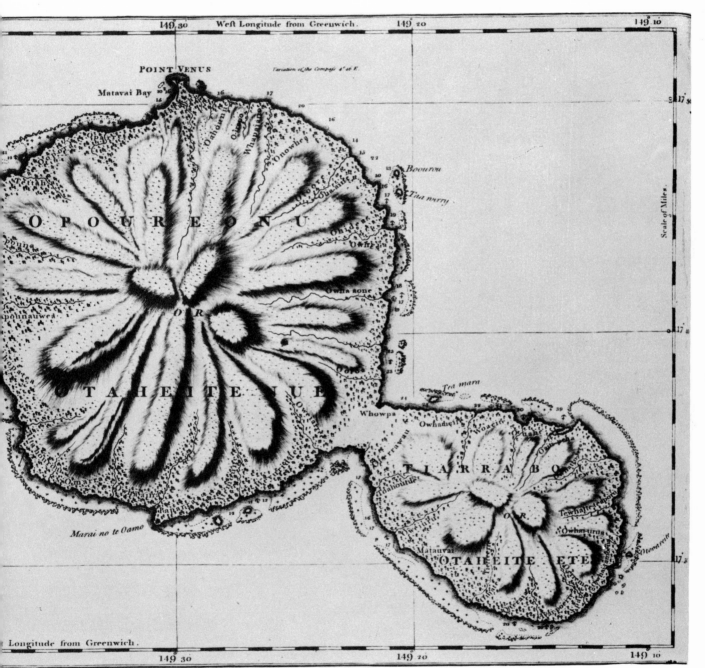

I therefore ordered the sergeant and one of the Marines to wound the two most resolute-looking fellows that were in the boat which first boarded us. This order was complied with and the one was killed which the sergeant fired at and the other was wounded in the thigh, and both fell overboard. When the other fellows in the canoe saw this they all jumped overboard, and the other two canoes immediately steered off. When we pointed the muskets to them they held up their paddles before their faces and dropped astern, clear of us. When they saw we gave them no more trouble, the crew of the canoe that first boarded us all jumped into their canoe and hauled in the two men that were wounded. One appeared quite dead. They tried to make him stand, and when they found he could not, they endeavored to make him sit, but found he was quite dead. They then laid him down in the bottom of the canoe, and one of them supported the other, and the rest made sail and stood in for the land.

22nd June 1767. Several canoes came off with hogs, fowl and fruit of various kinds, such as plantains, bananas, breadfruit and some other fruits whose name I know not. We purchased the whole for nails and other trifling things. Most of the natives traded very honestly, but a few of them were very great rogues and frequently attempted to defraud our men. But pointing a musket or even a spyglass at them they would return the nails, etc., or give value. They now understood the use of musketry and made signs that they had killed two of their partners. The way they took to make us understand was this: they called loudly, "*Bon-bon*," then smote their breasts and foreheads and laid back with their eyes fixed and without motion. The market price for this day was a twenty-penny nail for a hog about twenty pounds, a ten-penny for a roasting pig, a six-penny for a fowl or a bunch of fruit. A string of beads would purchase a fowl or some fruit, but all of them seemed most fond of nails.

This day Mr. Gore was ordered to take the barge and cutter, manned and armed, and to sound the coast to find out a watering place and to land if possible. If the natives gave him trouble he was ordered to come off immediately and the ship was to fire some round shot amongst them. Our boats set out and found regular soundings from seventeen to five fathoms, but saw no place to land, the surf running very high. None of the native canoes attempted to come near our boats but great numbers of men and women assembled on the beach. Some of these ventured off through the surf with large bunbows [casks] and calabashes [gourds] filled with water. They swim like fish and dive much quicker than any can believe.

Mr. Gore was ordered to take gang-casks and breakers [small barrels] in the boats and do all he could to get the natives to bring off water. For that purpose he got nails of all sorts and pieces of iron hoops to pay them with. At 4 P.M. the boats returned with only four breakers of water. When they got in to shore the natives came off and took six breakers ashore to fill but could not be prevailed on to bring more than four off. Our men made all the friendly signs they could think of for them to return the breakers, but all in vain. They would not, but made signs for our men to land and they would haul their boats up in the woods. When our people could not prevail on them by fair means they began to threaten them by pointing muskets, but that they made game of and laughed very hearty not knowing the muskets could hurt them at so great a distance. This made Mr. Gore fire a musketoon along shore, that they might see the balls take the water at a greater distance than they were from the boats. This he thought would make them sensible of the danger they were in, but they soon found none of them were hurt and all returned back to the waterside.

They brought a good many young girls down of different colors, some a light copper color, others mulatto, and some almost if not altogether white. This attracted our men a good deal, and the natives observed it and made the young girls play a great

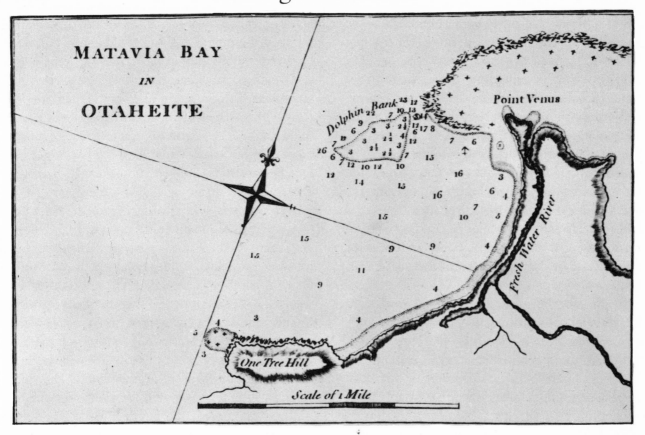

Cook's chart of Matavai Bay, showing the river where the crew of the Dolphin collected water and traded with the natives, Skirmish or One Tree Hill, and Dolphin Bank, where the ship went aground.

many droll, wanton tricks. The men made signs of friendship to entice our people ashore, but they very prudently deferred going ashore until we were better acquainted with the temper of these people.

Our boats returned with only four breakers, which is about forty gallons at most. We found it impossible to water by the assistance of the natives. Our water was now very short and not sufficient to carry us to any known place. Therefore, some said it was absolutely necessary to get water at any event, while others said it was impossible as the natives must now be greatly enraged against us, especially as we had killed two of them.

The Captain now being very bad, and not able to keep the deck, he consulted with his officers what was best to be done. Our First Lieutenant was likewise ill and not able to do duty upon deck, but thought himself very able to advise. What advice he gave the Captain at this time I know not, but I afterwards found it was opposite to mine—this at a time when it hurt me greatly. But I believe it turned out to be for the good of us all, as it made me do what I should not have done so willingly at another time.

The most of us thought it best to weigh anchor and run down to leeward of the low point, where we saw the appearance of an anchoring ground and smooth water to land with our boats. Here no man needed to be afraid of wetting his feet, much less his arms. This was agreed on, and we weighed.

When we got near the point we went ahead with the boats. I kept nearest the shore in the barge and Mr. Gore kept about two cable-lengths between me in the cutter. We both kept constantly sounding. When we got a little round the point we saw several thousands of the natives assembled on the shore, and a great number of canoes in the bay which we intended to sound. This made the ship stand close in after us, to prevent the canoes from hindering us to sound the bay. This surprised me greatly as the ship was not to come near us nor a mile until I made the signal for anchoring. By this time she was so near that I called to them to keep off as I had only three fathoms, but they being nearer the cutter, which had plenty of water, did not observe what I said. Soon after the ship struck and stood fast on a reef of rocks, which put all on board in great confusion. When I got on board I found she had struck several times very hard, and all the sails aback or shaking in the wind.

By this time the Captain had given orders to clear the decks of all lumber which was immediately done and the people were busy in getting in the stream cable and anchor to heave the ship off. The Captain and the First Lieutenant were now on deck giving orders. I therefore applied to the Captain for orders to do that which was best for the safety of the ship, but before the Captain could give me a proper answer, Mr. Knowall [Lieutenant Clarke] interrupted him, and told me on the public quarter-deck, that this misfortune was entirely owing to my wholesome advice, and now I should know the danger of contradicting him; that when we were soon in the enemy's power I should know better. This speech made my heart ache, but the time was improper to answer him as he deserved. I therefore told him we would find another time to dispute that point, but now was the time to study the safety of the ship. I therefore desired the seamen to fill all the sails, as the ship's head was to the sea; at the same time I asked the Captain if he approved of what I did. He said he did. Mr. Knowall disapproved of this and laid hold of the weather fore brace to haul it in, but his strength was not equal to his ill nature, and no man assisted him.

At this instant the men at the lead said the ship drew ahead. This gave great joy to all on board but to me in particular. In a few minutes we got clear off and run out about a mile. We frequently sounded the pumps but found she made but very little water more than usual. While we were on the reef we fired a few guns to prevent the natives from attempting to come near the ship. When we got clear off from the shore we lay to and I went down to the Captain and earnestly solicited him to let me make another trial of sounding the bay which he readily agreed to and sent up orders to man the boats.

While I was getting orders from the Captain, Mr. Knowall ordered Mr. Gore to go in the barge and sound off the low point, and ordered the cutter for some other use, and told me there was the jolly boat for me to go where I wanted to go. At first I resolved to acquaint the Captain but he then being so bad in his health and greatly the worse for being upon deck, I thought it wrong to hurt him more. I went down to my cabin to write a few lines, as I was some doubtful of returning back to the ship. In a few minutes I was sent for and told the boat was ready. I immediately put on a pair of good pistols and took my broadsword in my hand without the scabbard. My friend Knowall met me and told me the boat had been waiting for some time. I told him it was very well; I was now ready to go in her small as she was. In this boat I had only five of the smallest lads in the ship, which was her proper crew, and no arms for any of the five, and two Marines with their muskets. With this stout crew I set out to sound what we afterwards called Port Royal Bay [Matavai Bay] — where there was about two hundred canoes.

I was amongst the natives in their canoes and all of them staring at me. Several canoes came round me and some were so near that I had not room to throw the lead. I then expected they would run us down or board us every minute — but in hopes to frighten them I ordered the two Marines to point their muskets at them. This made them shear off a little, but soon after one old cross-looking fellow began to call out to his fellows and sheared close to us. I threatened him by pointing the muskets at

George Robertson

him but he held up his paddle and sheared off again, so that I was able to sound. I found fine regular soundings within a cable-length of the shore. This made me very happy and all that were in the boat. The poor youngsters said there was no danger to be feared from the natives. I then gave them a dram of good old rum each but the instant we turned towards the ship, which was now without gun shot of us, a great number of the canoes surrounded us and seemed resolved to attack us.

I then expected the barge would come down to our assistance, and ordered one of the Marines to fire amongst the thickest of the canoes. This made the most of them shear off but one fellow who

A drawing by George Pinnock, one of the midship-men on the Dolphin, of the ship at anchor in Matavai Bay. At the right is Skirmish or One Tree Hill.

threw a stone at us but luckily hurt none of us. I immediately fired a pistol at this fellow, which I believe went through his paddle which he held up before his face, as I afterwards saw him show the paddle to several other canoes. This made them all keep off, but the barge never came near us which surprised me greatly. But fortunately the Captain observed us with his glass out of the cabin window. He ordered the ship to stand in and fired several signal shot at the barge in order to make her come down to us, but they say they did not understand that signal. However, it was of great use to me and the poor little jolly boat's crew. The natives were again surrounding us which obliged me to order another musket to be fired amongst them, which with the great guns so terrified them that they all dispersed.

In the meantime the Captain ordered the cutter manned and armed to my assistance. By the time

she reached me I crossed the bay twice and found it all good ground. I therefore ordered the young gentleman in the cutter to take the jolly boat, and row up to the barge and order her to come down and lie on the end of the shoal which the ship struck on, in order to be a mark for me to steer in by. At the same time I rowed off to the ship in the cutter and acquainted Captain Wallis what sort of a bay I had found. He desired to know the reason that I went down without the barge, and I told him Mr. Knowall knowed that best, but if he pleased I would take charge of the ship, and carry her into the finest bay I ever saw, where there appeared to be a small river, where we could have no manner of difficulty completing getting our water. This pleased him a good deal but he was still doubtful about the shoal. I told him the barge and jolly boat were now upon the outer end of the shoal, so that there was no kind of danger in going into the bay. He then ordered me to take charge of the ship and carry her in. I then ordered them to steer right in, keeping the two boats a little open on the larboard bow and I stood at the foretop masthead where I saw the shoal as plain as if I had been upon it. In a short time we anchored in seventeen fathoms of water with fine white sandy ground.

24th June. At sunrise about three hundred canoes came off and lay round the ship. As many as could conveniently lay alongside. They traded very fair and took nails and toys for their hogs, fowl and fruit. By eight o'clock there was upwards of five hundred canoes round the ship, and at a moderate computation there was near four thousand men. Most of the trading canoes which lay round the ship, and dealt with our people, had a fair young girl in each canoe, who played a great many droll and wanton tricks, which drew all our people upon the gunwales to see them. When they seemed to be most merry and friendly some of our people observed great numbers of stones in every canoe. This created a little suspicion in several of our people, but the most of us could not think they had any bad intention against us, especially as the whole traded very fair and honest, and all the men seemed as hearty and merry as the girls.

At this time the whole bay was all lined round with men, women and children, to see the onset which was now near at hand. But they still behaved friendly until a large double canoe came off from the shore, with several of the principal inhabitants in her. This canoe lay some time on the larboard side but kept a good distance from all the rest, and was observed to hoist some signal by some of our men. The very instant that this signal was made all trade broke up, and in a few seconds of time all our decks was full of great and small stones, and several of our men cut and bruised. This was so sudden and unexpected by the most of us, that we were some time before we could find out the cause. We then ordered the sentries to fire amongst them, in hopes that would frighten them, but this had not the desired effect. They all gave another shout and flung the stones like hail amongst us which hurt a great many of our men. We then found lenity would not do, and therefore applied to the great guns and gave them a few round and grape shot, which struck such terror among the poor unhappy crowd that it would require the pen of Milton to describe, therefore too much for mine.

When any of the round shot took their canoes it carried all before it. The poor unhappy creatures that escaped immediately jumped overboard and hung by the remaining part of the canoe, until some of their friends took them up or towed off the broken canoe. When we found they had all pulled off, we gave over firing for some time, and enquired how this affair began.

In the meantime all the canoes began to assemble together at about a mile distant from the ship, thinking themselves safe from all danger, not knowing how far our shot could reach. By this time we all found out how this affair happened and several of the young gentlemen and common seamen pointed out the great canoe which gave the signal to the rest to begin the attack. We afterwards

George Robertson

found out that the King of the island and several of the grandees were in this canoe. The King now began to rally his forces at about a mile distance without the ship, and several other large double canoes rallied the canoes at about a mile distance within us. We then thought it full time to disperse them, and make them sensible of the danger they were in, in order to deter them from making any more attempts upon the ship. As the poor unfortunate King was in the boat which first attracted us, we resolved to prevent him and his friends in the boat from attempting any such thing again. Therefore we pointed two great guns at this great canoe, well loaded with round and grape shot, which soon drove her in two and I believe few that was in her escaped with life.

But what surprised me most was the resolution of five or six small canoes, with only four and six men in each, who constantly lay close by their King, and great men, when all the rest fled as fast as they could paddle off. These few poor fellows behaved so brave, that they not only carried off the lame and dead men, but they even towed off the two shattered ends of the canoe to the end of a reef.

We fired a few shot at the remaining part of the great canoe, after she was in tow, and one of the round shot struck on part of her, but even this did not make this handful of brave men give over their good offices to their chiefs and leaders. When they landed on the reef, we gave over firing and the poor men carried up the lame and dead men, and I suppose gave them a decent burial.

While this was being done the great canoes inshore had assembled above three hundred canoes and began to paddle towards the ship. I believe these leaders knew nothing of the fate of their King, or they would not have made another attempt. We let them come within about three or four hundred yards of the ship, then fired a three pounder loaded with seventy musket balls amongst

The Dolphin's guns repel the attack by the natives.

the thickest of them. This made them all shear off not without a considerable loss, and to add the more to the terror they were in we fired two round shot amongst them when they were about a mile from the ship, which made them all paddle off with all their strength, and the whole of them landed. We gave over firing and got up the light guns which we formerly stowed in the hold, and mounted them in their proper places and cleared ship for action, expecting another onset from them the first favorable opportunity that they could think of.

While this skirmish lasted all the bays and tops of the hills round were full of men, women and children to behold the onset. I dare say they were in great hopes of sharing all our nails and toys, besides the pleasure of calling our great canoe their own, and having all of us at their mercy, to ill or well use us as they thought most proper. But in place of that, when they came all running down to receive their victorious friends, how terrible must have been their shock to see their nearest and dearest of friends dead, and torn to pieces in such a manner as I am certain they never beheld before. To attempt to say what these poor ignorant creatures thought of us, would be taking more upon me than I am able to perform.

25th June. At sunrise we found all our new acquaintances had employed themselves ashore as there was not one canoe to be seen in the water. We then unmoored and hove up and warped up towards the river, where we moored in nine fathom water fine soft sandy ground to be ready to heave her broadside up to make it bear on the watering place, in order to cover the people when filling the water. Notwithstanding the skirmish that we had yesterday a few canoes ventured off about noon, with the tops of plantain trees set up in the bows of their canoes, and small branches in their hands, as emblems of peace and friendship.

We this day behaved very haughty to them and only suffered two or three to come alongside at one time. When they disposed of what they had we ordered them off, and let two or three more come

alongside. The poor creatures used a great deal of ceremony this day. Before they came within a hundred yards of the ship, they all stood up and looked hard at us and held up the plantain boughs in their hands, and one of them made a long talk, and all the rest seemed very attentive until he had done. Then they all threw their boughs to the sea, and began to paddle nearer the ship still keeping their eyes fixed on us, and if any of us looked surly they immediately held up the top of the plantain tree, and forced a sort of smile, then laid down the plantain tree top and showed us what they had got to sell. If we wanted what they brought, we made signs for them to come alongside.

Then they began another part of their ceremony by pointing to the green plantain tree top. They made a long talk and put their bodies in several postures. Sometimes he who made the talk would look up to the heavens seemingly very serious, then look at us and hold up the tree top for some time, then turn round and point to the shore and to all his partners in the canoe, after that they again looked at us and talked a little, then threw the tree top on board the ship. Then pointed to their hogs, pigs, fowl and fruit and began to trade very fair and honestly. But one of our seamen who was wounded in the head by some of the stones the day before, took an opportunity to defraud one of the natives of two fowl and when the poor fellow wanted to be paid he struck at the man, in place of paying him. This the poor fellow resented by making a great noise and shaking his fist at the sailor, which was soon observed by some of our young gentlemen, who informed Captain Wallis what had happened, and he immediately ordered the seaman to be punished with a dozen lashes, in order to deter others from attempting to defraud any of the natives. The Captain gave strict orders to punish every man that was found guilty of the like offense.

26th June. We now prepared for landing at the watering place, to take possession of this beautiful island in His Majesty's name. We first hove to upon the spring and brought the ship's broadside

George Robertson

to bear on the head of the bay, then manned and armed the barge, cutter and launch, and quartered all the hands on board at the great guns, to be ready to fire upon the natives if they attempted to prevent our boats from landing. When all this precaution was taken Mr. Furneaux, the Second Lieutenant, was ordered to take the command of the party, and to land with the sergeant and twelve Marines and eighteen able seamen besides three young gentlemen to assist him. Mr. Molleneux, one of the mates, had the command of the three boats, with orders to bring them all three to anchor, with their grapnels in a line along shore. The instant Lieutenant Furneaux landed he was to keep four men in each boat ready to fire the musketoons upon the natives, if they attacked our men, and if the party was obliged to retreat to the boats, Mr. Molleneux was to take care to keep the boats in about four foot water that the men might be able to jump in.

After all this, orders were given, the boats set out, and in a few minutes landed and formed on the beach, and took possession of the island in His Majesty's name, and honored it with the name of our most gracious sovereign King George the Third.

Soon after they landed about four or five hundred of the natives assembled within musket shot of our men and began to advance slowly towards the river side, every man carrying the bough of a plantain tree in his hand as an emblem of peace. When they got to the river side they all stopped and made several friendly signs to our people but none of them attempted to cross the river until Lieutenant Furneaux made a sign for some of them to come over. Then three elderly men set out directly and crossed the river, with a small pig in one hand and an emblem of peace in the other. When they got over the river Lieutenant Furneaux made signs for one of the three to come up to him, and he advanced about twenty yards from his party to meet the old man.

When the old man came within a few yards of the Lieutenant he made a full stop, and talked for some time then laid down the pig and laid the plantain bough on the top of it. Then the Lieutenant

Tahitian sailing canoes.

made a short talk to the old man and ordered one of the seamen to receive the peace offering, and the Lieutenant paid the old man with nails and toys, and let him know that we wanted water, which he made signs for us to take as much as we wanted. Then the Lieutenant ordered our men to roll two small casks into the river, and fill them, which was immediately done. At the same time he ordered some men to fix a long pole in the ground, and hoisted a pennant on it in token of our having taken possession of that place.

While this was doing several of the natives brought over small hogs, and pigs and some fruit, and laid them down with an emblem of peace with each, and immediately returned back to their friends on the other side of the river. They waited there until the Lieutenant ordered our men to carry all on board the boats, and laid down toys, nails, and two billhooks for the hogs, pigs and fruit, which the old man came over and took up. The Lieutenant and he shook hands and parted very good friends, then our boats returned on board with the hogs, pigs, fruit and two casks of as good water as ever was drunk.

When the natives saw our boats return great numbers of them came over the river to the place where our men stood, and every man brought over a plantain branch in his hand, and viewed the place all round, but was a considerable time before they ventured near the pennant. They all seemed afraid of it not knowing what it was put there for. At last a few of them approached the pennant. I then had the curiosity to view them with a very good spyglass, and saw two old men advance first, with two large plantain tree tops in their hands. They seemed to approach it with as much ceremony as if it had been a demigod. They made a stop at every eight or ten passes and seemed to talk some time looking up very attentively to the flag which was hoisted on a very long spar.

While these two old men were alongside some of our people observed two men throw some stones at the pennant and drive off all their countrymen

from it, that was laying down plantain tree boughs, and using the same ceremony as the others did. But this I saw not. However, the very instant that the old men landed they went and struck the pennant and carried it clear off.

At daylight we manned and armed all the boats the same as yesterday and carried a few water casks ashore to fill with some spare hands besides the thirty armed men. In two hours time we got off three tuns of exceeding good water, and filled about three tuns more, which we intended to bring off. But at half past 7 A.M. we observed a great number of large canoes, coming towards the ship from the S.W. side of the bay, and all full of men. At the same time we saw several thousands of men coming along shore toward the river. The first great body of men came over the top of a hill in the bottom of the bay, with our pennant flying at the end of a long pole, amongst the middle of them. He that carried the pennant appeared to be a tall brisk young man and the most of them appeared to be armed with spears and sticks or some such thing. This sight alarmed us all and we soon expected another skirmish, therefore the Captain ordered the jolly boat to go and order Mr. Furneaux with all our men from the shore. By the time our men embarked there were several hundreds of the natives within gun shot of them, and several thousands coming through the woods towards the watering place. There were a great many of them that had no sort of arms, but we supposed they were for throwing stones, as we saw great numbers of stones piled up like shot all along the river side. When our men were fairly embarked the Captain gave orders to fire a few random shot into the woods, in order to frighten them and make them disperse—but this had not the desired effect, until we fired a few round and grape shot amongst the thickest of them then they began to run to the top of the hill, where they supposed they were safe. This we called Skirmish Hill.

By this time about a hundred large canoes lay by abreast of the north end of Skirmish Hill, and some of their party were sent ashore to get information on how those on shore fared. We observed some of them return from the shore and hold some sort of counsel. Soon after they began to paddle towards us but at a very slow rate. We supposed they were waiting a great number of more canoes paddling up from the S.W. point of the bay to join them, before they attacked us. When we observed their intention we let them come within a short mile of us, then fired a round shot amongst them in hopes they would give over their design. But they still persisted as the shot hurt none of them, and we therefore fired some round and grape shot amongst them. This soon put them to flight, and the most of them ran their canoes ashore, and ran

into the woods thinking themselves safe there, but we soon convinced them that the woods would not protect them from our round and double-headed shot. The shot brought down several of the trees, and great numbers of the branches about their heads, which they afterwards showed us when we became good friends. This so terrified them that they all fled to the top of Skirmish Hill, where a great number of them sat down and thought themselves very safe. All the canoes that were coming up from the S.W. end of the bay had put ashore, but about five or six which pulled close in shore until they got amongst those who put ashore at the north end of Skirmish Hill.

We then fired one gun loaded with round and

One Tree Hill, called by Robertson Skirmish Hill.

The handsome, regular features of the Tahitians astonished Europeans of the eighteenth century. Some surmised that here might be the fabled lost tribe of Israel.

grape shot at them, that soon sent them after their friends to the top of the hill. By that time there were upward of seventy or eighty large canoes at the north end of Skirmish Hill capable of carrying from eight to ten hundred men, and all ready to launch in a minute's warning, in the dark of the night. To prevent their attempting any such plan, the Captain gave orders to man and arm all the boats, and to carry ashore all the carpenters and those who could use an axe to destroy all the canoes. This order was soon complied with, and in about two or three hours our people rendered about eighty canoes uncapable of floating, several of them from forty to fifty foot long and capable of

carrying upwards of thirty men. This a few of the natives observed and went and informed the rest, and several of them ventured down through the wood, I suppose with an intention to prevent our men from disabling their canoes. The guard, which landed to protect the carpenters, fired upon them and soon put them to the flight—and obliged them to retire to the top of Skirmish Hill, where they still thought they were safe until we threw a round shot close by them which made the dirt fly so that they could not help looking at the hole it made. After that they all retired to the back of the Hill and never attempted to molest us any more.

This day the Captain gave orders to let every man in the ship have as many cocoanuts, and other fruit as they thought proper to eat. Likewise he ordered hogs and pigs to be killed to make broth for all hands. Several of the men had fine fowl which they purchased before—in short all hands now lived so well that they began to revive their sunken spirits, and the most of the sick began to crawl upon deck.

27th June 1767. This day we had fine pleasant weather with a regular sea breeze all day and a land breeze at night. The instant that our boat returned from disabling all the canoes at the north end of Skirmish Hill, we saw a large body of men and women assembling on the beach to the northward of the watering place, and bringing down green boughs with hogs, pigs, fowl, and fruits, and a great quantity of white cloth. We supposed these people wanted to make peace with us, and what they were bringing down was intended for a peace offering to prevent us from destroying their canoes as we did those to the southward of the watering place.

Immediately after dinner the Second Lieutenant took the barge and cutter, manned and armed, and the launch loaded with empty water casks. He first brought the launch to anchor off the watering place, then landed where the peace offering was laid down, and walked a few steps towards the place where their canoes were hauled up on the

George Robertson

beach, as if he meant to destroy them as he did those to the southward. When the natives saw him going towards the canoes they seemed greatly afraid, and made all the signs of friendly[ness] that they could think of and pointed to the peace offering, which consisted of eight large hogs, four pigs, a dozen fowls, some fruit, and six large bales of the country cloth, from six to eight yards in each bale —besides two fine fat dogs with their forefeet tied on their backs; all this they made signs for our people to take. Then the Lieutenant ordered the men to take the hogs, pigs, fowl, and fruit and put them in the boat, but cast loose the two poor dogs who ran a mile before they stopped to look back at their deliverers. The cloth he made signs for the natives to take back, as it was of very little use to us and certainly a great loss to them. But they seemed greatly afraid when they saw he left the cloth and made signs for him to take it away. He thought it better to let it alone and laid down hatchets, billhooks, nails, and some toys and made signs for the natives to take these things and their cloth, but none of them would come near or accept of anything.

Because the cloth was not received by our people they thought the peace was not concluded, but the Lieutenant, not thinking that was their reason, went to the watering place and sent off about six tun. All returned on board without being molested by any of the natives, but still observed the poor people to the northeast of the watering place bringing down green boughs, and waving them around their heads. We therefore judged the reason and sent the two armed boats for the cloth. The instant our men laid hold of the cloth, there appeared joy in every one of the natives' faces. When the cloth was put in the boats, our people made signs for the natives to take the things which we laid down. This they complied with and brought down some more hogs, pigs, and fruit, which our men received and paid them with nails and toys.

But our young men seeing several very handsome young girls, they could not help feasting their eyes with so agreeable a sight. This was observed by some of the elderly men, and several of the young girls were drawn out—some a light copper color, others a mulatto, and some almost white. The old men made them stand in a row, and made signs for our people to take whom they liked best, and as many as they liked, and for fear our men had been ignorant and not known how to use the poor young girls, the old men made signs how we should behave to the young women. This all the boat's crew seemed to understand perfectly well, and begged the officer would receive a few of the young women on board. At same time they made signs to the young girls, that they were not so ignorant as the old men supposed them. This seemed to please the old men greatly when they saw our people merry, but the poor young girls seemed a little afraid, but soon after turned better acquainted.

The officer in the boat having no orders to bring off any of the natives, would not receive the young girls but made signs that he would see them afterwards, and ordered all our men on board the boats, and returned on board the ship. When our boats returned to the ship all the sailors swore they never saw more handsome women in their lives, and declared they would, all to a man, live on two-thirds allowance, rather than lose so fine an opportunity of getting a girl apiece. This piece of news made all our men madly fond of the shore; even the sick which had been on the Doctor's list for some weeks before now declared they would be happy if they were permitted to go ashore. At the same time they said a young girl would make an excellent nurse, and they were certain of recovering faster under a young girl's care for all the Doctor would do for them. We passed this night very merry, supposing all hostilities were now over, and to our great joy it so happened.

28th June 1767. None of the canoes came to trade with us this day—but several of the natives ventured to carry off the great double canoes, which we cut down at the last skirmish. The method that they took was this: First one man stole down and launched a single canoe and paddled her close along shore, still keeping his eye upon the ship for fear of being fired at; when this poor fellow got clear off without our seeming to take notice of him about ten of them crawled down to the beach upon their hands and feet, and launched off one of the double canoes; the instant she was afloat two stout fellows jumped on board of her and paddled off to the southward as fast as they could run. In this manner they carried off all that was not fairly cut in two except two which we brought on board and cut up for fire wood. It was once resolved to take the whole for fire wood, but we thought that would be too cruel, and would distress the poor people too much—we therefore let them carry the rest all off without any trouble from us.

At sunrise we manned and armed the boats and got off about three tuns of water. While the launch crew was filling the water, and getting it off, eight Marines and eight seamen stood on the river side all under arms to protect the waterers. At the same time about two hundred of the natives came down to the other side of the river and brought down a good many fowl and several large bundles of fruits and made signs that they wanted to trade with our men. The gunner being commanding officer made signs for one of them to bring the fowl and fruit over, but they were a long time before any of them would venture and the whole of them kept staring at the men under arms and seemed greatly afraid until the men grounded their arms. Then several of them ventured into the river but the gunner only allowed one old man to bring a fowl and some fruit over and waved the others back—the old man delivered the fowl and fruit, and Mr. Harrison the gunner gave him a ten-penny nail for the fowl, and a six-penny nail for the bundle of fruit. This pleased the old man and he went for a few more fowls and some bundles of fruit. At noon the boats was always ordered to come off to dinner so that we got but a few fowls this day and but very little fruit, as Mr. Harrison allowed none but the old man to bring any trade over the river.

This day the Captain gave strict orders to the gunner not to let any of our men go across the river, nor to allow above two or three of the natives to come on our side, neither was he to allow any of the men to trade with the natives, but to carry on all the trade himself. This made our trade to go on but slowly and prevented discoveries of all kinds for some time.

30th June. We carried ashore a tent for the coopers to set up some water casks, and a sail to make a shed for the guard to shelter themselves from the sun. The natives traded very peaceably this day and no murmuring was made.

We now began to think the natives would continue peaceable and the Doctor told Captain Wallis that the sick ought now to go ashore every day for the recovery of their health. This the Captain agreed to, and ordered [a sail] to be carried

The beautiful women of Tahiti, immortalized by Gauguin.

ashore to shelter the sick men from the sun, at same time giving strict orders that no man should straggle away into the woods for fear of accidents.

1st July 1767. At night we had fine pleasant weather with refreshing showers, which brought a very agreeable smell from the land. At sunrise the traders and waterers went ashore, and about twenty liberty men, the most of them in the sick list, but all able to walk about a little. The sick tent was pitched upon a small island in the middle of the river, and the sick were carried through the smallest branch of the river to the tent, and all those who were able had a cutlass to defend themselves with, and two of the young gentlemen with four Marines stood guard over the sick tent, to prevent the people from strolling away from the island.

3rd July. Sent all our traders, waterers and liberty men ashore and scrubbed the ship betwixt wind and water, and payed the bends with warm tar. Our copper bottom looked as well as the first day we came out of England. At noon our people all returned on board and brought one hog and six small pigs. One of the young gentlemen that was along with the guard told me that a great many of the principal people of the island came down to the river side with servants attending them, carrying stools for their masters and mistresses to sit down on along the river side. Several of them brought down large hogs to trade with us for nails and other things, which they wanted, but the gunner would permit none of them to cross the river but the old man and his son. When any of the others set their foot in to cross the river, he ordered some of the guard to point their muskets at them, which frightened them greatly and made them return back trembling to their own side, and very often go off into the woods and not return again.

4th July. We had fine pleasant clear weather and were employed completing our rigging and overhauling our sea provisions, and making a thorough clean all over the ship. We now got up our yards and topmasts and tarred all our yards and standing rigging. At night we had a fine pleasant

land breeze which never failed to bring a sweet and agreeable smell of various sorts of fruits and herbs. At sunrise we sent all the boats ashore with the traders, waterers, and liberty men. We ordered all the liberty men that were able to cut grass, to make hay for our sheep, there being a great plenty of very fine grass on the island. This was a very good moderate exercise for the sick and gave them a little more liberty to walk about in order to find proper grass for cutting. Before they were never suffered to go to the nearest end of the island, but this day they strolled about a good way, and all returned on board greatly refreshed. The men say all the natives appear to be very peaceable and friendly inclined. Several of them wanted to come over to the liberty men with hogs, fowl and fruit, but none were permitted. This day our people were served salt provisions, there not being a sufficient quantity of fresh pork on board. This was entirely owing to the treatment we gave the natives, who it is reasonable to think had some sense of good and bad ways, as well as we.

5th July. We sent our traders, waterers and liberty men ashore as usual, and the gunner allowed the people to bring their stock to market themselves, but the instant he paid for them he made them return back and by this means he brought off eight hogs, four pigs, eighteen fat fowl and plenty of fruit. All the natives seemed very cheerful and merry, and some of the young girls brought fowl to market, which was paid with tenpenny nails, but to encourage trade the young gentlemen gave them some earrings and the gunner gave them beads, which he tied about their neck and wrists. This pleased the young girls much, and made trade go on well.

6th July. Some of the young girls ventured over to the liberty men, and our honest-hearted tars received them with great cheerfulness, and made them some little presents which gained the hearts of the young girls and made them give our men a signal, which they would have willingly obeyed, had they not been immediately ordered on board.

George Robertson

At noon we returned on board and found our traders had but very indifferent success, they only brought off four pigs, a few fowls and some fruit. I was told by one of the young gentlemen that a new sort of trade took up the most of their attention this day, but it might be more properly called the old trade. He says a dear Irish boy, one of our Marines, was the first that began the trade, for which he got a very severe cobbing from the liberty men for not beginning in a more decent manner, in some house or at the back of some bush or tree. Paddy's excuse was the fear of losing the honor of having the first.

7th July. After dinner we sent the trading party ashore to endeavor to produce some more hogs, but they got none, and returned on board with only a few bunches of plantains and bananas, but the old trade went on merrily. At sunrise we sent the traders, waterers and liberty men ashore, and for fear of their not succeeding better nor yesterday, Mr. Gore was sent with a party of twenty armed men to trade along shore from house to house, beginning at the foot of Skirmish Hill and to come up to the watering place. At noon all hands returned on board but neither party had great success, the old traders brought off but three small pigs, some fowls and a little fruit, and Mr. Gore's party brought off four small hogs and two pigs with some very fine red and white yams. We this day served all the seamen fresh pork and good broth and all the warrant and petty officers were served two fowls among three men and as much fruit as they chose to take. Our First Lieutenant now turned very sick when the Captain began to recover, but the most of the seamen are now pretty well. All those who are able to go ashore recover fast.

9th July. I went ashore for the first time, and walked about a mile up the river, with two of the young gentlemen along with me, and one of the seamen with a musket. In returning back to the boats, three very fine young girls accosted us, and one of them made a signal and smiled in my face.

This made me stop to enquire what the young lady wanted and supposing the young gentlemen better acquainted than me, who had never seen any of the young ladies before, but at a great distance, I desired one of them to explain the meaning of the signal. They both put on a very grave look and told me they did not understand her signs. I then supposed she had something for sale, made signs for her to show her goods, but this seemed to displease her and another repeated the same signal, which was this: She held up her right hand and first finger of the right hand straight, then laid hold of her right wrist with the left hand, and held the right hand and first finger up straight and smiled, then crooked all her fingers and kept playing with them and laughed very hearty, which set my young friends laughing as heartily as the young girl. This made me insist upon their explaining the sign, and they told me the young girls only wanted a long nail each, but they never before saw them make a sign for one longer nor their fingers. They supposed the young girls thought I carried longer nails than the rest because I was dressed in a different manner. I wanted them to explain the other part of the signal, that I might understand the whole. But the young men begged to be excused. I therefore gave the young girls a nail each, and parted good friends. We then walked down to see how the traders went on, and told the gunner what had happened betwixt us and the young girls, and he explained the whole matter in a few words, and told me my young friends were not so very ignorant as they pretended to be. He likeway told me that the price of the old trade is now fixed at a thirty-penny nail each time, and he told me that the liberty men dealt so largely in that way that he was much afraid of losing his trade of hogs, pigs, fowls and fruit.

He said the people of this country deal very cunningly. If they bring down three or four different things to sell, they always endeavor to sell the worst first, and if they get what they want for any trifling thing that they can easily spare they carry back their hogs, pigs and fowl. He likeways says he has often seen them conceal their best things, until he purchased the other things of less value. This made him afraid that the natives would purchase all the nails and toys by means of the old trade, and of course bring no other goods to market, therefore advised me to endeavor to put a stop to it when I went on board by preventing the liberty men from coming ashore. This I told him was out of my power, as the most of them were on the sick list. He then told me the sickest of them traded a little, therefore could not be so very bad as they pretended. I then promised to represent the case to the Commanding Officer.

When I returned on board I acquainted the Second Lieutenant who was then Commanding Officer, the Captain and First Lieutenant then being sick. I then let him and the Doctor and our good merry friend the purser know how trade went on ashore. We then consulted what was best to be done. Some were of the opinion it would be best to detain the liberty men some days; others said it would be ruining all trade to keep them on board, and the Doctor, who was certainly a man that took the greatest care of his patients, affirmed that the keeping of the liberty men confined on board the ship would ruin their health and constitution, for, said he, anything that depresses the mind and spirits of men must certainly hurt them. We sent for a few who were on the sick list, and examined them, and threatened to stop their liberty for spoiling the gunner's trade. This affected the poor unthinking fellows so much, that we immediately saw a visible change in their countenance, which plainly confirmed what the Doctor said. We therefore agreed to prevent them as much as possible from taking nails and toys ashore with them. We likeways put a very necessary question to the Doctor, who affirmed upon his honor that no man on board was affected with any sort of disorder, that they could communicate to the natives of this beautiful island. [Written in red ink and different hand at the botton of the page — *No Venereal.*]

128

10th July 1767. At noon all the traders, wooders and liberty men came off and brought two of the natives to dine with them. One was the old man's son who assisted the gunner and the other was one of their chiefs or great men. He appeared to be a sensible, well-behaved man, about thirty years of age, and about five foot nine, well made and very good features of a dark Mustee color. We showed him the ship, and he took very particular notice of everything we showed him, and seemed greatly surprised at the construction of our ship.

This day the Captain and the First Lieutenant were both able to sit up, and we all dined in the gun room, with the chief along with us. After spreading the cloth we all set down and made him sit down in a chair, but before he sat down he viewed the chair all around. Then he sat down and viewed the plates, knives and forks with great attention, but the instant he saw the dinner set down, he laid down his plate and touched nothing until he was helped. We had a very excellent dinner, which consisted of broth made with two fine fat fowl, two roasted fowl, roast pig, yams, plantains, bananas, soft bread, apple pudding and apple pie — all of this he ate a part of, and took very great notice of the way we used our spoons, knives and forks, and used them in the same manner that we did and helped himself with fowl, pig, yams, etc., the same as we did.

We had very good claret, Madeira, port, rum and brandy, grog and excellent good London porter, but his choice was water. He smelt and tasted the wine and grog but liked neither but water and seemed greatly pleased when we all touched glasses with him. He observed us wipe our mouths before we drank, with our pocket handkerchiefs. This made him a little uneasy he having nothing of that kind, and seemed unwilling to use his clothes. I therefore gave him the corner of the tablecloth to wipe his mouth, which so shocked the delicate Mr. Clarke that he could neither eat nor drink any more at that time, but kept growling at the chief and me

A Tahitian dance, as portrayed by John Webber, an artist accompanying Captain Cook.

George Robertson

for being so very undelicate all the time we sat at dinner. He took up the cloth several times, and endeavored to make the man understand how unpolite it was to use the cloth. This made the man unhappy for some time, as he could not comprehend this meaning. He still thought he had done something very bad which began to make me uneasy, knowing myself to be the original author of this man's trouble.

I therefore, in order to please the chief, sat with him and used the corner of the cloth, and made him do the same and began to be very merry with him which pleased the man so much that he made signs to poor "Growel," who was still on the fret, that he would bring him a fine young girl to sleep with him. This merry thought put an end to growling and pleased the fretter, who was pleased to say, "Well done, Jonathan; if you perform your promise you shall be rewarded." This being the first Christian name that was ever bestowed on any of the natives of this island, we always after called this man Jonathan.

After dinner we showed Jonathan a looking glass which surprised him a little at first, but he soon began to pull his beard which is the custom of his country. Then he got a pair of tweezers which he applied to the proper use and began to pull his beard and the hairs out of his nose. But the thing which pleased and astonished Jonathan the most of all, was the picture of a very handsome well-dressed young lady, in miniature, which the Doctor showed him. We made him understand that this was the picture of the women in our country and if he went with us he should have one of them always to sleep with. This put him in such raptures of joy that it impossible for me to describe. He hugged the picture to his breast and kissed it twenty times, and made several other odd motions, to show us how happy he would be with so fine a woman. We all supposed Jonathan to be one of the first-rank people of the island, from the respect that the rest showed him, but had he been King of this and all the high mountains to the southward, let them reach or extend ever so far even to the Dutch Spice

Islands, I am certain Jonathan would have made this young lady Queen. Had the substance been here in place of the shadow, I really believe he would have come to England for her had we been willing to take him with us, and his friends contented to let him go.

11th July 1767. At noon all hands came on board to dinner, and our friend Jonathan came off in a canoe with four men paddling him and two very handsome young girls, which he brought off to dine with us. We immediately got in Jonathan and the two Mustee girls, and carried them all through the ship, and showed them everything that was curious, supposing them to be his two sisters. But when he came down to the gun room, he made us understand that he brought them off agreeable to his promise. In order to make up matters with Mr. Clarke he offered him the choice of either.

13th July. Our old friend Jonathan came off to pay us another visit and brought two fine roasted pigs from him and some fruit. Mr. Furneaux and I rigged out Jonathan with a complete suit of clothes, shoes, etc. We had plenty of diversion showing him how to put all the clothes on, especially the britches as they puzzled him worst of all, but after he found out how to use them he seemed more fond of them than all the rest except the shoes. These pleased him greatly and he walked up and down the deck with great spirits. After dinner he went ashore in his English dress and seemed extremely happy when our boat landed him. He called to some of the country people to carry him out for fear of wetting his shoes, and when he came to the river he made two of his servants carry him over. When he got across the river a great many of his country people came round him and he took great pleasure of showing himself. What became of this jolly young fellow afterwards we know not, as we never saw nor heard anything more of him. We supposed the young man's friends were afraid of his going off with us, and had ordered him back into the country to prevent him.

130

16th July. The first part of the day we sent no boats ashore except the barge which the Captain and Lieutenant Furneaux went in to get the air. At the north side of the bay there is a very long house with several small ones round it that the inhabitants have forsaken ever since we arrived here. This long house was built more like a shade than one of our houses, therefore the more open and airy and the more suitable to this climate. Captain Wallis and the Lieutenant walked up and down within the house not being able to bear the heat of the sun until he was near set. While they kept under the shade with a guard to attend them, the other gentlemen who went along with them sometimes walked a little way into the woods where there were several little houses, but never attempted to go any great distance. By this time the natives and all our people were very sociable, and the instant our boats landed numbers of them came flocking round, especially the young girls who seldom failed to carry off a nail from every man of the party.

I was told by a gentleman of the party that he had seen a very handsome little woman, who lived near to this long house, and he says he made her several little presents at different times that he saw her ashore, but could never find her so kind as the other young girls. This day he gave her some very considerable presents, at least they appeared so to her, and she gave him the usual signal, which he readily obeyed, and walked after her into the woods. When she got clear out of sight of the rest, she pointed to a little house, and made him understand that he should be happily rewarded for all his presents, but just as my friend was going in he observed a strong well-made man coming towards the house. This made him stop and the woman observed him waiting at the door, ran out and saw it was her husband, she immediately looked frightened and called out "*takena takena*" which made my friend suppose it was her husband. She soon returned to the door with a very fine fowl and some fruit, and when the husband came she was selling the fowl and my friend was offering

George Robertson

double the price that any other fowl cost, but she could not agree until her husband came. Then she talked to him and he began to smile, and offered the fowl and fruit for what was offered to his wife, and my friend gladly accepted and seeing the husband was a carpenter, he gave him several nails which gained the poor man's heart so much that he would have given him all that he had except his handsome wife.

My friend returned to his party very unhappy at so great a disappointment, but I told him I thought he had double reason to be happy, that the strong fellow did not catch him and give him a good drubbing. He allows he was well able if he had got hold of him without his sword. He told me the guard relieved one another regularly and got value for their nails, and returned back to their duty. Some of the fellows were so extravagant that while he was ashore they spent two nails. He says this was owing to the great variety of goods which came to market.

17th July. The first part of the day we sent no boats ashore to trade, but the Captain went to take the air at the long house on the north side of the bay where numbers of the natives assembled as usual, and trade went on the same as yesterday, every man laid out his nail and some two.

The handsome little woman brought my friend a fine large pig, and her husband brought a large bundle of fruit, and wanted to make him a present of all, but he obliged them to take triple value, and made signs for them to come on board the ship. But the man seemed unwilling to come on board, but the little woman pointed to the ship and called out "*Mettaccow, Mettaccow, Mettaccow*," which in their language signifies tomorrow.

A little after 9 A.M. the handsome little woman came off in a canoe with her husband, father and mother, and a young girl which we supposed to be her sister. We showed them all the different parts of the ship, and the husband took very great notice of everything he saw, especially the chairs, chests and tables. He observed every joint in the chairs and tables, and measured the length and breadth of every joint of our chairs and the gun room table, and marked his measures on a piece of line, which he brought with him. I observed him make different knots for the length and breadth. He appears to be a very sensible fellow and I dare say will be able to make a chair or table when he has a mind.

While the honest carpenter and I were taking the dimensions of the chairs and tables, my friend and the wife were endeavoring to get clear of the old man and his wife, and another hand took care of the sister and showed her some curious things which pleased the young lass, but the instant the carpenter saw his wife and my friend go into his cabin, he immediately went after them to see what curiosities they had there. This disappointment cost my friend a suit of old clothes to the honest carpenter, and a shirt to the wife, besides the trouble of showing the curious man everything in his cabin.

At this time the woman slipped out of the cabin, and cast loose the canoe which she came off in, and let her run a good way from the ship. The wind being a head soon carried her near sixty yards from the ship. She then looked round and saw her father and mother was out of the gun room, and one of the young gentlemen entertaining her sister. She then called out loudly to her husband and told him the canoe was gone adrift. This made the poor man throw off his clothes to jump into the water to save his canoe. This alarmed my friend who desired me to be so good as order a boat to go after the canoe. Meantime he laid hold of the carpenter to prevent him from jumping overboard, but the little artful creature immediately put herself in such a passion that her husband twisted himself out of my friend's hands and jumped out at the gun room port and swam after his canoe.

The instant that he was in the water, she immediately stepped into my friend's cabin and laid hold of his coat and pulled him in. While she was

131

enjoying the reward of her art and cunning, the poor man's life was running the greatest risk imaginable, not knowing but he might be devoured any minute by some large shark such as we caught about a fortnight before. But the honest carpenter had better luck, in about ten minutes' time he brought his canoe back and made her fast to the gun room port where his wife cast her loose from, and jumped into the gun room where his wife received him, and gave him a few large nails which she gained in his absence, to make up for the loss he sustained. This greatly pleased the good man, as he knew nothing of the way and manner the nails were procured.

A somewhat fanciful view of the "surrender" of Tahiti to Captain Wallis by "Queen Oberea" (actually Purea, a tribal chieftainess). In the background is the long house where she entertained Robertson and other members of the Dolphin's crew.

The gunner now told me that there was a great alteration of the prices at market, what he now buys is a hundred per cent dearer than the first week that we landed. This he says is chiefly owing to the liberty men, who give too high a price for all sorts of curiosities that they deal in.

19th July. While the rest was at dinner, Mr. Pickersgill and the sergeant strolled a great way into the woods, where they fell in with a great number of the natives assembled together at a very long house where there was a very great entertainment preparing for all the assembly. The Queen of the Country was present. At first they were both afraid, and would have willingly come off without going too near the assembly, but several of the natives came towards them, and invited them to the feast. They were both afraid to disoblige them, knowing that they were a great way from the guard and scarce knew their way back, therefore accepted of the invitation and sat down along with the natives.

George Robertson

They all formed a ring and sat down around the Queen, who was seated on a very fine mat, with two very handsome young ladies standing by her. In the middle of the ring, when the dinner was laid down before the Queen, all the servants that brought it stood round, and the Queen ordered the two young ladies who stood by her to serve it out in dishes, then delivered it to the servants, who served those who sat round, beginning at them who sat next the Queen. They appeared to be the people of the first rank. When they were served, every one of them seemed a little grave, and muttered a few words with their faces toward the sun, then laid or rather threw a small portion out of each dish. After that they began to eat very heartily.

The Queen ordered the two young ladies to feed her which they did; the one stood at the right hand and the other at the left, and fed her by turns with their hands only. She that stood at the right hand put her hand in a basin of clean water, then took up a part of the meat, and put it in the Queen's mouth, with her right hand, and she ate the meat from her fingers. Then the young lady washed her hand in another basin of clean water, and stood ready to give her another mouthful, after she on the left went through the same ceremony.

20th July 1767. After all had dined the Queen stood up and made a talk to her people, then ordered two of her people to conduct our people to the landing place, which they did and was paid with nails for their trouble. Soon after the Queen came on board with six of her chief men, which we entertained in the gun room. The Captain being very poorly at the time she came on board, we could not carry Her Majesty to the Great Cabin. She brought a very good present of livestock on board, which served all hands two days, and the Captain ordered a present in return. The principal part of her attendance ate and drank very heartily with us in the gun room but the Queen did neither. She was well entertained with viewing our curiosities, while her great men were busy in eating and drinking. Each of them ate hearty and drank two glasses of Madeira and a tumbler of water, but would not drink either rum or brandy or grog.

They examined the cook's coppers which were extremely clean, and shone as brightly as any tea kettle in London. This seemed to surprise them the most of anything which we showed them. They tried to haul off a small piece of the copper but could not, then they had a long talk and the Queen put her hand in to both coppers, and seemed greatly surprised. We endeavored to explain the use of the coppers which they seemed to understand. We walked aft to the quarterdeck where we showed them geese and turkeys in the coops. They had never seen any of the kind in the country for which reason we gave them a breed of each some days before we sailed.

In my opinion the whole were smart, sensible people and very curious in observing everything which they saw, but the Queen was rather more so than any of the rest. She is a strong well-made woman about five foot ten inches high, and very plainly dressed without either shoes, stockings or head dress, and no kinds of jewels or trinkets about her. The sergeant says she had three large pearls in each ear, when he first saw her, but she soon after took them out of her ears. Her clothes were different from the rest, but worn after the same manner, her under garments were white which I shall call her shirt, her petticoat was white and yellow, and her gown was red. She appeared very cheerful and merry all the time she was on board.

21st July 1767. After dinner we sent the traders and waterers ashore. When I was ordering the liberty men into the boat the carpenter came and told me every cleat in the ship had been drawn, and all the nails carried off. At the same time the boatswain informed me that most of the hammock nails were drawn, and two-thirds of the men obliged to lie on the deck for want of nails to hang their hammocks.

I immediately stopped the liberty men, and called all hands, and let them know that no man on the ship should have liberty to go ashore until they informed me who drew out the nails and cleats, and let me know what use they made of them. Not one would acknowledge that they knew anything about the nails and cleats, but all said they knew what use they went to. I told them it was very surprising because they knew the use they were put to, but knew none of the men.

Then some of the young gentlemen told me that all the liberty men carried on a trade with the young girls, who had now increased their price for some days past, from a twenty- or thirty-penny nail, to a forty-penny. Some were so extravagant as to demand a seven- or nine-inch spike. This was plain proof of the way the large nails went. I then acquainted the Captain with what had happened, and he ordered me to stop their liberty until I found out some of those who had drawn the cleats, and he would order them all to be punished. I then went upon deck and told all the ship's company that there was no man to have liberty, to set his foot upon shore, until I was informed who drew the nails and cleats. I then ordered off the boats who had pretty good success in the trading way.

This evening I observed a great murmuring amongst the people. I went forward to see if I could find out who had drawn the nails and cleats. At this time they were preparing their supper at the galley and some blamed one, some another. It being dark none of them observed me, therefore told their mind plain. At last I found out that the most of them were concerned, and several said they had rather receive a dozen lashes than to have their liberty stopped. At last there was a trial amongst them, and six were condemned for spoiling the old trade by giving large spike nails, when others had only a hammock nail, which three declared were refused, they being much smaller than the spikes. Two cleared themselves by proving that they got double value for the spikes. After that a battle ensued about the one interfering with the other in the way of trade. I was obliged to call out what was the matter: all was quiet immediately.

134

At sunrise I sent all the boats ashore, but sent no liberty men. At noon the boats returned and brought ten hogs, six fowl and plenty of fruit. I told the traders they were to go ashore after dinner, but none should go on liberty unless some of them who drew the nails were found out.

At last three witnesses proved him to be a poor fellow, flogged some time before for thieving, had drawn one of the cleats. This unhappy fellow was a proper object to make an example of. I therefore acquainted the Captain, who ordered me to cause him to run the gauntlet three times round the ship. I then called all hands and placed the men in proper order with a nettle in each of their hands. I several times asked him if there was any of the rest concerned with him but he still said no. This made the men very merciful the first round, but when I ordered him the second round he began to impeach some of the rest, and hoped to be excused himself. I told him it was then too late, and sent him the second round. The poor fellow got a hard drubbing that time, which made me excuse him from going the third time. At the same time I acquainted the whole that if any such complaint came again they might rely on a much more severe punishment and none of them would ever be allowed to go on liberty any more. Then they all declared to a man that they should take care that no such thing should ever be done again.

22nd July 1767. At 8 A.M. the Queen paid us another visit and brought off a very good present of livestock, for which the Captain gave her another present in return. I convoyed her and one of her principal attendants into the great cabin, where the Captain ordered breakfast to be got immediately and made her and the chief both sit down to tea and bread and butter. Before the chief touched the bread and butter he rose up and made a long speech looking all round the cabin, then went to the quarter gallery and looked out towards the sun and kept still talking which makes me suppose they worship the sun. When his talk or speech was over he sat down on the Queen's left hand and took up a piece of soft bread and smelt it, then began to eat hearty.

We gave him a knife and showed him how to spread the butter on the bread. He mistook our meaning and laid down the knife, and took up a little of the butter, with the nails of his two fingers and smelt it, then threw it down, I suppose according to the custom of his country, as they were always observed to throw away a little of everything they ate. This put one that was present [Lieutenant Clarke] out of humor and was so rude that he snatched the butter away, and ordered the Captain's servant to bring clean butter. This behavior surprised the chief and prevented him from eating any more; it likewise made the Queen very grave, who was very merry before. This made the Captain very uneasy but he said nothing to old Growl, and soon after made the Queen a present which made her good-humored, but she neither ate nor drank while she was on board.

After breakfast I carried her all round betwixt decks, where she took very particular notice of everything she saw, and seemed highly pleased. I then carried her into every cabin of the gun room, where I showed her everything that was curious, and made her a present of any trinket that she seemed fond of, such as looking glass, a wine glass, buttons and earrings, etc. But what she seemed most fond of was linen cloth. I therefore gave a very good ruffled shirt, and showed her how to put it on. This trifling present gained her heart, and I convoyed her to the Captain's cabin, where I left her in great spirits and the Captain showed her all his courtesies, but the Queen looking upon him as our king wanted him to sign a treaty of peace in order to settle all differences betwixt her people and ours. But Captain Wallis at that time being very poorly and having a little paralytic disorder in his hand could not hold the pen, therefore excused himself until another opportunity.

They have a very peculiar custom in this country. At the age of sixteen they paint all the men's thighs black, and soon after paint curious figures on their legs and arms, and the ladies seem not to exceed the age of twelve or thirteen when they go through that operation. I suppose they look upon themselves as men and women at the age of sixteen and twelve.

When I again went into the Captain's cabin the Queen took it in her head that I was painted after the manner of her country therefore wanted to see my legs, thighs and arms. Rather than disoblige her I showed her all, which greatly surprised her and she would not believe that I showed my skin until she felt it with her own hands. She then wanted to see my breast which I likeways showed her, but it surprised her most of all my breast being full of hair. She supposed I was a very strong man and certainly of age, although not painted. She then began to feel my thighs and legs to know if they had the strength that they seemed to have. I then put my legs in position that they both felt stiff and strong which made her look very hard in my face, and call out with admiration, "Oh! Oh! Oh!" and desired the chief to feel my legs, which I allowed him to do and he seemed greatly astonished as she. After that they had a long talk, and the Queen laid hold of me to lift me up, but I prevented her, without her being sensible of the reason why she could not lift me up. This surprised her most of all and she called, "Oh! Oh!" and talked again for some time to the chief, who made a sign for me to lift her, which I did with one arm and carried her round the cabin. This seemed to please her greatly and she eyed me all round and began to be very merry and cheerful. If I am not mistaken Her Majesty's behavior is the way the ladies here try the men, before they admit them to be their lovers.

When I landed the Queen there were some hundreds of her subjects standing ready on the shore to receive her. After we were carried over the river she laid hold of my hand, and introduced me to all the principal people, and made them all shake hands with me, and one of the young gentlemen that I took along with me. After that cere-

The breadfruit.

care to keep one of my pistols cocked ready in my hand. The young fellow inspected it and felt the edge, then began to cut capers not unlike one of the Moorfields Cudgel players. This made me a little uneasy and I held out my hand to get the sword back, but the stout young fellow laughed at me and cut another caper. I then caught hold of his wrist, and took the sword out of his hand, but not without some trouble. This made him look a little surly. I therefore gave him a stroke with the flat of the sword, and immediately turned round and struck at a plantain tree which was growing close by where we stood, and had the good luck to cut it through, which so frightened the fellow that he marched off directly. The Queen and the old lady laughed very hearty and all the rest smiled and seemed pleased.

I went to take my leave of the Queen but they obliged me to sit down again and the Queen cut me out a suit of the country cloth, and wanted me to throw off my own, but I declined that and put them on over my own. There was no great trouble in making this suit. She only cut off about ten feet of the piece of cloth, which was about five feet wide, and cut a hole in the middle which was where I put my head, and she then tied it round my waist with a sash of much finer cloth.

By that time dinner was near ready and the Queen insisted on our staying for dinner, but as I had positive orders from Captain Wallis I was obliged to deprive myself of the honor of dining with her. When she found I was positive to go she spoke to the old woman which I cannot help thinking was her mother as she suffered none other to take the least liberty with her. Then the old lady laid hold of me, and endeavored to detain me, and when she found nothing would prevail on me to stay for dinner, she made me understand with very plain signs that I should have her daughter to sleep with, and when that had not the desired effect, the old lady pointed to two very handsome young ladies, and made us understand that the young gentleman and I should have them to sleep with,

mony was over I ordered six of the barge men armed to come up after us. We then set out for the palace.

I then walked around the palace to view it, and measured the length of it with my broadsword and found it to be a house of three hundred and twenty-one feet in length, and thirty-six feet in breadth, neatly built and supported with fourteen large pillars of wood in the middle of the house. Every pillar was about fifteen or sixteen inches in diameter and about twenty-four feet high, several of them neatly carved, considering the tools which we saw them have.

While I was viewing the palace a brisk young man came up to me and held out his hand and I shook hands with him. He then wanted to look at my broadsword, which I was rather unwilling to give him, but on the Queen making a sign to let him have it, I gave it out of my hands, but took thinking that would tempt us to stay. I then excused myself in the best manner I could, and laid hold of the Queen's hand, and the old lady's to take my leave. At the same time I made them understand that I would soon come back from my own country and sleep with her in my arms. This pleased both and I parted with the old lady, who seemed extremely well pleased, but the Queen laid hold of my arm, and came along with me down to the waterside.

Between the palace and the shore there were several houses full of the principal people of the island, which I suppose had come down the country to see our ship. She obliged me to call at every house, and I shook hands with all the old people, and was very merry with the young, as was my young friend. The country people seeing us both dressed after the country fashion, appeared to be very cheerful and happy and all paid a very great respect to the Queen.

At the last house where we called, there were two of the handsomest young ladies that I ever saw upon the island. One in particular was fully as fair and had as good features as the women in England. Had she been dressed after the English manner, I am certain no man would have thought her of another country. I first shook hands with two fine jolly old people, who I suppose was the young lady's parents. They were both of a mulatto color. I then shook hands with the young ladies who were both fine brisk-spirited women. The fairest of these two, seeing that I took more notice of her than the other, began to be very merry and we compared skins and hers was rather fairer and more white than mine. In short I took so much notice of this fine young lady that I almost forgot Her Majesty who was conversing with the old people.

Her looking round and observing my young friend deeply engaged with the other young lady and me seemingly so fond of her who was so very fair, put the Queen a little out of humor, and she immediately broke up the conversation with the old people and said something to the young lady whom I was talking with that made her very unhappy. I was sorry to see the young lady uneasy and took her in my arms to comfort her, but the instant I laid hold of her, the Queen laid hold of my arm, and gave the poor young lady so cross a look in the face, that I really believe she soon after fainted. Knowing it was my duty to please the Queen, I endeavored to recover my surprise, and did all I could to please Her Majesty but after that she would enter no house, but in a manner led me to the boat side, where she waited until I went off to the ship.

24th July 1767. This day I chanced to look to an Ephemerides which informed me that there was an eclipse of the sun on the 25th Inst. which was said to be visible in Mexico and Peru, but not in any part of Europe. It was also said to be new moon at Paris as seven hours eight minutes in the

A Tahitian burial shed. A native at the right climbs a breadfruit tree.

afternoon, for which reason I found it must be visible where we were about seven or eight next morning, therefore acquainted the Captain, who ordered me to fix the reflecting telescope and see if it was fit to observe by. This I did but found there was no dark glass belonging to the telescope so that it was impossible to observe the eclipse. But on recollecting we found a dark glass in a small telescope belonging to a sextant which the Captain had. This I fitted to the largest telescope and told the Captain, and he ordered me to take the barge and go to observe the eclipse at the proper time.

25th July 1767. "Mr. Growl" came on deck at sunrise as we prepared to leave the ship. He told me I could not use the barge, despite the Captain's orders. He gave me a disdainful sneer and ordered Mr. Gore with a party of twenty armed men into the barge, cutter and launch, then told me I might take the jolly boat if I wanted to look at the sun with an instrument that I knew nothing about. I thanked him for his civility and ordered up the jolly boat's crew to shift the things out of the barge into the jolly boat, but "Old Growl" found ways and means to detain us too long. Knowing him to be a ill-natured, ignorant sort of man, I said nothing more to him but got ashore as fast as possible to the northernmost point of the bay, where I desired Mr. Pinnock to take the altitude of the sun, and work the true time of the day.

At the same time Mr. Harrison and I took the instant of time that he observed the sun's altitude by our watches, which were regulated the night before. When that was done Mr. Harrison began to look at the sun with a very good spyglass and told me he thought the eclipse was beginning. In the meantime, I was fixing the reflecting telescope, and bid him observe the time by his watch, which he did and found it to be about 6:51′:50″. At the same time Mr. Pinnock took the sun's altitude which corresponded with the watch. About two minutes after Mr. Harrison first observed the eclipse, I got the reflecting telescope fixed and saw

that the emersion had been commenced some minutes sooner than Mr. Harrison had observed it. This was owing to our being so long detained by "Old Growl." I must own I was very unhappy as was both my companions for fear of our not being able to determine the emersion, as the weather was beginning to be very cloudy, but we chanced to have better fortune, for the weather proved very clear all the time of the eclipse. When the eclipse was near ended I deserted Mr. Pinnock to run and acquaint the Captain that it was near over. He being at that time coming along shore in his barge with "Old Growl" along with him, who I dare say prevailed on him to come ashore to laugh at my ignorance, in pretending to know what time the eclipse happened.

When Mr. Pinnock informed Captain Wallis, "Old Growl" gave a disdainful sneer, and said he supposed the Captain would come time enough to see it ended as it was not yet began because he could not discover it with his sickly eyes; but the young gentleman told the Captain that he saw it for some time himself, and that if he wanted to look at it, he must make haste. Then they all came up, and saw it both with the telescope, and the common spyglass. This made the Captain very happy, and he desired me to be very exact in observing the end of the eclipse which I did with the greatest exactness, but not without some difficulty with "Old Growl," who declared that I saw nothing of the eclipse with the reflecting telescope, because he could not see with so nice an instrument, but he owned that he saw it very plain with Mr. Harrison's spyglass. I begged of him to have a little patience until the eclipse was over.

I then told Mr. Pinnock to be ready to take the sun's altitude, at the same instant that I called to him. At the same time desired Mr. Harrison to be very exact in observing the end by his common glass, which he did and called out directly. As I had so fine an instrument I could see it continue about a minute longer before the tops of the mountains disappeared on the verge of the sun.

George Robertson

Just as we had done with the observation the Queen and one of her chiefs came to us, and I gave her a sight of the sun with the dark glass, which surprised beyond expectation both her and her chief who likewise had a sight. The chief wanted to have another look at the sun. I set the telescope but neglected putting in the dark glass, which almost blinded the poor man. To keep him from knowing the trick I put in the dark glass and looked as long as he, then looked him full in the face as if I had been surprised at his not being able to look.

27th July 1767. The first part of the day we completed getting in seventy-eight tuns of water and got everything clear for sea. After dinner we sent the trading party ashore who brought off ten large hogs, several fowl and a great quantity of fruit. At 4 P.M. the Queen came on board to endeavor to make us stay for some days longer than we intended. The instant that the Captain made her understand that we were to sail at sunrise, she appeared greatly concerned and made signs for us to stay ten days before we took our departure from her fruitful, pleasant island. Captain Wallis

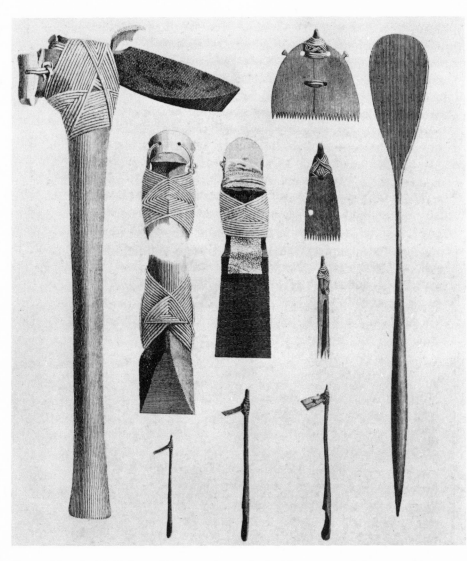

Tools used by the Tahitians. The small, toothed objects are prickers used in tattooing.

was positive to sail the next morning and therefore ordered the ship to be unmoored, that we might be ready to sail the sooner in the morning.

When this great woman could not prevail with the Captain to stay ten days, she came down to nine, eight, seven, six and five days, and when she found that he still was for going in the morning at sunrise, she immediately wept and cried for some minutes, then made all the friendly signs that she could possibly think of to induce us to stay only two days longer, but the Captain would not be prevailed on by her entreaties, but still made signs that he would sail at sunrise. This positive resolution of the Captain's affected this great woman beyond expectation. When she found that all her entreaties had no effect she immediately burst out in tears and cried and wept in such a manner that few men could have helped pitying her.

At 5 A.M. we hove short and sent the launch for some water. It being calm we could not weigh the anchor until a fresh breeze sprung up. When the launch and cutter got close to the watering place, our people observed several hundred people on the beach, which made them unwilling to land, as they never saw them come down before until the sun was up. This made our people suppose they were now ready to be revenged for the loss of their countrymen who had been killed when the poor, unthinking people thought to have made a prize of the only ship that ever surrounded the globe twice. Therefore our men lay on their oars for some time until they should see how the natives behaved, but in a few minutes the Queen came down, and made signs for our men to land, but they would not until she ordered her people to the other side of the river. Then they landed and filled what casks they had, and soon got them into the boats and ready to come off.

While this was being done the Queen made the officer understand that she had laid on the beach all night, with all the people he saw there along with her. This was with no other intention but to see us again before we sailed from her fruitful country. When the officer stepped into the boat, the Queen with a few of her principal attendants wanted to come with him, but he had orders from the Captain to take none of the natives on board, therefore came off without her. This he told me made her very unhappy and she immediately ordered a few of her people to bring her a large double canoe, which was lying at some distance on the shore.

We then weighed anchor and made sail, but there was so little wind that we were obliged to tow the ship with the boats. The instant that we got under sail the Queen came under the stern with a large double canoe, and brought us a great quantity of more livestock and the Captain made her some presents in return, but this great friendly woman took no manner of notice of what she got from us, but shook hands with all that she could come near. She wept and cried and in my opinion, with as much tenderness and affection as any wife or mother could do at the parting with their husband or children.

At 10 A.M. we got a fine light breeze easterly. We lay to about half an hour and then made sail and steered away to the westward, toward the Duke of York Island, and left all the country people who came out with us, in great sorrow, especially the Queen and the most part of our acquaintance belonging to the bay where we lay. I really do believe there was a vast many of these country people who would have willingly come home with us if we could have taken them, and there was some of our men who said they would stay at this place, if they were sure of a ship to come home within a few years.

Adventure 10

A Captive of the Indians

from A Narrative of the Adventures and Sufferings of John R. Jewitt

NOT all mariners were able to bring about so cordial a relationship with the natives in remote parts of the world as Captain Wallis and the crew of the *Dolphin*. Many voyagers successfully braved the dangers of uncharted seas only to fall victim to the hostile natives of the distant shores they reached. Both Magellan and Cook—the greatest sea explorers of their time—met death at the hands of the inhabitants of island kingdoms; sailors engaged in the *bêche-de-mer* and sandalwood trades, shipwrecked in the Fijis, were lucky if they escaped being killed and eaten by the cannibals; whalers were often beaten to death on coral atolls by apparently friendly natives; and well into the nineteenth century the tea and opium clippers had to run a gauntlet of pirates approaching the Malay Straits or the China coast.

One of the most bloodcurdling accounts of such combat is the narrative of John R. Jewitt—a young Englishman who was one of the two survivors of the massacre of an entire ship's company by Indians of the Northwest Coast in 1803. It was compiled from an original journal kept in secret by Jewitt during his captivity.

It is necessary to know something of the background of this adventure to understand how it came about. During the critical years following the Revolution, restless American mariners had sought the rich markets of the Far East through the spice and tea trade. The chief trading commodity America could offer in the competitive Canton market (aside from ginseng) was the pelt of the sea otter native to the Northwest Pacific. New England merchants were quick to take part in this lucrative business, with the celebrated "Nor-west Trade" a result. By 1792 the route from Boston to the Northwest Coast, thence to Canton, and back to Boston, was well established. Captain Gray discovered the Columbia River, Captain Ingraham had found new islands in the northern Marquesas, and Nootka Sound had become a household word from Newburyport to New Haven.

In 1802, the ship *Boston* left that seaport under Captain John Salter on a voyage for the Northwest Coast by way of England. She was a well-built craft of 280 tons, ninety feet long by twenty-five feet in beam. Sailing first to Hull, the ship took aboard English cloth, Dutch blankets, looking glasses, beads, knives, sugar, rum, and three thousand muskets and fowling pieces with a quantity of ammunition—trading goods for the Indians. While at Hull, Captain Salter agreed to ship as armorer John R. Jewitt, son of a shipsmith working on the vessel and then nineteen years old. Captain Salter started the passage to the Northwest Coast on September 3, 1802. On December 28 he rounded

Cape Horn, made his way up the western coast of South and North America and reached Nootka Sound on Vancouver Island on March 12, 1803.

They anchored near the village, close by a place called, ironically enough, Friendly Cove. For a decade this had been the most important harbor on the coast between California and Alaska. Accounts by Captain Cook and John Meares had served to introduce the fur traders to the area, and ships from Spain, Russia, England, and America had found their way here. When John Jewitt visited Nootka, the aboriginal life was little changed from Cook's day—but through contact with the newcomers the natives had suffered humiliation and insult; they had become fierce as well as suspicious. Degraded by white men's vices and frequently cheated, their warlike spirit became a smoldering spark, ready for such a trifling incident as occurred aboard the *Boston* to set it afire.

Jewitt was by temperament better qualified for his ordeal than the bitter sailmaker, Thompson, who shared his captivity. Originally spared by the Indian Maquina because his trade as an armorer or blacksmith provided the shrewd chief an artisan who could fix muskets, the narrative makes clear that Jewitt's quick wit as well as his skill managed to save him and his companion. Their escape, engineered by Jewitt, rivals the wildest yarns of fiction.

Nootka Sound was a popular harbor for explorers and traders of the Pacific Northwest.
An artist with George Vancouver's expedition provided this view
of the Indian village at Friendly Cove in 1793.

"I expected every moment to share the wretched fate of my companions"

WE pursued our voyage to the northward until the twelfth of March 1803, when we made Woody Point in Nootka Sound on the Northwest Coast of America. We immediately stood up the Sound for Nootka, where Captain Salter had determined to stop, in order to supply the ship with wood and water before proceeding up the coast to trade. But in order to avoid the risk of any molestation or interruption to his men from the Indians while thus employed, he proceeded with the ship about five miles to the northward of the village, which is situated on Friendly Cove, and sent out his chief mate with several of the crew in the boat to find a good place for anchoring her. After sounding for some time they returned with information that they had discovered a secure place for anchorage on the western side of an inlet or small bay at about half a mile from the coast, near a small island which protected it from the sea, and where there was a plenty of wood and excellent water. The ship accordingly came to anchor in this place, at twelve o'clock at night, in twelve fathom water, muddy bottom, and so near the shore that to prevent the ship from winding we secured her by a hawser to the trees.

On the morning of the next day, the thirteenth, several of the natives came on board in a canoe from the village of Nootka, with their king, called Maquina, who appeared much pleased on seeing us, and with great seeming cordiality welcomed Captain Salter and his officers to his country. As I had never before beheld a savage of any nation, it

may readily be supposed that the novelty of their appearance, so different from any people that I had hitherto seen, excited in me strong feelings of surprise and curiosity. I was, however, particularly struck with the looks of their king, who was a man of a dignified aspect, about six feet in height and extremely straight and well proportioned; his features were in general good and his face was rendered remarkable by a large Roman nose, a very uncommon form of feature among these people; his complexion was of a dark copper hue, though his face, legs, and arms were on this occasion so covered with red paint that their natural color could scarcely be perceived, his eyebrows were painted black in two broad stripes like a new moon, and his long black hair, which shone with oil, was fastened in a bunch on the top of his head and strewed or powdered all over with white down, which gave him a most curious and extraordinary appearance. He was dressed in a large mantle or cloak of the black sea-otter skin, which reached to his knees and was fastened around his middle by a broad belt of the cloth of the country, wrought, or painted with figures of several colors; this dress was by no means unbecoming, but on the contrary had an air of savage magnificence.

From his having frequently visited the English and American ships that traded to the coast, Maquina had learned the signification of a number of English words, and in general could make himself pretty well understood by us in our own language. He was always the first to go on board such ships as came to Nootka, which he was much pleased in visiting, even when he had no trade to offer, as he almost always received some small present, and was in general extremely well treated by the commanders. He remained on board of us for some time during which the captain took him into the cabin and treated him with a glass of rum, these people being very fond of distilled spirits, and some biscuit and molasses, which they prefer to any kind of food that we can offer them.

On the fifteenth the king came on board with several of his chiefs; he was dressed as before in his magnificent otter-skin robe, having his face highly painted, and his hair tossed off with the white down which looked like snow; his chiefs were dressed in mantles of the country cloth of its natural colour, which is a pale yellow; these were ornamented with a broad border painted or wrought in figures of several colors representing men's heads, various animals, etc., and secured around them by a belt like that of the king, from which it was distinguished only by being narrower: the dress of the common people is of the same fashion and differs from that of the chiefs in being of a coarser texture and painted red, of one uniform color.

Captain Salter invited Maquina and his chiefs to dine with him, and it was curious to see how these people (when they eat) seat themselves (in their country fashion upon our chairs) with their feet under them crossed like Turks. They cannot endure the taste of salt, and the only thing they would eat with us was the ship bread which they were very fond of, especially when dipped in molasses; they had also a great liking for tea and coffee when well sweetened. As iron weapons and tools of almost every kind are in much request among them, whenever they came on board they were always very attentive to me, crowding around

me at the forge as if to see in what manner I did my work, and in this way became quite familiar — a circumstance, as will be seen in the end, of great importance to me.

The salmon which they brought us furnished a most delicious treat to men who for a long time had lived wholly on salt provisions excepting such few sea fish as we had the good fortune occasionally to take. We indeed feasted most luxuriously, and flattered ourselves that we should not want while on the coast for plenty of fresh provisions, little imagining the fate that awaited us, and that this dainty food was to prove the unfortunate lure to our destruction! On the nineteenth, the king came again on board and was invited by the Captain to dine with him. He had much conversation with Captain Salter, and informed him that there were plenty of wild ducks and geese near Friendly Cove, on which the Captain made him a present of a

A Spanish chart of Vancouver Island, showing the entrance to Nootka Sound (Entrada de Nutka) on the west coast. Friendly Cove is labeled Puerto (Pto.) de Macuina.

144

double-barreled fowling piece with which he appeared to be greatly pleased, and soon after went on shore.

On the twentieth we were nearly ready for our departure, having taken in what wood and water we were in want of.

The next day Maquina came on board with nine pair of wild ducks as a present; at the same time he brought with him the gun, one of the locks of which he had broken, telling the Captain that it was *peshak*, that is, bad. Captain Salter was very much offended at this observation and, considering it as a mark of contempt for his present, he called the king a liar, adding other opprobrious terms, and taking the gun from him tossed it indignantly into the cabin and calling me to him said, "John, this fellow has broken this beautiful fowling piece, see if you can mend it"; on examining it I told him that it could be done.

As I have already observed, Maquina knew a number of English words, and unfortunately understood but too well the meaning of the reproachful terms that the Captain addressed to him. He said not a word in reply, but his countenance sufficiently expressed the rage he felt, though he exerted himself to suppress it, and I observed him while the Captain was speaking repeatedly put his hand to his throat and rub it upon his bosom, which he afterwards told me was to keep down his heart which was rising into his throat and choking him. He soon after went on shore with his men, evidently much discomposed.

On the morning of the twenty-second the natives came off to us as usual with salmon, and remained on board, when about noon Maquina came alongside with a considerable number of his chiefs and men in their canoes, who, after going through the customary examination, were admitted into the ship. He had a whistle in his hand, and over his face a very ugly mask of wood representing the head of some wild beast. [He] appeared to be remarkably good-humored and gay, and while his people sang and capered about the deck, entertaining us with a variety of antic tricks and gestures, he blew his whistle to a kind of tune which seemed to regulate their motions. As Captain Salter was walking on the quarterdeck amusing himself with their dancing, the king came up to him and inquired when he intended to go to sea. He answered, "Tomorrow." Maquina then said, "You love salmon—much in Friendly Cove, why not go then and catch some?" The Captain thought that it would be very desirable to have a good supply of these fish for the voyage, and on consulting with Mr. Delouisa it was agreed to send part of the crew on shore after dinner with the seine in order to procure a quantity.

Maquina and his chiefs stayed and dined on board, and after dinner the chief mate went off with nine men in the jolly boat and yawl to fish at Friendly Cove, having set the steward on shore at our watering place to wash the Captain's clothes.

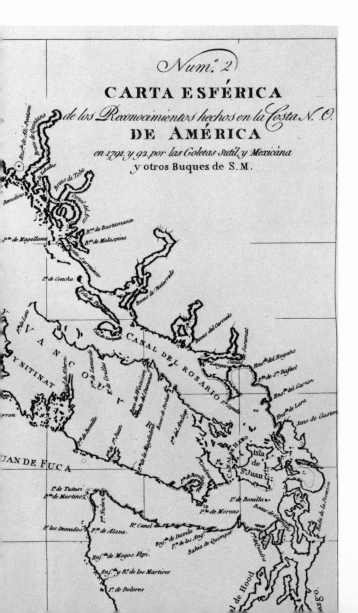

Chief Maquina, after a drawing by the Spanish artist Tomas de Suria, who was a member of the Malaspina expedition of 1792.

Shortly after the departure of the boats I went down to my vise-bench in the steerage, where I was employed in cleaning muskets. I had not been there more than an hour when I heard the men hoisting in the long boat, which, a few minutes after, was succeeded by a great bustle and confusion on deck. I immediately ran up the steerage stairs, but scarcely was my head above deck when I was caught by the hair by one of the savages and lifted from my feet; fortunately for me, my hair being short, and the ribbon with which it was tied slipping, I fell from his hold into the steerage. As

146

I was falling, he struck at me with an axe, which cut a deep gash in my forehead and penetrated the skull, but in consequence of his losing his hold, I luckily escaped the full force of the blow which, otherwise, would have cleft my head in two. I fell, stunned and senseless upon the floor—how long I continued in this situation I know not, but on recovering my senses the first thing that I did was to try to get up; but so weak was I, from the loss of blood, that I fainted and fell. I was however soon recalled to my recollection by three loud shouts or yells from the savages, which convinced me that they had got possession of the ship. It is impossible for me to describe my feelings at this terrific sound. Some faint idea may be formed of them by those who have known what it is to half waken from a hideous dream and still think it real. Never, no, never, shall I lose from my mind the impression of that dreadful moment. I expected every instant to share the wretched fate of my unfortunate companions, and when I heard the song of triumph by which these infernal yells was succeeded, my blood ran cold in my veins.

Having at length sufficiently recovered my senses to look around me after wiping the blood from my eyes, I saw that the hatch of the steerage was shut. This was done, as I afterwards discovered, by order of Maquina, who, on seeing the savage strike at me with the axe, told him not to hurt me, for that I was the armorer and would be useful to them in repairing their arms; while at the same time to prevent any of his men from injuring me, he had the hatch closed. But to me this circumstance wore a very different appearance, for I thought that these barbarians had only prolonged my life in order to deprive me of it by the most cruel tortures. I remained in this horrid state of suspense for a very long time, when at length the hatch was opened, and Maquina, calling me by name, ordered me to come up. I groped my way up as well as I was able, being almost blinded with the blood that flowed from my face, which having done, I was able to see distinctly with one of my eyes, but the other was so swollen from my wound that it was closed. But what a terrific spectacle met my eyes; six naked savages, standing in a circle around me, covered with the blood of my murdered comrades, with their daggers uplifted in their hands, prepared to strike. I now thought my last moment had come, and recommended my soul to my Maker.

The king, who, as I have already observed, knew enough of English to make himself understood, entered the circle, and placing himself before me, addressed me nearly in the following words—"John—I speak—you no say no—You say no—daggers come!" He then asked me if I would be his slave during my life—If I would fight for him in his battles—If I would repair his muskets and make daggers and knives for him—with several other questions, to all of which I was careful to answer yes. He then told me that he would

spare my life, and ordered me to kiss his hands and feet to show my submission to him, which I did. In the meantime his people were very clamorous to have me put to death, so that there should be none of us left to tell our story to our countrymen and prevent them from coming to trade with them; but the king in the most determined manner opposed their wishes, and to his favor am I wholly indebted for my being yet among the living.

As I was busy at work at the time of the attack, I was without my coat, and what with the coldness of the weather, my feebleness from loss of blood, the pain of my wound, and the extreme agitation and terror that I still felt, I shook like a leaf, which the king, observing, went into the cabin and bringing up a greatcoat that belonged to the Captain, threw it over my shoulders, telling me to drink some rum from a bottle which he handed me at the same time, giving me to understand that it would

A primitive but graphic illustration from Jewett's account of his adventures,
showing the slaughter of the Boston's crew.

147

be good for me and keep me from trembling as I did. I took a draught of it, after which, taking me by the hand, he led me to the quarterdeck, where the most horrid sight presented itself that ever my eyes witnessed—the heads of our unfortunate Captain and his crew, to the number of twenty-five, were all arranged in a line, and Maquina, ordering one of his people to bring a head, asked me whose it was. I answered, "The Captain's." In like manner the others were showed me, and I told him the names, excepting a few that were so horribly mangled that I was not able to recognize them.

I now discovered that all our unfortunate crew had been massacred, and learned that after getting possession of the ship the savages had broken open the arms chest and magazine, and supplying themselves with ammunition and arms, sent a party on shore to attack our men who had gone thither to fish, and being joined by numbers from the village, without difficulty overpowered and murdered them, and cutting off their heads, brought them on board after throwing their bodies into the sea. On looking upon the deck, I saw it entirely covered with the blood of my poor comrades, whose throats had been cut with their own jackknives, the savages having seized the opportunity while they were busy hoisting in the boat to grapple with them and overpower them by their numbers; in the scuffle the Captain was thrown overboard and dispatched by those in the canoes, who immediately cut off his head. What I felt on this occasion may be more readily conceived than expressed.

After I had answered his questions, Maquina took my silk handkerchief from my neck and bound it around my head, placing over the wound a leaf of tobacco, of which we had a quantity on board. This was done at my desire, as I had often found from personal experience the benefit of this application to cuts.

Maquina then ordered me to get the ship under weigh for Friendly Cove. This I did by cutting the cables and sending some of the natives aloft to loose the sails, which they performed in a very

bungling manner. But they succeeded so far in loosing the jib and topsails, that, with the advantage of a fair wind, I succeeded in getting the ship into the Cove, where, by order of the king, I ran her ashore on a sandy beach, at eight o'clock at night.

We were received by the inhabitants of the village, men, women, and children, with loud shouts of joy, and a most horrible drumming with sticks upon the roofs and sides of their houses, in which they had also stuck a great number of lighted pine torches, to welcome their king's return and congratulate him on the success of his enterprise.

Maquina then took me on shore to his house, which was very large and filled with people—where I was received with much kindness by the women, particularly those belonging to the king, who had no less than nine wives, all of whom came around me expressing much sympathy for my misfortune, gently stroking and patting my head in an encouraging and soothing manner, with words expressive of condolence. How sweet is compassion, even from savages! Those who have been in a similar situation can alone truly appreciate its value.

In the meantime, all the warriors of the tribe, to the number of five hundred, had assembled at the king's house to rejoice for their success. They exulted greatly in having taken our ship, and each one boasted of his own particular exploits in killing our men, but they were in general much dissatisfied with my having been suffered to live, and were very urgent with Maquina to deliver me to them to be put to death, which he obstinately refused to do, telling them that he had promised me my life and would not break his word; and that besides, I knew how to repair and to make arms, and should be of great use to them.

The king then seated me by him and ordered his women to bring him something to eat. They set before him some dried clams and train oil, of which he ate very heartily and encouraged me to follow his example, telling me to eat much and take a great deal of oil, which would make me strong and fat; notwithstanding his praise of this new kind of food, I felt no disposition to indulge in it, both the smell and taste being loathsome to me; and had it been otherwise, such was the pain I endured, the agitation of my mind, and the gloominess of my reflections that I should have felt very little inclination for eating.

Not satisfied with his first refusal to deliver me up to them, the people again became clamorous that Maquina should consent to my being killed, saying that not one of us ought to be left alive to give information to others of our countrymen and prevent them from coming to trade or induce them to revenge the destruction of our ship, and they at length became so boisterous that he caught up a large club in a passion and drove them all out of the house. During this scene a son of the king, of about eleven years old, attracted no doubt by the singularity of my appearance, came up to me; I caressed him; he returned my attentions with much apparent pleasure, and considering this as a fortunate opportunity to gain the good will of the father, I took the child on my knee, and cutting the metal buttons from off the coat I had on, I tied them around his neck. At this he was highly delighted, and became so much attached to me that he would not quit me.

The king appeared much pleased with my attention to his son, and telling me that it was time to go to sleep, directed me to lie with his son next to him, as he was afraid lest some of his people would come while he was asleep and kill me with their daggers. I lay down as he ordered me, but neither the state of my mind nor the pain I felt would allow me to sleep. About midnight I was greatly alarmed by the approach of one of the natives, who came to give information to the king that there was one of the white men alive, who had knocked him down as he went on board the ship at night. This Maquina communicated to me, giving me to understand that as soon as the sun rose he should kill him. I endeavored to persuade him to spare his

life, but he bade me be silent and go to sleep. I said nothing more but lay revolving in my mind what method I could devise to save the life of this man. What a consolation, thought I, what a happiness would it prove to me in my forlorn state among these heathen, to have a Christian and one of my own countrymen for a companion, and how greatly would it alleviate and lighten the burden of my slavery. As I was thinking of some plan for his preservation, it all at once came into my mind that this man was probably the sailmaker of the ship, named Thompson, as I had not seen his head among those on deck and knew that he was below at work upon the sails not long before the attack. The more I thought of it the more probable it appeared to me, and as Thompson was a man nearly forty years of age, and had an old look, I conceived it would be easy to make him pass for my father, and by this means prevail on Maquina to spare his life. Towards morning I fell into a doze, but was awakened with the first beams of the sun by the king, who told me that he was going to kill the man who was on board the ship and ordered me to accompany him. I rose and followed him, leading with me the young prince his son.

On coming to the beach I found all the men of the tribe assembled. The king addressed them, saying that one of the white men had been found alive on board the ship, and requested their opinion as to putting him to death or saving his life. They were unanimously for the first. This determination he made known to me. Having arranged my plan, I asked him, pointing to the boy whom I still held by the hand, if he loved his son; he answered that he did; I then asked the child if he loved his father, and on replying in the affirmative, I said "and I also love mine." I then threw myself on my knees at Maquina's feet and implored him with tears in my eyes to spare my father's life, if the man on board should prove to be him, telling him that if he killed my father it was my wish that he should kill me too, and that if he did not I would kill myself—and that he would thus lose my services;

whereas, by sparing my father's life he would preserve mine, which would be of great advantage to him by my repairing and making arms for him.

Maquina appeared moved by my entreaties and promised not to put the man to death if he should be my father. He then explained to his people what I had said, and ordered me to go on board and tell the man to come on shore. To my unspeakable joy, on going into the hold I found that my conjecture was true. Thompson was there; he had escaped without any injury, excepting a slight wound in the nose, given him by one of the savages with a knife as he attempted to come on deck during the scuffle. Finding the savages in possession of the ship, as he afterwards informed me, he secreted himself in the hold, hoping for some chance to make his escape—but that the Indian who came on board in the night approaching the place where he was, he supposed himself discovered, and being

A man of Nootka Sound.

determined to sell his life as dearly as possible, as soon as he came within his reach he knocked him down, but the Indian immediately springing up, ran off at full speed.

I informed him in a few words that all our men had been killed; that the king had preserved my life and had consented to spare his on the supposition that he was my father, an opinion which he must be careful not to undeceive them in, as it was his only safety. After giving him his cue, I went on shore with him and presented him to Maquina, who immediately knew him to be the sailmaker and was much pleased, observing that he could make sails for his canoe. He then took us to his house and ordered something for us to eat.

On the twenty-fourth and twenty-fifth the natives were busily employed in taking the cargo out of the ship, stripping her of her sails and rigging, cutting away the spars and masts, and in short rendering her as complete a wreck as possible, the muskets, ammunition, cloth, and all the principal articles taken from her being deposited in the king's house.

While they were thus occupied, each one taking what he liked, my companion and myself being obliged to aid them, I thought it best to secure the accounts and papers of the ship, in hopes that on some future day I might have it in my power to restore them to the owners. With this view I took possession of the Captain's writing desk, which contained the most of them, together with some paper and implements for writing. I had also the good fortune to find a blank account book, in which I resolved, should it be permitted me, to write an account of our capture and the most remarkable occurrences that I should meet with during my stay among these people, fondly indulging the hope that it would not be long before some vessel would arrive to release us. I likewise found in the cabin a small volume of sermons, a Bible, and a common prayer book of the Church of England, which furnished me and my comrade great consolation in the midst of our mournful

John R. Jewitt

servitude, and enabled me, under the favor of Divine Providence, to support with firmness the miseries of a life which I might otherwise have found beyond my strength to endure. As these people set no value upon things of this kind, I found no difficulty in appropriating them to myself, by putting them in my chest, which though it had been broken open and rifled by the savages, as I still had the key I without much difficulty secured.

On the twenty-sixth, two ships were seen standing in for Friendly Cove. At their first appearance the inhabitants were thrown into great confusion, but soon collecting a number of muskets and blunderbusses, ran to the shore, from whence they kept up so brisk a fire at them that they were evidently afraid to approach nearer, and after firing a few rounds of grape shot which did no harm to anyone, they wore ship and stood out to sea. These ships, as I afterwards learned, were the *Mary* and *Juno* of Boston.

They were scarcely out of sight when Maquina expressed much regret that he had permitted his people to fire at them, being apprehensive that they would give information to others in what manner they had been received, and prevent them from coming to trade with him.

A few days after hearing of the capture of the ship, there arrived at Nootka a great number of canoes filled with savages from no less than twenty tribes to the north and south. Maquina, who was very proud of his new acquisition, was desirous of welcoming these visitors in the European manner. He accordingly ordered his men, as the canoes approached, to assemble on the beach with loaded

The most famous explorer of the eighteenth century, James Cook, also visited Nootka Sound, and this view is after a drawing by his artist John Webber.

muskets and blunderbusses, placing Thompson at the cannon which had been brought from the ship and laid upon two long sticks of timber in front of the village, then taking a speaking trumpet in his hand he ascended with me the roof of his house and began drumming or beating upon the boards with a stick most violently. Nothing could be more ludicrous than the appearance of this motley group of savages collected on the shore, dressed as they were, with their ill-gotten finery, in the most fantastic manner, some in women's smocks, taken from our cargo, others in *Kotsacks* (or cloaks), of blue, red or yellow broadcloth, with stockings drawn over their heads and their necks hung round with numbers of powder-horns, shot-bags, and cartouche-boxes, some of them having no less than ten muskets apiece on their shoulders and five or six daggers in their girdles. Diverting indeed was it to see them all squatted upon the beach, holding their muskets perpendicularly, with the butt pressed upon the sand instead of against their shoulders, and in this position awaited the order to fire.

Maquina at last called to them with his trumpet to fire, which they did in the most awkward and timid manner, with their muskets hard pressed upon the ground as above mentioned. At the same moment the cannon was fired by Thompson, immediately on which they threw themselves back and began to roll and tumble over the sand as if they had been shot, when suddenly springing up they began a song of triumph and running backward and forward upon the shore, with the wildest gesticulations, boasted of their exploits and exhibited as trophies what they had taken from us. Notwithstanding the unpleasantness of my situation and the feelings that this display of our spoils excited, I could not avoid laughing at the strange appearance of these savages, their awkward movements and singular contrast of their dress and arms.

When the ceremony was concluded, Maquina invited the strangers to a feast at his house, consisting of whale blubber, smoked herring spawn, and dried fish and train oil, of which they ate most plentifully. The feast being over, the trays out of which they ate and other things were immediately removed to make room for the dance which was to close the entertainment. This was performed by Maquina's son, the young prince Sat-sat-sok-sis, whom I have already spoken of, in the following manner: Three of the principal chiefs, dressed in their otter-skin mantles, which they wore only on extraordinary occasions and at festivals, having their heads covered over with white down and their faces highly painted, came forward into the middle of the room, each furnished with a bag filled with the white down, which they scattered around in such a manner as to represent a fall of snow. These were followed by the young prince who was dressed in a long piece of yellow cloth, wrapped loosely around him and decorated with small bells, with a cap on his head, to which was fastened a curious mask in imitation of a wolf's head, while the rear was brought up by the king himself in his robe of sea-otter skin, with a small whistle in his mouth and a rattle in his hand, with which he kept time to a sort of tune on his whistle. After passing very rapidly in this order around the house, each of them seated himself, except the prince, who immediately began his dance, which principally consisted in springing up into the air in a squat posture, and constantly turning around on his heels with great swiftness in a very narrow circle.

This dance, with a few intervals of rest, was continued for about two hours, during which the chiefs kept up a constant drumming with sticks of about a foot in length on a long hollow plank, which was, though a very noisy, a most doleful kind of music. This they accompanied with songs, the king himself acting as chorister, while the women applauded each feat of activity in the dancer by repeating the words *Wocash! Wocash Tyee!*—That is good! very good prince. As soon as the dance was finished Maquina began to give presents to the strangers in the name of his son Sat-sat-sok-sis. These were pieces of European

John R. Jewitt

cloth generally of a fathom in length, muskets, powder, shot, etc. Whenever he gave them anything, they had a peculiar manner of snatching it from him with a very stern and surly look, repeating each time the words *Wocash Tyee*. This I understood to be their custom, and was considered as a compliment which if omitted would be supposed as a mark of disregard for the present. On this occasion Maquina gave away no less than one hundred muskets, the same number of looking glasses, four hundred yards of cloth, and twenty casks of powder, besides other things.

After receiving these presents, the strangers retired on board their canoes, for so numerous were they that Maquina would not suffer any but the chiefs to sleep in the houses; and in order to prevent the property from being pillaged by them, he ordered Thompson and myself to keep guard during the night, armed with cutlasses and pistols.

In this manner tribes of savages from various parts of the coast continued coming for several days, bringing with them blubber, oil, herring spawn, dried fish and clams, for which they received in return presents of cloth, etc., after which they in general immediately returned home. I observed that very few if any of them, except the chiefs, had arms, which I afterwards learned is the custom with these people whenever they come upon

A dance by the Indians on the beach at Friendly Cove.
Attributed to Tomás de Suria.

153

a friendly visit or to trade, in order to show, on their approach, that their intentions are pacific.

Early on the morning of the eighteenth the ship was discovered to be on fire. This was owing to one of the savages having gone on board with a firebrand at night for the purpose of plunder, some sparks from which fell into the hold and communicating with some combustibles soon enveloped the whole in flames. The natives regretted the loss of the ship the more as a great part of her cargo still remained on board. To my companion and myself it was a most melancholy sight, for with her disappeared from our eyes every trace of a civilized country; but the disappointment we experienced was still more severely felt for we had calculated on having the provision to ourselves, which would have furnished us with a stock for years, as whatever is cured with salt, together with most of our other articles of food, are never eaten by these people. I had luckily saved all my tools excepting the anvil and the bellows which was attached to the forge and from their weight had not been brought on shore. We had also the good fortune in looking over what had been taken from the ship to discover a box of chocolate and a case of port wine, which as the Indians were not fond of it proved a great comfort to us for some time, and from one of the natives I obtained a nautical almanac which had belonged to the Captain and which was of great use to me in determining the time.

About two days after, on examining their booty, the savages found a tierce of rum with which they were highly delighted, as they have become very fond of spirituous liquors since their intercourse with the whites. This was towards evening and Maquina, having assembled all the men at his house, gave a feast at which they drank so freely of the rum that in a short time they became so extremely wild and frantic that Thompson and myself, apprehensive for our safety, thought it prudent to retire privately into the woods, where we continued till past midnight. On our return we found the women gone, who are always very temperate, drinking nothing but water, having quitted the house and gone to the other huts to sleep, so terrified were they at the conduct of the men, who all lay stretched out on the floor in a state of complete intoxication.

How easy in this situation would it have been for us to have dispatched or made ourselves masters of our enemies, had there been any ship near to which we could have escaped, but as we were situated, the attempt would have been madness. The wish of revenge was however less strongly impressed on my mind than what appeared to be so evident an interposition of Divine Providence in our favor. How little can man penetrate its designs, and how frequently is that intended as a blessing which he views as a curse. The burning of our ship, which we had lamented so much as depriving us of so many comforts, now appeared to us in a very different light, for had the savages got possession of the rum, of which there were nearly twenty puncheons on board, we must inevitably have fallen a sacrifice to their fury in some of their moments of intoxication. This cask fortunately and a case of gin was all the spirits they obtained from the ship. To prevent the recurrence of similar danger I examined the cask, and finding still a considerable quantity remaining, I bored a small hole in the bottom with a gimlet, which before morning to my great joy completely emptied it.

By this time the wound in my head began to be much better, so that I could enjoy some sleep, which I had been almost deprived of by the pain, and though I was still feeble from the loss of blood and my sufferings, I found myself sufficiently well to go to work at my trade, in making for the king and his wives bracelets and other small ornaments of copper or steel and in repairing the arms, making use of a large square stone for the anvil and heating my metal in a common wood fire. This was very gratifying to Maquina and his women particularly, and secured me their good will.

John R. Jewitt

It was now past midsummer, and the hopes we had indulged of our release became daily more faint, for though we had heard of no less than seven vessels on the coast, yet none appeared inclined to venture to Nootka. The destruction of the *Boston*, the largest, strongest, and best equipped ship, with much the most valuable cargo of any that had ever been fitted out for the northwest trade, had inspired the commanders of others with a general dread of coming thither lest they should share the same fate; and though in the letter I wrote (imploring those who should receive them

Interior of an Indian house at Friendly Cove, after John Webber.

to come to the relief of two unfortunate Christians who were suffering among heathen) I stated the cause of the *Boston*'s capture and that there was not the least danger in coming to Nootka, provided they would follow the directions I laid down, still I felt very little encouragement that any of these letters would come to hand, when on the morning of the nineteenth of July, a day that will be ever held by me in grateful remembrance of the mercies of God, while I was employed with Thompson in forging daggers for the king, my ears were saluted with the joyful sound of three cannon and the cries of the inhabitants exclaiming *Weena, weena—Mamethlee*—that is, strangers—white men.

Soon after, several of our people came running into the house to inform me that a vessel under

full sail was coming into the harbor. Though my heart bounded with joy, I repressed my feelings, and affecting to pay no attention to what was said told Thompson to be on his guard and not betray any joy, as our release and perhaps our lives, depended on our conducting ourselves so as to induce the natives to suppose we were not very anxious to leave them. We continued our works as if nothing had happened, when in a few minutes after Maquina came in, and seeing us at work appeared much surprised and asked me if I did not know that a vessel had come. I answered in a careless manner that it was nothing to me. How, John, said he, you no glad go board. I replied that I cared very little about it, as I had become reconciled to their manner of living, and had no wish to go away. He then told me that he had called a council of his people respecting us, and that we must leave off work and be present at it.

The men having assembled at Maquina's house, he asked them what was their opinion should be done with Thompson and myself now a vessel had arrived, and whether he had not better go on board himself, to make a trade, and procure such articles as were wanted. Each one of the tribe who wished gave his opinion. Some were for putting us to death and pretending to the strangers that a different nation had cut off the *Boston*, while others, less barbarous, were for sending us fifteen or twenty miles back into the country until the departure of the vessel. These, however, were the sentiments of the common people, the chiefs opposing our being put to death or injured, and several of them, among the most forward of whom were Yealthlower and the young chief Toowinnakinnish, were for immediately releasing us; but this, if he could avoid it, by no means appeared to accord with Maquina's wishes.

With regard, however, to Maquina's going on board the vessel, which he discovered a strong inclination to do, there was but one opinion, all remonstrating against it, telling him that the captain would kill him or keep him a prisoner, in consequence of his having destroyed our ship. When Maquina had heard their opinions, he told them that he was not afraid of being hurt from going on board the vessel, but that he would, however, in that respect be guided by John, whom he had always found true. He then turned to me, and asked me if I thought there would be any danger in his going on board. I answered that I was not surprised at the advice his people had given him, unacquainted as they were with the manners of the white men, and judging them by their own, but if they had been with them as much as I had, or even himself, they would think very differently. That he had almost always experienced good and civil treatment from them, nor had he any reason to fear the contrary now, as they never attempted to harm those who did not injure them, and if he wished to go on board he might do it, in my opinion, with security. After reflecting a few moments, he said, with much apparent satisfaction, that if I would write a letter to the captain, telling him good of him, that he had treated Thompson and myself kindly since we had been with him, and to use him well, he would go. It may readily be supposed that I felt much joy at this determination; but knowing that the least incaution might annihilate all my hopes of escape, I was careful not to manifest it and to treat his going or staying as a matter perfectly indifferent to me. I told him that if he wished me to write such a letter, I had no objection, as it was the truth, otherwise I could not have done it.

I then proceeded to write the recommendatory letter, which the reader will naturally imagine was of a somewhat different tenor from the one he had required; for if deception is in any case warrantable, it was certainly so in a situation like ours, where the only chance of regaining that freedom of which we had been so unjustly deprived depended upon it; and I trust that few, even of the most rigid, will condemn me with severity for making use of it on an occasion which afforded me the only hope of ever more beholding a Christian

John R. Jewitt

country and preserving myself, if not from death, at least from a life of continued suffering.

The letter which I wrote was nearly in the following terms:

To Captain ———,
of the Brig ———,
Nootka, July 19, 1805.

Sir,

THE *bearer of this letter is the Indian king by the name of Maquina. He was the instigator of the capture of the ship* BOSTON, *of Boston in North America, John Salter captain, and of the murder of twenty-five men of her crew, the two only survivors being now on shore—Wherefore I hope you will take care to confine him according to his merits, putting* [him] *in your dead lights, and keeping so good a watch over him, that he cannot escape from you. By so doing we shall be able to obtain our release in the course of a few hours.*

JOHN R. JEWITT

Armourer of the BOSTON, *for himself and* JOHN THOMPSON, *Sail-maker of said ship.*

I have been asked how I dared to write in this manner: my answer is that from my long residence among these people I knew that I had little to apprehend from their anger on hearing of their king being confined while they knew his life depended upon my release, and that they would sooner have given up five hundred white men than have had him injured. This will serve to explain the little apprehension I felt at their menaces afterwards, for otherwise, sweet as liberty was to me, I should hardly have ventured on so hazardous an experiment.

On my giving the letter to Maquina, he asked me to explain it to him. This I did line by line, as [he] pointed them out with his finger, but in a sense very different from the real, giving him to understand that I had written to the captain that as he had been kind to me since I had been taken by

him, that it was my wish that the captain should treat him accordingly, and give him what molasses, biscuit, and rum he wanted. When I had finished, placing his finger in a significant manner on my name at the bottom, and eyeing me with a look that seemed to read my inmost thoughts, he said to me, "John, you no lie?" Never did I undergo such a scrutiny, or ever experience greater apprehensions than I felt at that moment, when my destiny was suspended on the slightest thread, and the least mark of embarrassment on mine or suspicion of treachery on his part would probably have rendered my life the sacrifice.

Fortunately I was able to preserve my composure, and my being painted in the Indian manner, which Maquina had required of me, prevented any change in my countenance from being noticed, and I replied with considerable promptitude, looking at him in my turn, with all the confidence I could muster, "Why do you ask me such a question, Tyee? Have you ever known me to lie?" "No." "Then how can you suppose I should tell you a lie now, since I have never done it." As I was speaking, he still continued looking at me with the same piercing eye, but observing nothing to excite his suspicion, he told me that he believed what I said was true and that he would go on board, and gave orders to get ready his canoe. His chiefs again attempted to dissuade him, using every argument for that purpose, while his wives crowded around him, begging him on their knees not to trust himself with the white men. Fortunately for my companion and myself, so strong was his wish of going on board the vessel that he was deaf to their solicitations, and making no other reply to them than "John no lie," left the house, taking four prime skins with him as a present to the captain.

Scarcely had the canoe put off when he ordered his men to stop, and calling to me, asked me if I did not want to go on board with him. Suspecting this as a question merely intended to ensnare me, I replied that I had no wish to do it, not having any desire to leave them.

157

On going on board the brig, Maquina immediately gave his present of skins and my letter to the captain, who on reading it asked him into the cabin, where he gave him some biscuit and a glass of rum, at the same time privately directing his mate to go forward and return with five or six of the men armed. When they appeared, the captain told Maquina that he was his prisoner and should continue so until the two men whom he knew to be on shore were released, at the same time ordering him to be put in irons and the windows secured, which was instantly done, and a couple of men placed as a guard over him. Maquina was greatly surprised and terrified at this reception; he however made no attempt to resist, but requested the captain to permit one of his men to come and see him. One of them was accordingly called, and Maquina said something to him which the captain did not understand, but supposed to be an order to release us when the man returning to the canoe, it was paddled off with the utmost expedition to the shore. As the canoe approached, the inhabitants, who had all collected upon the beach, manifested some uneasiness at not seeing their king on board, but when on its arrival they were told that the captain had made him a prisoner and that John had spoke bad about him in a letter, they all, both men and women, set up a loud howl and ran backward and forward upon the shore like so many lunatics, scratching their faces and tearing the hair in handfuls from their heads.

After they had beat about in this manner for some time, the men ran to their huts for their weapons, as if preparing to attack an invading enemy; while Maquina's wives and the rest of the women came around me and throwing themselves on their knees begged me with tears to spare his life, and Sat-sat-sak-sis, who kept constantly with me, taking me by the hand, wept bitterly, and joined his entreaties to theirs that I would not let the white men kill his father. I told them not to afflict themselves, that Maquina's life was in no danger, nor would the least harm be done to him.

The men were, however, extremely exasperated with me, more particularly the common people, who came running in the most furious manner towards me, brandishing their weapons and threatening to cut me in pieces no bigger than their thumbnails, while others declared they would burn me alive over a slow fire, suspended by my heels. All this fury, however, caused me but little alarm, as I felt convinced they would not dare to execute their threats while the king was on board the brig. The chiefs took no part in this violent conduct, but came to me and enquired the reason why Maquina had been thus treated and if the captain intended to kill him. I told them that if they would silence the people, so that I could be heard, I would explain all to them. They immediately put a stop to the noise, when I informed them that the captain in confining Maquina had done it of his own accord, and only in order to make them release Thompson and myself, as he well knew we were with them, and if they would do that, their king would receive no injury but be well treated; otherwise he would be kept a prisoner. As many of them did not appear to be satisfied with this, and began to repeat their murderous threats, "Kill me," said I to them, "if it is your wish," throwing open the bear skin which I wore; "here is my breast, I am only one among so many, and can make no resistance, but unless you wish to see your king hanging by his neck to that pole," pointing to the yardarm of the brig, "and the sailors firing at him with bullets, you will not do it." "O no," was the general cry, "that must never be; but what must we do?" I told them that their best plan would be to send Thompson on board to desire the captain to use Maquina well till I was released, which would be soon. This they were perfectly willing to do, and I directed Thompson to go on board. But he objected, saying he would not leave me alone with the savages. I told him not to be under any fear for me, for that if I could get him off I could manage well enough for myself, and that I wished him immediately on getting on board the brig to see the captain and request him to keep Maquina close till I was released, as I was in no danger while he had him safe.

When I saw Thompson off, I asked the natives what they intended to do with me. They said I must talk to the captain again, in another letter, and tell him to let his boat come on shore with Maquina, and that I should be ready to jump into the boat at the same time Maquina should jump on shore. I told them that the captain, who knew that they had killed my shipmates, would never trust his men so near the shore for fear they would kill them too, as they were so much more numerous; but that if they would select any three of their number to go with me in a canoe, when we came within hail I could desire the captain to send his boat with Maquina, to receive me in exchange for him.

This appeared to please them, and after some whispering among the chiefs, who from what words I overheard concluded that if the captain should refuse to send his boat with Maquina, the three men would have no difficulty in bringing me back with them, they agreed to my proposal and selected three of their stoutest men to convey me. Fortunately having been for some time accustomed to see me armed, and suspecting no design on my part, they paid no attention to the pistols that I had about me.

As I was going into the canoe, little Sat-sat-sak-sis, who could not bear to part with me, asked me, with an affecting simplicity, since I was going away to leave him, if the white men would not let his father come on shore, and not kill him. I told him not to be concerned, for that no one should injure his father, when taking an affectionate leave of me and again begging me not to let the white men hurt his father, he ran to comfort his mother, who was at a little distance, with the assurances I had given him.

On entering the canoe, I seated myself in the prow facing the three men, having determined if it was practicable, from the moment I found Maquina was secured, to get on board the vessel before he

was released, hoping by that means, to be enabled to obtain the restoration of what property belonged to the *Boston* still remaining in the possession of the savages, which I thought, if it could be done, a duty that I owed to the owners. With feelings of joy impossible to be described, did I quit this savage shore, confident now that nothing could thwart my escape or prevent the execution of the plan I had formed, as the men appointed to convey and guard me were armed with nothing but their paddles. As we came within hail of the brig, they at once ceased paddling, when presenting my pistols at them, I ordered them instantly to go on, or I would shoot the whole of them. A proceeding so wholly unexpected threw them into great consternation, and resuming their paddles, in a few moments, to my inexpressible delight, I once more found myself alongside of a Christian ship, a happiness which I had almost despaired of ever again enjoying. All the crew crowded to the side to see me as the canoe came up, and manifested much joy at my safety. I immediately leaped on board, where I was welcomed by the captain, Samuel Hill, of the brig *Lydia* of Boston, who congratulated me on my escape, informing me that he had received my letter off Kla-iz-zart from the chief Mackee Ulatilla, who came off himself in his canoe to deliver it to him, on which he immediately proceeded hither to aid me. I returned him my thanks in the best manner I could for his humanity, though I hardly knew what I said, such was the agitated state of my feelings at that moment, with joy for my escape, thankfulness to the Supreme Being who had so mercifully preserved me, and gratitude to those whom he had rendered instrumental in my delivery, that I have no doubt, what with my strange dress, being painted with red and black from head to foot, having a bearskin wrapped around me, and my long hair, which I was not allowed to cut, fastened on the top of my head in a large bunch with a sprig of green spruce, I must have appeared more like one deranged than a rational creature, as Captain Hill afterwards told me that he never saw any thing in the form of man look so wild as I did when I first came on board.

The captain then asked me into the cabin, where I found Maquina in irons, with a guard over him. He looked very melancholy, but on seeing me his countenance brightened up, and he expressed his pleasure with the welcome of "Wocash John"; when taking him by the hand, I asked the captain's permission to take off his irons, assuring him that, as I was with him, there was no danger of his being in the least troublesome. He accordingly consented, and I felt a sincere pleasure in freeing from fetters a man who, though he had caused the death of my poor comrades, had nevertheless always proved my friend and protector, and whom I had requested to be thus treated only with a view of securing my liberty. Maquina smiled and appeared much pleased at this mark of attention from me. When I had freed the king from his irons, Captain Hill wished to learn the particulars of our capture, observing that an account of the destruction of the ship and her crew had been received at

Boston before he sailed, but that nothing more was known except that two of the men were living, for whose rescue the owners had offered a liberal reward, and that he had been able to get nothing out of the old man, whom the sailors had supplied so plentifully with grog as to bring him too much by the head to give any information.

I gave him a correct statement of the whole proceeding, together with the manner in which my life and that of my comrade had been preserved. On hearing my story, he was greatly irritated against Maquina and said he ought to be killed. I observed that however ill he might have acted in taking our ship, yet it would, perhaps, be wrong to judge an uninformed savage with the same severity as a civilized person, who had the light of religion and the laws of society to guide him. That Maquina's conduct in taking our ship arose from an insult that he thought he had received from Captain Salter, and from the unjustifiable conduct of some masters of vessels, who had robbed him and without provocation killed a number of his people. Besides that, a regard for the safety of others ought to prevent his being put to death, as I had lived long enough with these people to know that revenge of an injury is held sacred by them, and that they would not fail to retaliate, should he kill their

Jewitt's ordeal made popular reading during the nineteenth century. These quaint illustrations, with their clean-cut hero and cigar-store Indians, come from an 1835 version of the story, written by the editor of Jewitt's own book, Richard Alsop.

king, on the first vessel or boat's crew that should give them an opportunity; and that, though he might consider executing him as but an act of justice, it would probably cost the lives of many Americans.

The captain appeared to be convinced from what I said of the impolicy of taking Maquina's life and said that he would leave it wholly with me whether to spare or kill him, as he was resolved to incur no censure in either case. I replied that I most certainly should never take the life of a man who had preserved mine, had I not other reason, but as there was some of the *Boston*'s property still remaining on shore, I considered it a duty that I owed to those who were interested in that ship to try to

save it for them, and with that view I thought it would be well to keep him on board till it was given up. He concurred in this proposal, saying if there was any of the property left, it most certainly ought to be got.

During this conversation Maquina was in great anxiety, as from what English he knew he perfectly comprehended the subject of our deliberation; constantly interrupting me to enquire what we had determined to do with him, what the captain said, if his life would be spared, and if I did not think that Thompson would kill him. I pacified him as well as I was able by telling him that he had noth-

ing to fear from the captain, that he would not be hurt, and that if Thompson wished to kill him, which was very probable, he would not be allowed to do it. He would then remind me that I was indebted to him for my life, and that I ought to do by him as he had done by me. I assured him that such was my intention, and I requested him to remain quiet, and not alarm himself, as no harm was intended him. But I found it extremely difficult to convince him of this, as it accorded so little with the ideas of revenge entertained by them. I told him however that he must restore all the property still in his possession belonging to the ship. This he was perfectly ready to do, happy to escape on such terms. But as it was now past five, and too late for the articles to be collected and brought off, I told him that he must content himself to remain on board with me that night, and in the morning he should be set on shore as soon as the things were delivered. To this he agreed, on condition that I would remain with him in the cabin. I then went upon deck, and the canoe that brought me having been sent back, I hailed the inhabitants, and told them that their king had agreed to stay on board till the next day, when he would return, but that no canoes must attempt to come near the vessel during the night, as they would be fired upon. They answered, *Woho, woho*—very well, very well. I then returned to Maquina, but so great were his terrors that he would not allow me to sleep, constantly disturbing me with his questions and repeating, "John, you know when you was alone, and more than five hundred men were your enemies, I was your friend and prevented them from putting you and Thompson to death, and now I am in the power of your friends, you ought to do the same by me." I assured him that he would be detained on board no longer than the property was released, and that as soon as it was done he would be set at liberty.

At daybreak I hailed the natives and told them that it was Maquina's order that they should bring off the cannon and anchors and whatever remained with them of the cargo of the ship. This they set about doing with the utmost expedition, transporting the cannon and anchors by lashing together two of their largest canoes and covering them with planks, and in the course of two hours they delivered everything on board that I could recollect, with Thompson's and my chest, containing the papers of the ship, etc.

When everything belonging to the ship had been restored, Maquina was permitted to return in his canoe, which had been sent for him with a present of what skins he had collected, which were about sixty, for the captain in acknowledgment of his having spared his life and allowed him to depart unhurt; such was also the transport he felt when Captain Hill came into the cabin and told him that he was at liberty to go, that he threw off his mantle, which consisted of four of the very best skins, and gave it to him as a mark of his gratitude; in return the captain presented him with a new greatcoat and hat, with which he appeared much delighted.

The captain then desired me to inform him that he should return to that part of the coast in November, and that he wished him to keep what skins he should get, which he would buy of him. This Maquina promised, saying to me at the same time, "John, you know I shall be then at Tashees, but when you come make *pow*, which means fire a gun to let me know, and I will come down." When he came to the side of the brig, he shook me cordially by the hand, and told me that he hoped I would come to see him again in a big ship, and bring much plenty of blankets, biscuit, molasses and rum, for him and his son who loved me a great deal, and that he would keep all the furs he got for me, observing at the same time that he should never more take a letter of recommendation from any one, or ever trust himself on board a vessel unless I was there. Then grasping both my hands with much emotion, while the tears trickled down his cheeks, he bade me farewell and stepped into the canoe, which immediately paddled him on shore.

A boat of the Northwest Indians, after a drawing by a member of the La Pérouse expedition.

Adventure 11

The Battle of Trafalgar

*from Authentic Narrative
of the Death of Lord Nelson, by William Beatty*

HORATIO, Lord Nelson, was forty-seven years old when he led the British fleet to a decisive victory over Napoleon's navy at Trafalgar, but he had lived already the lifetimes of several ordinary men before his last battle. He had lost his right eye during the storming of Calvi in Corsica; his right arm had been amputated after the Battle at Santa Cruz. His gallantry in the action with the Spanish off Cape St. Vincent in 1797 gained him the rank of rear admiral. The following year he ended Napoleon's plans for an eastern empire by annihilating the French fleet in the Battle of the Nile, for which he was made a baron. After his victory over the Danes at Copenhagen in 1801, he was made Viscount Nelson, commander-in-chief of the Royal Navy. He was the darling of his people, who studiously overlooked his open liaison with Lady Emma Hamilton and accepted the fiction of the "adoption" of their daughter Horatia.

The brilliant stars of Nelson and Napoleon met for the last time at Trafalgar. For both the English and French this was the most crucial of the many naval engagements between them; upon its outcome, and the resulting command of the English Channel, depended Napoleon's plans for the invasion of England.

Nelson selected the scene of this battle: some sixty miles to the west of Cadiz, near Cape St. Mary. From this distance he hoped to decoy the combined French and Spanish fleets under Admiral Villeneuve from Cadiz while he guarded against being driven within the Straits of Gibraltar by the prevailing westerlies. Nelson developed an unorthodox and characteristically audacious strategy against the French. It was the general custom of fleets of this time to position themselves in well-organized lines that pounded away broadside to broadside as they sailed past one another. Nelson abandoned this strategy entirely. He planned to break into the enemy's fleet by two bold frontal attacks, and then to engage the ships individually, counting upon the superior discipline and gunnery of his crews to overpower their adversaries.

On the morning of October 21, 1805, the French fleet appeared, answering his challenge from Cadiz. The combined fleets of his enemy consisted of thirty-seven ships of the line and four frigates. His opponents were not only numerically superior but also had greater size and weight in armament—and four thousand troops aboard, including expert riflemen for the tops.

Signals were hoisted to attack. The wind was steady from the west, with a heavy ground swell. In his flagship, the *Victory*, Nelson led the weather line of his fleet—fourteen ships—in an assault upon the center itself. His second-in-command, Admiral Collingwood, led the leeward line of thirteen vessels in the *Royal Sovereign* against the enemy's rear. At the commencement of the attack Nelson retired to his cabin, where Lady Hamilton's miniature was a prominent decoration, to write his memorable prayer: "May the great God whom I worship, grant to my country, and for the benefit of Europe in general, a great and glorious victory. . . ."

The carnage in sea battles of this period was truly dreadful—especially at the close quarters in which Nelson chose to fight. The aim was not so much to sink the enemy's ships as to render them unmanageable by destroying their rigging and steering gear, setting them afire, and annihilating their crews with concentrated gunfire. The English put most of their reliance on their well-manned cannon, augmented on the main deck by Marines with muskets, but the French also liked to station men in the tops, where they could direct a murderous fire upon the open decks of the enemy. It was one of these that gave Nelson his last wound—a ball through the shoulder epaulette that clouded the great English victory with the death of their hero.

The principal chronicler of Nelson's death was the surgeon William Beatty. Some of the events on the main deck he had to report by hearsay, but after Nelson was carried below Beatty attended him in his last hours and recorded his last words.

Nelson's *Victory* was a "first-rater," so termed because she carried between 100 and 120 guns—in this case actually manning 104 guns. She was an old vessel, having been launched at Chatham in 1765, and had been rebuilt several times. The *Victory* was 186 feet long on her gun deck, with a beam of 51 feet 10 inches at the widest part of her hull. To many who visit this remarkable ship, still preserved in England, it comes as a surprise that Nelson died not in the stern quarters, or just below the gun deck, but among the other wounded three decks down—in the depths of the *Victory*, just abaft the mainmast.

"Thank God, I have done my duty"

AS the *Victory* drew near to the Enemy, His Lordship, accompanied by Captain Hardy, and the Captains of the four frigates (*Euryalus, Naiad, Sirius,* and *Phœbe*) who had been called on board by signal to receive instructions, visited the different decks of the ship. He addressed the crew at their several quarters, admonishing them against firing a single shot without being sure of their object; and expressed himself to the Officers highly satisfied with the arrangements made at their respective stations.

The Battle of Trafalgar.

It was now plainly perceived by all on board the *Victory*, that from the very compact line which the Enemy had formed, they were determined to make one great effort to recover in some measure their long-lost naval reputation. They wore in succession about twenty minutes past seven o'clock; and stood on the larboard tack, with their heads toward Cadiz. They kept a good deal of sail set; steering about two points from the wind, with top-sails shivering. Their van was particularly closed, having the *Santissima Trinidada* and the *Bucentaure* the ninth and tenth ships, the latter the flag-ship of Admiral Villeneuve; but as the Admirals of the Combined Fleets declined shewing their flags till the heat of the battle was over, the former of these ships was only distinguished from the rest by her having four decks; and Lord Nelson ordered the *Victory* to be steered for her bow.

Several Officers of the ship now communicated to each other their sentiments of anxiety for His Lordship's personal safety, to which every other consideration seemed to give way. Indeed all were confident of gaining a glorious victory, but the apprehensions for His Lordship were great and general; and the Surgeon made known to Doctor Scott his fears that His Lordship would be made the object of the Enemy's marksmen, and his desire that he might be entreated by somebody to cover the stars on his coat with a handkerchief. Doctor Scott and Mr. Scott (Public Secretary) both observed, however, that such a request would have no effect; as they knew His Lordship's sentiments on the subject so well, that they were sure he would be highly displeased with whoever should take the

165

liberty of recommending any change in his dress on this account: and when the Surgeon declared to Mr. Scott that he would avail himself of the opportunity of making his sick-report for the day, to submit his sentiments to the Admiral, Mr. Scott replied, "Take care, Doctor, what you are about; I would not be the man to mention such a matter to him." The Surgeon notwithstanding persisted in his design, and remained on deck to find a proper opportunity for addressing His Lordship; but this never occurred: as His Lordship continued occupied with the Captains of the frigates (to whom he was explaining his intentions respecting the services they were to perform during the battle) till a short time before the Enemy opened their fire on the *Royal Sovereign*, when Lord Nelson ordered all persons not stationed on the quarter-deck or poop to repair to their proper quarters; and the Surgeon, much concerned at this disappointment, retired from the deck with several other Officers.

About half an hour before the Enemy opened their fire, the memorable telegraphic signal was made, that "England Expects Every Man Will Do His Duty," which was spread and received throughout the Fleet with enthusiasm. It is impossible adequately to describe by any language, the lively emotions excited in the crew of the *Victory* when this propitious communication was made known to them: confidence and resolution were strongly portrayed in the countenance of all; and the sentiment generally expressed to each other was, that they would prove to their Country that day, how well

The Victory sailing into battle, an aquatint by R. Dodd

William Beatty

British seamen could "do their duty" when led to battle by their revered Admiral. The signal was afterwards made to "prepare to anchor after the close of the day," and union-jacks were hoisted at the fore-top-mast and top-gallant-stays of each ship, to serve as a distinction from the Enemy's, in conformity with orders previously issued by the Commander in Chief. By His Lordship's directions also, the different divisions of the Fleet hoisted the St. George's or white ensign, being the colours of the Commander in Chief: this was done to prevent confusion from occurring during the battle, through a variety of national flags.

The *Royal Sovereign* now made the signal by telegraph, that "the Enemy's Commander in Chief was in a frigate." This mistake arose from one of their frigates making many signals. Lord Nelson ordered his line to be steered about two points more to the northward than that of his Second in Command, for the purpose of cutting off the retreat of the Enemy's van to the port of Cadiz; which was the reason of the three leading ships of Admiral Collingwood's line being engaged with the Enemy previously to those of the Commander in Chief's line.

The Enemy began to fire on the *Royal Sovereign* at thirty minutes past eleven o'clock; in ten minutes after which she got under the stern of the *Santa Anna*, and commenced a fire on her. Lieutenant Pasco, Signal Officer of the *Victory*, was heard to say while looking through his glass, "There is a top-gallant-yard gone." His Lordship eagerly asked, "Whose top-gallant-yard is that gone? Is it the *Royal Sovereign*'s?" and on being answered by Lieutenant Pasco in the negative, and that it was the Enemy's, he smiled, and said: "Collingwood is doing well."

At fifty minutes past eleven the Enemy opened their fire on the Commander in Chief. They shewed great coolness in the commencement of the battle; for as the *Victory* approached their line, their ships lying immediately ahead of her and across her bows fired only one gun at a time, to ascertain whether she was yet within their range. This was frequently repeated by eight or nine of their ships, till at length a shot passed through the *Victory*'s main-top-gallant-sail; the hole in which being discovered by the Enemy, they immediately opened their broadsides, supporting an awful and tremendous fire. In a very short time afterwards, Mr. Scott, Public Secretary to the Commander in Chief, was killed by a cannon-shot while in conversation with Captain Hardy. Lord Nelson being then near them, Captain Adair of the Marines, with the assistance of a Seaman, endeavoured to remove the body from His Lordship's sight: but he had already observed the fall of

Lord Nelson, an aquatint by W. Barnard after the famous painting by Lemuel F. Abbott. In the background is the Battle of the Nile.

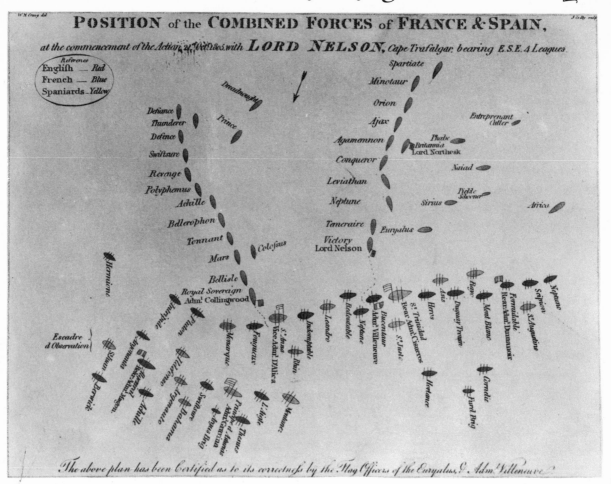

his Secretary; and now said with anxiety, "Is that poor Scott that is gone?" and on being answered in the affirmative by Captain Adair, he replied, "Poor fellow!"

Lord Nelson and Captain Hardy walked the quarter-deck in conversation for some time after this, while the Enemy kept up an incessant raking fire. A double-headed shot struck one of the parties of Marines drawn up on the poop, and killed eight of them; when His Lordship, perceiving this, ordered Captain Adair to disperse his men round the ship, that they might not suffer so much from being together. In a few minutes afterwards a shot struck the fore-brace-bits on the quarter-deck, and passed between Lord Nelson and Captain Hardy; a splinter from the bits bruising Captain Hardy's foot, and tearing the buckle from his shoe. They both

Nelson's strategy was to break the French line in two places, as may be seen in both the diagram of the battle and the bird's eye view of the attack. In the latter, Admiral Collingwood in the Royal Sovereign is already breaking the line, as Nelson in the Victory sails toward Admiral Villeneuve's Bucentaure. The small ship in the left foreground is probably the schooner Pickle, which brought to England the news of Nelson's triumph and death.

instantly stopped; and were observed by the Officers on deck to survey each other with inquiring looks, each supposing the other to be wounded. His Lordship then smiled, and said: "This is too warm work, Hardy, to last long"; and declared that "through all the battles he had been in, he had

never witnessed more cool courage than was displayed by the *Victory*'s crew on this occasion."

The *Victory* by this time, having approached close to the Enemy's van, had suffered very severely without firing a single gun: she had lost about twenty men killed, and had about thirty wounded. Her mizzen-topmast, and all her studding-sails and their booms, on both sides were shot away; the Enemy's fire being chiefly directed at her rigging, with a view to disable her before she could close with them. (The Enemy's fire continued throughout the engagement, that the *Victory* did not lose a man on her lower deck; and had only two wounded on that deck, and these by musket-balls.) At four minutes past twelve o'clock she opened her fire, from both sides of her decks, upon the Enemy; when Captain Hardy represented to His Lordship, that

"it appeared impracticable to pass through the Enemy's line without going on board some one of their ships." Lord Nelson answered, "I cannot help it: it does not signify which we run on board of; go on board which you please; take your choice."

At twenty minutes past twelve, the tiller-ropes being shot away, Mr. Atkinson, the Master, was ordered below to get the helm put to port; which being done, the *Victory* was soon run on board the *Redoutable* of seventy-four guns. On coming alongside and nearly on board of her, that ship fired her broadside into the *Victory*, and immediately let down her lower-deck ports; which, as has been since learnt, was done to prevent her from being boarded through them by the *Victory*'s crew. She never fired a great gun after this single broadside. A few minutes after this, the *Téméraire* fell likewise on board

169

Nelson is fatally wounded on the deck of the Victory.

of the *Redoutable*, on the side opposite to the *Victory*; having also an Enemy's ship, said to be *La Fougueux*, on board of *her* on her other side: so that the extraordinary and unprecedented circumstance occurred here, of *four* ships of the line being *on board of each other* in the heat of battle; forming as compact a tier as if they had been moored together, their heads lying all the same way. The *Téméraire*, as was just before mentioned, was between the *Redoutable* and *La Fougueux*. The *Redoutable* commenced a heavy fire of musketry from the tops, which was continued for a considerable time with destructive effect to the *Victory*'s crew: her great guns however being silent, it was supposed at different times that she had surrendered; and in consequence of this opinion, the *Victory* twice ceased firing upon her, by orders transmitted from the quarter-deck.

At this period, scarcely a person in the *Victory* escaped unhurt who was exposed to the Enemy's musketry; but there were frequent huzzas and cheers heard from between the decks, in token of the surrender of different of the Enemy's ships. An incessant fire was kept up from both sides of the *Victory:* her larboard guns played upon the *Santissima Trinidad* and the *Bucentaur*; and the starboard guns of the middle and lower decks were depressed, and fired with a diminished charge of powder, and three shot each, into the *Redoutable*. This mode of firing was adopted by Lieutenants Williams, King, Yule, and Brown, to obviate the danger of the *Téméraire*'s suffering from the *Victory*'s shot passing through the *Redoutable;* which must have been the case if the usual quantity of powder, and the common elevation, had been given to the guns.—A circumstance occurred in this situation, which shewed in a most striking manner the cool intrepidity of the Officers and men stationed on the lower deck of the *Victory*. When the guns on this deck were run out, their muzzles came into contact with the *Redoutable*'s side; and consequently at every discharge there was reason to fear that the Enemy would take fire, and both the *Victory* and

172

the *Téméraire* be involved in her flames. Here then was seen the astonishing spectacle of the firemen of each gun standing ready with a bucket full of water, which as soon as his gun was discharged he dashed into the Enemy through the holes made in her side by the shot.

It was from this ship [the *Redoutable*] that Lord Nelson received his mortal wound. About fifteen minutes past one o'clock, which was in the heat of the engagement, he was walking the middle of the quarter-deck with Captain Hardy, and in the act of turning near the hatchway with his face towards the stern of the *Victory*, when the fatal ball was fired from the Enemy's mizzen-top; which, from the situation of the two ships (lying on board of each other), was brought just abaft, and rather below, the *Victory*'s main-yard, and of course not more than fifteen yards distant from that part of the deck where His Lordship stood. The ball struck the epaulette on his left shoulder, and penetrated his chest. He fell with his face on the deck. Captain Hardy, who was on his right (the side furthest from the Enemy) and advanced some steps before His Lordship, on turning round, saw the Serjeant Major (Secker) of Marines with two Seamen raising him from the deck; where he had fallen on the same spot on which, a little before, his Secretary had breathed his last, with whose blood His Lordship's clothes were much soiled. Captain Hardy expressed a hope that he was not severely wounded; to which the gallant Chief replied: "They have done for me at last, Hardy."—"I hope not," answered Captain Hardy. "Yes," replied His Lordship; "my backbone is shot through."

Captain Hardy ordered the Seamen to carry the Admiral to the cockpit; and now two incidents occurred strikingly characteristic of this great man, and strongly marking that energy and reflection which in his heroic mind rose superior even to the immediate consideration of his present awful condition. While the men were carrying him down the ladder from the middle deck, His Lordship observed that the tiller-ropes were not yet replaced;

William Beatty

and desired one of the Midshipmen stationed there to go upon the quarter-deck and remind Captain Hardy of that circumstance, and request that new ones should be immediately rove. Having delivered this order, he took his handkerchief from his pocket and covered his face with it, that he might be conveyed to the cockpit at this crisis unnoticed by the crew.

Several wounded Officers, and about forty men, were likewise carried to the Surgeon for assistance just at this time; and some others had breathed their last during their conveyance below. Among the latter were Lieutenant William Andrew Ram, and Mr. Whipple, Captain's Clerk. The Surgeon had just examined these two Officers, and found that they were dead, when his attention was arrested by several of the wounded calling to him, "Mr. Beatty, Lord Nelson is here: Mr. Beatty, the Admiral is wounded." The Surgeon now, on looking round, saw the handkerchief fall from His Lordship's face; when the stars on his coat, which also had been covered by it, appeared. Mr. Burke the Purser, and the Surgeon, ran immediately to the assistance of His Lordship, and took him from the arms of the Seamen who had carried him below. In conveying him to one of the Midshipmen's berths, they stumbled, but recovered themselves without falling. Lord Nelson then inquired who were supporting him; and when the Surgeon informed him, His Lordship replied, "Ah, Mr. Beatty! you can do nothing for me. I have but a short time to live: my back is shot through." The Surgeon said, "he hoped the wound was not so dangerous as His Lordship imagined, and that he might still survive long to enjoy his glorious victory." The Reverend Doctor Scott, who had been absent in

Nelson is carried below.

173

another part of the cockpit administering lemonade to the wounded, now came instantly to His Lordship; and in the anguish of grief wrung his hands, and said: "Alas, Beatty, how prophetic you were!" alluding to the apprehensions expressed by the Surgeon for His Lordship's safety previous to the battle.

His Lordship was laid upon a bed, stripped of his clothes, and covered with a sheet. While this was effecting, he said to Doctor Scott, "Doctor, I told you so. Doctor, I am gone"; and after a short pause he added in a low voice, "I have to leave Lady Hamilton, and my adopted daughter Horatia, as a legacy to my Country." The Surgeon then examined the wound, assuring His Lordship that he would not put him to much pain in endeavouring to discover the course of the ball; which he soon found had penetrated deep into the chest, and had probably lodged in the spine. This being explained to His Lordship, he replied, "he was confident his back was shot through." The back was then examined externally, but without any injury being perceived; on which His Lordship was requested by the Surgeon to make him acquainted with all his sensations. He replied, that "he felt a gush of blood every minute within his breast: that he had no feeling in the lower part of his body: and that his breathing was difficult, and attended with very severe pain about that part of the spine where he was confident that the ball had struck; for," said he, "I felt it break my back." These symptoms, but more particularly the gush of blood which His Lordship complained of, together with the state of his pulse, indicated to the Surgeon the hopeless situation of the case; but till after the victory was ascertained and announced to His Lordship, the true nature of his wound was concealed by the Surgeon from all on board except only Captain Hardy, Doctor Scott, Mr. Burke, and Messrs. Smith and Westemburg, the Assistant Surgeons.

The *Victory*'s crew cheered whenever they observed an Enemy's ship surrender. On one of these occasions, Lord Nelson anxiously inquired what was the cause of it; when Lieutenant Pasco, who lay wounded at some distance from His Lordship, raised himself up, and told him that another ship had struck, which appeared to give him much satisfaction. He now felt an ardent thirst; and frequently called for drink, and to be fanned with paper, making use of these words: "Fan, fan," and "Drink, drink." This he continued to repeat, when he wished for drink or the refreshment of cool air, till a very few minutes before he expired. Lemonade, and wine and water, were given to him occasionally. He evinced great solicitude for the event of the battle, and fears for the safety of his friend Captain Hardy. Doctor Scott and Mr. Burke used every argument they could suggest, to relieve his anxiety. Mr. Burke told him "the Enemy were decisively defeated, and that he hoped His Lordship would still live to be himself the bearer of the joyful tidings to his country." He replied, "It is nonsense, Mr. Burke, to suppose I can live: my sufferings are great, but they will all be soon over." Doctor Scott entreated His Lordship "not to despair of living," and said "he trusted that Divine Providence would restore him once more to his dear Country and friends."—"Ah, Doctor!" replied His Lordship, "it is all over, it is all over."

Many messages were sent to Captain Hardy by the Surgeon, requesting his attendance on His Lordship; who became impatient to see him, and often exclaimed: "Will no one bring Hardy to me? He must be killed: he is surely destroyed." The Captain's Aide-de-camp, Mr. Bulkley, now came below, and stated that "circumstances respecting the Fleet required Captain Hardy's presence on deck, but that he would avail himself of the first favourable moment to visit His Lordship." On hearing him deliver this message to the Surgeon, His Lordship inquired who had brought it. Mr. Burke answered, "It is Mr. Bulkley, my Lord."—"It is his voice," replied His Lordship: he then said to the young gentleman, "Remember me to your father."

An hour and ten minutes however elapsed, from

William Beatty

The death of Lord Nelson, as painted by Arthur W. Devis, who went aboard the Victory before she reached England. The Reverend Dr. Scott is shown rubbing Nelson's chest, while the purser, Mr. Burke, supports his head, and Dr. Beatty feels for his pulse.

the time of His Lordship's being wounded, before Captain Hardy's first subsequent interview with him; the particulars of which are nearly as follow. They shook hands affectionately, and Lord Nelson said: "Well, Hardy, how goes the battle? How goes the day with us?"—"Very well, my Lord," replied Captain Hardy: "we have got twelve or fourteen of the Enemy's ships in our possession; but five of their van have tacked, and shew an intention of bearing down upon the *Victory*. I have therefore called two or three of our fresh ships round us, and have no doubt of giving them a drubbing."—"I hope," said His Lordship, "none of *our* ships have struck, Hardy."—"No, my Lord," replied Captain Hardy; "there is no fear of that." Lord Nelson then said: "I am a dead man, Hardy. I am going fast: it will be all over with me soon. Come nearer to me. Pray let my dear Lady Hamilton have my hair, and all other things belonging to me." Mr. Burke was about to withdraw at the commencement of this conversation; but His Lordship, perceiving his intention, desired he would remain.

Captain Hardy observed, that "he hoped Mr. Beatty could yet hold out some prospect of life."—"Oh! no," answered His Lordship; "it is impossible. My back is shot through. Beatty will tell you so." Captain Hardy then returned on deck, and at parting shook hands again with his revered friend and commander.

His Lordship now requested the Surgeon, who had been previously absent a short time attending Mr. Rivers, to return to the wounded, and give his assistance to such of them as he could be useful to; "for," said he, "you can do nothing for me." The Surgeon assured him that the Assistant Surgeons were doing everything that could be effected for those unfortunate men; but on His Lordship's several times repeating his injunctions to that purpose, he left him surrounded by Doctor Scott, Mr. Burke, and two of His Lordship's domestics. After the Surgeon had been absent a few minutes attending Lieutenants Peake and Reeves of the Marines, who were wounded, he was called by Doctor Scott to His Lordship, who said: "Ah, Mr. Beatty! I

Three "Delineations of Nautical Characters" of Nelson's time by Thomas Rowlandson:
a midshipman, a lieutenant, and a cabin boy.

176

have sent for you to say, what I forgot to tell you before, that all power of motion and feeling below my breast are gone; and *you*," continued he, "very well *know* I can live but a short time." The emphatic manner in which he pronounced these last words, left no doubt in the Surgeon's mind, that he adverted to the case of a man who had some months before received a mortal injury of the spine on board the *Victory*, and had laboured under similar privations of sense and muscular motion. The case had made a great impression on Lord Nelson: he was anxious to know the cause of such symptoms, which was accordingly explained to him; and he now appeared to apply the situation and fate of this man to himself. The Surgeon answered, "My Lord, you told me so before": but he now examined the extremities, to ascertain the fact; when His Lordship said, "Ah, Beatty! I am too certain of it: Scott and Burke have tried it already. You know I am gone." The Surgeon replied: "My Lord, unhappily for our Country, nothing can be done for you," and having made this declaration he was so much affected that he turned round and withdrew a few steps to conceal his emotions. His Lordship said: "I know it. I feel something rising in my breast," putting his hand on his left side, "which tells me I am gone." Drink was recommended liberally, and Doctor Scott and Mr. Burke fanned him with paper. He often exclaimed, "God be praised, I have done my duty"; and upon the Surgeon's inquiring whether his pain was still very great, he declared, "it continued so very severe, that he wished he was dead. Yet," said he in a lower voice, "one would like to live a little longer, too": and after a pause of a few minutes, he added in the same tone, "What would become of poor Lady Hamilton, if she knew my situation!"

The Surgeon, finding it impossible to render His Lordship any further assistance, left him, to attend Lieutenant Bligh, Messrs. Smith and Westphall, Midshipmen, and some Seamen, recently wounded. Captain Hardy now came to the cockpit to see His Lordship a second time, which was after

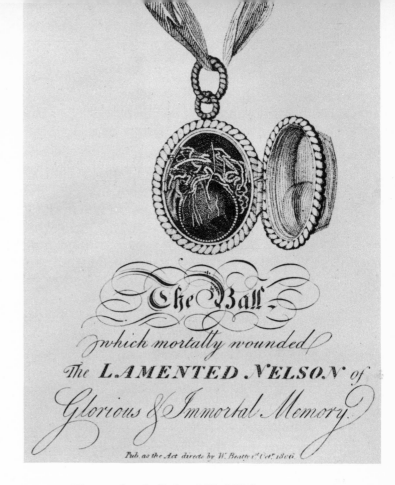

The musket ball that killed Nelson,
with bits of his coat and epaulet sticking to it.

an interval of about fifty minutes from the conclusion of his first visit. Before he quitted the deck, he sent Lieutenant Hills to acquaint Admiral Collingwood with the lamentable circumstance of Lord Nelson's being wounded. — Lord Nelson and Captain Hardy shook hands again: and while the Captain retained His Lordship's hand, he congratulated him even in the arms of Death on his brilliant victory; "which," he said, "was complete; though he did not know how many of the enemy were captured, as it was impossible to perceive every ship distinctly. He was certain however of fourteen or fifteen having surrendered." His Lordship answered, "That is well, but I bargained for twenty:" and then emphatically exclaimed, "*Anchor*, Hardy, *anchor!*" To this the Captain replied: "I suppose, my Lord, Admiral Collingwood will now take upon himself the direction of affairs." — "Not while I live, I hope, Hardy!" cried the dying Chief; and at that moment endeavoured ineffectually to raise

177

himself from the bed. "No," added he; "do *you* anchor, Hardy." Captain Hardy then said: "Shall *we* make the signal, Sir?"—"Yes," answered His Lordship; "for if I live, I'll anchor." [Meaning that in case of His Lordship's surviving till all resistance on the part of the Enemy had ceased, Captain Hardy was then to anchor the British Fleet and the prizes, if it should be found practicable.] The energetic manner in which he uttered these his last orders to Captain Hardy, accompanied with his efforts to raise himself, evinced his determination never to resign the command while he retained the exercise of his transcendant faculties, and that he expected Captain Hardy still to carry into effect the suggestions of his exalted mind; a sense of his duty overcoming the pains of death. He then told Captain Hardy, "he felt that in a few minutes he should be no more"; adding in a low tone, "Don't throw me overboard, Hardy." The Captain answered, "Oh! no, certainly not."—"Then," replied His Lordship, "you know what to do: and," continued he, "take care of my dear Lady Hamilton, Hardy; take care of poor Lady Hamilton. Kiss me, Hardy." The Captain now knelt down, and kissed his cheek; when His Lordship said, "Now I am satisfied. Thank God, I have done my duty." Captain Hardy stood for a minute or two in silent contemplation: he then knelt down again, and kissed His Lordship's forehead. His Lordship said: "Who is that?" The Captain answered: "It is Hardy"; to which His Lordship replied, "God bless you, Hardy!" After this affecting scene Captain Hardy withdrew, and returned to the quarter-deck, having spent about eight minutes in this his last interview with his dying friend.

Lord Nelson now desired Mr. Chevalier, his Steward, to turn him upon his right side; which being effected, His Lordship said: "I wish I had not left the deck, for I shall soon be gone." He afterwards became very low; his breathing was oppressed, and his voice faint. He said to Doctor Scott, "Doctor, I have *not* been a *great* sinner;" and after a short pause, "*Remember*, that I leave Lady Hamilton and my Daughter Horatia as a legacy to my Country: and," added he, "never forget Horatia." His thirst now increased; and he called for "Drink, drink," "Fan, fan," and "Rub, rub": addressing himself in the last case to Doctor Scott, who had been rubbing His Lordship's breast with his hand, from which he found some relief. These words he spoke in a very rapid manner, which rendered his articulation difficult: but he every now and then, with evident increase of pain, made a greater effort with his vocal powers, and pronounced distinctly these last words: "Thank God, I have done my duty"; and this great sentiment he continued to repeat as long as he was able to give it utterance.

His Lordship became speechless in about fifteen minutes after Captain Hardy left him. Doctor Scott and Mr. Burke, who had all along sustained the bed under his shoulders (which raised him in nearly a semi-recumbent posture, the only one that was supportable to him), forbore to disturb him by speaking to him; and when he had remained speechless about five minutes, His Lordship's Steward went to the Surgeon, who had been a short time occupied with the wounded in another part of the cockpit, and stated his apprehensions that His Lordship was dying. The Surgeon immediately repaired to him, and found him on the verge of dissolution. He knelt down by his side, and took up his hand; which was cold, and the pulse gone from the wrist. On the Surgeon's feeling his forehead, which was likewise cold, His Lordship opened his eyes, looked up, and shut them again. The Surgeon again left him, and returned to the wounded who required his assistance; but was not absent five minutes before the Steward announced to him that "he believed His Lordship had expired." The Surgeon returned, and found that the report was but too well founded: His Lordship had breathed his last, at thirty minutes past four o'clock; at which period Doctor Scott was in the act of rubbing His Lordship's breast, and Mr. Burke supporting the bed under his shoulders.

178

Adventure 12

"Stove in"

from Whale Hunt, by Nelson Cole Haley

At the Marine Historical Association's Stillman Library in Mystic, Connecticut, is a manuscript account in faded brown ink containing the reminiscences of the first voyage of a New Bedford whaleman named Nelson Cole Haley. Written as a continuous narrative and put together in the later years of its author's life, it remained generally unknown until 1944. At this time the whale ship *Charles W. Morgan*, the ship on which Haley had gone to sea, found a new and permanent home at Mystic Seaport, and Haley's heirs deemed Mystic an appropriate repository for the work. Edited by Carl P. Cutler and Sumner Putnam, it was published in 1948 under the title *Whale Hunt*.

Haley was seventeen when he signed aboard the *Morgan*, not an unusual age for young men of that time to go to sea. His writing conveys a keen sense of adventure happily combined with an equally keen sense of humor. These capacities served him well, for whaling voyages were long, often tedious, and sometimes dangerous, and this one, lasting from 1849 to 1853, was no exception.

Haley's account is full of fascinating and authentic detail of life aboard the *Morgan:* the day-to-day routine of the forecastle; the lining up of boat crews and the pursuit of whales, the toilsome cutting-in of the blubber and boiling of the oil; the perils of storms, uncharted reefs, wounded whales, and even cannibals. But it is the jaunty exuberance and unfailing good humor of the author which give the narrative its real distinction, and best serve to recapture the spirit of this great era in American seamanship.

The episode that follows climaxed Haley's adventures, and was his narrowest escape from death on the whole voyage. It was also the climax of a minor feud between Haley, the harpooner of his boat and hence second in command, and the second mate, in nominal control of the boat. The events described here healed the quarrel once and for all. This is a rousing story made all the more striking by the fact that Haley's experiences were not in the least unusual at this time.

The Charles W. Morgan at Mystic Seaport.

"*The few hours of hope and despair was enough to answer a lifetime*"

HEN in about the Lat. of 5° South, Long. 170° East, all hands were made happy one morning, just as seven bells struck, by the pleasing sound from the masthead of "T-h-e-r-e s-h-e b-l-o-w-s!" The answer to the Captain's question of "Where away? And how far off?" being "Four points on the lee bow, two and a half miles off," the main-yard was hove aback, lines were placed in the boats, and all hands but those to keep ship went to a hurried breakfast, which was soon finished, and the boats lowered away.

The weather for the past two or three days had been squally. Squalls of wind and rain would blow for an hour at a time, with rain coming down in torrents, obscuring everything but a narrow circle of darkened waters half a mile around the ship. When the squall would pass over, the sun would shine out and the sky become quite clear until another squall forming would cover all up again, sometimes two or three hours apart, at other times not so long. It was in between two of these squalls that the whale we lowered for was sighted; and the weather continued so good that before another squall came on we caught sight of him again: a large lone bull whale, who no doubt had been driven off from a school of cows by one more vigorous than he.

Two large bull whales in one school of whales at the same time is unknown without they would be fighting, when the conquered one would leave instantly. They fight with terrific fury, using their jaws in rushing at each other, something like two men fencing with swords; and cases have been known of whales having their jaw twisted quite out of shape and sometimes broken entirely asunder. I have seen one or two instances of the first kind myself.

Before the whale went down again, we had got so good a run of him that by the time the next squall cleared off we sighted him no great distance from our boat, and although drenched to the skin by the rain, we started for him with glee. As we were some two or three ship's lengths nearer to him when he broke water than any other boat, and square in after him, the chance was ours, and with our sail and oars we improved it for all it was worth.

The whale was heading to the leeward with the wind about four points on his quarter, and as there was a fresh breeze blowing, we shot up across the corner of his flukes with a free sheet, and when the boat's stern passed clear of his flukes a quick stroke with the steering oar caused the boat's head to shoot to windward (as it is always the rule to go on the lee side of a sperm whale when approaching to strike or lance). Bringing the boat's head within two or three feet of his side, I let him have the first iron, which I had been holding in my hand since ordered to stand up by the 2d Mate when crossing the whale's flukes. The second iron was planted into his huge body, no great distance from the first, a second after. Throwing overboard the coil of stray line, I turned around and commenced to roll up the sail.

181

This job was none too easy, as the whale, instead of sounding as is almost always the first thing they do when fastened to, took to running to the windward. This caused the sail to slat and bang so much that at times the sprit would slip out of my hands when I had the folds of the sail wound around it almost to the mast, and away the whole thing would fly, adrift again. With the assistance of the bow oarsman, I secured it at last; and unshipping the mast out of the thwart, I passed it to the 2d Mate, who shoved the heel of the mast under the after thwart, with the upper part resting on the gunwale and the covering board over the stern sheets on the starboard side of the boat, all clear of the line and steering oar, leaving everything clear for working on the whale.

As soon as the mast was out of the way, the 2d Mate took his place in the head of the boat and I went aft to the steering oar. By the time everything was straightened in the boat, we had run quite a distance away from the other boats and were as far to the windward as the ship, but some mile and a half ahead of her, the whale showing no signs of slacking his speed; so all we could do was to hold our line, trim boat and keep the water bailed out

that now and then rolled over her sides and bows when she pitched into a larger sea than common.

This thing went on for an hour or more, when big dark masses of clouds could be seen to the windward, making up into a mess that denoted a squall of unusual severity and continuance. The ship saw it and took in her main-topgallant sail and flying jib.

Not much had been said out of the usual line by either the 2d Mate or myself up to this time, but now we both expressed ourselves in regard to the whale and the look of the weather. If the confounded whale would only give us a show to lance him, though, we did not care much about what might be in that impenetrable mass of black matter that was fast rolling down on our unprotected heads from the windward.

About the time the clouds had gathered overhead so thick that all signs of blue had vanished and the first pattering drops of rain began to hit us, the whale milled a little to the leeward; and by the time full force of the squall was on us, he was running at the rate of ten knots an hour with the wind abaft the starboard beam. Keeping this course and speed for half an hour, he suddenly stopped

and commenced to roll and tumble, snap his jaws and strike with his flukes. This was what we wanted, in one way, since now might be a chance to get a lance into him; whereas there would be none when he was running like he had been.

But of all the different views of whaling that it has been my lot to see, this beat them all. Here we were in the midst of a raging tempest, rain pouring down in torrents, the sea and wind combined in a roar that was accompanied now and then by the sound of the whale's flukes as he struck the water, after raising them fifteen or twenty feet above the surface, sending the foam flying in every direction when he brought them down in his rage.

All the world was lost to our view, a little space in the world of waters in which a battle was going on; a whaleboat with six men in it, a whale and a gale, each trying to win. We did not pay much heed to anything but the whale, and watching a chance the whale gave us, we sent the boat ahead and with a skilled aim the 2d Mate drove his lance deep into the life of the whale, and the thick blood that came pouring out from his spout hole told of our battle won. "Stern all! Stern all hard!!" was the cry from both of us to the men, as the whale turned towards us with his head and just missed the boat with his wide-open jaw. Sterning off a safe distance from him, as he was tumbling about too much for us to do any fooling just then, we watched him in his struggles for a few minutes. Raising his head at last well out of water, he shot ahead and turned flukes.

"Look out for the line!" was the order from the 2d Mate to me. "He is going to sound."

"Aye, aye, sir," was my reply and at the same time I took an extra turn around the loggerhead and reached for a canvas nipper to shield my hands from burning by the friction of the line passing through them when grasping it to prevent its running any faster around the loggerhead in the stern of the boat than safety obliged.

Down he went, dragging flake after flake out of the tub until more than one-half had rapidly disappeared; I holding the line at times hard enough to pitch the head of the boat under water, and getting a sharp word of warning to be careful from the officer. Still the line ran out, and the 2d Mate was calling for the drags. (These are boards nailed together, about eighteen inches square, with a block of wood in the center, through which a hole is bored for splicing a piece of towline long enough to fasten around the whale line with a rolling hitch. They answer to retard the whale's progress, in a degree, when there is danger of his taking a boat's line.) The 2d Mate fastened on the two drags we had in the boat. By the time he had done this, our line was run out to the last two flakes; about one hundred and eighty fathoms being gone of the two hundred and twenty that is the length of a whale line.

We commenced to look blue, as, if he took our line, we should have but little chance of ever seeing any more of him. We knew he had his death wound;

and if he did not take our line, when he came again to the surface his life would be short. Just then the strain on the line slackened. This made our hearts rejoice, and when our officer gave the order "Haul line," every man faced around forward on his thwart, and with both hands pulled hard together and brought a little line back into the boat, gaining on it faster and faster as the whale approached the surface, which he now was doing. Coming to the drags, the lanyards to them were cast off from where they had been made fast to the line, and they were taken into the boat.

By the time he broke water, some three or four hundred feet from us, we had hauled into the boat about two-thirds of our line, and as he was only moving very slowly through the water the boys hauled so lively on the line that I had hard work to coil it fast enough in the open part of the stern sheets to keep up with them. The whale was throwing out thick clots of blood by the barrelful at each spouting, and hardly moving through the water, and the boat shot towards him as fast as four men could haul the line.

When we had approached within a short distance of him, the 2d Mate, much to my astonishment, ordered the men to take the oars, and at the same time he told me: "Put the boat on the whale, so that I can lance him again." He and I had had so many bouts with each other that I hardly liked to say anything against any more orders he might give, but in this case I could not keep still, for our lives were to be placed in jeopardy very foolishly.

Lowering the boats to pursue a whale.

Nelson Cole Haley

The look of astonishment he had on his face when he turned from looking forward, towards me at the steering oar, on my saying to him that I thought he had made a mistake, as he certainly could not think under the existing conditions of wanting to lance that whale, would have made me laugh if it were not a too serious time for levity. The men had stopped pulling, no doubt at my great breach of discipline in asking him such a question, so the boat almost stopped.

"Pull ahead!" he yelled at the top of his voice.

"Hold on a minute, Mr. Griffin, let me say a few words first," was my reply, and then as rapidly as possible I called his attention to the fact that the whale was about dead and would soon go into his flurry. Also, that though the worst part of the squall was over, nothing could be seen yet any great distance from the boat and the ship could not tell our position, as the whale had changed his course so much, from what it was when we were last seen by her, that if our boat should get stoven the chance of her finding the whale or us would be mighty slim when the weather cleared up again. "This is all I have to say in the matter, except, if you are bound to lance that whale, let me put the boat on his lee side, instead of going to him as we are now, heading on to windward of him."

The only answer he made to any of the reasons or requests made by me was that he did not think I was such a coward, and to put the boat on to the whale the way she was headed; the quicker I did it, the better.

Going on the whale. The spirited drawings that follow are the work of Robert Weir, crew member of another New Bedford whaler, the Clara Bell, from 1855 to 1858. They are part of a private journal similar to Haley's.

Telling the men to pull ahead, I told him he would not find me far behind him in any danger that any reasonable man had to face. A few strokes of the oars, and the heave of the seas sent the boat on to the whale. He set his lance over its shoulder blade and, holding by the pole, thrust it up and down two or three times, and then sung out: "Stern all!"

The men did their level best to obey the order, but even with the 2d Mate assisting at the harpooner's oar when he saw the four men failed to stern off the whale, nothing more could be done than to get the boat a short distance away from him to the windward, and then be swept back by the next heavy sea. This happened three or four times, and the boat had worked aft on the whale quite a piece, when the whale, with a blow from his flukes, knocked the bottom half out of her and tumbled us all into the water.

The 2d Mate, who could not swim a stroke, managed to be amongst the first to grasp hold of some part of the boat and so keep afloat; and before he had hardly got the salt water out of his mouth, he was giving orders for securing the oars and lashing them across the gunwales of the boat, to keep her from rolling over and over in the seaway, and drowning us all. He was a brick, in many ways, when a pinch came.

The situation we were now in was rather critical, to say the least, and how it would end would be hard to say. We had lashed the oars across the boat by pieces of small throat-seizing stuff fastened under each gunwale for just such an emergency as this, and so we kept the boat on her keel, thus affording us a good resting-place for our arms over the gunwales on each side. Of course, our bodies and legs hung in the water, which would afford an easy meal for the sharks that abound in the sea in those Latitudes. Of these we felt somewhat nervous, but had hopes the whale would attract them by the blood from his carcass, that lay dead on the water some hundred yards away; for soon after he stove us, he had gone into his flurry and turned fin out.

Just before we took our bath, the clouds began to break, and an hour afterwards the sun was

A sperm whale smashing a boat in its jaws.

First Fort Dauphin Whale

shining brightly. The wind went down to a light royal breeze and the sea in two hours was so smooth that it ceased to break over us. The last squall had been the most severe of any in the last twenty-four hours and seemed to have exhausted itself and brought good weather with it, much to our satisfaction in more ways than one. When the weather cleared, the ship could be seen some eight or ten miles away, but no signs of any boats to cheer us with hopes of relief. They had lost all run of us as well as the ship had, and when it cleared up they went to the ship and added their eyes to the others on board, in the vain effort to catch sight of our boat on the waste of waters.

As the time we got stove was about 10 A.M., we felt not much apprehension but that long before

A "gallied" whale sounding.

Darting the second iron.   More than one harpoon was ordinarily needed to penetrate the whale's blubber and attach him firmly to the boat. A lance was also used, for the kill.

dark we would be found. We made the best of our surroundings. The water was not very cold, and until our legs became almost as wrinkled as a washerwoman's thumb, we suffered but little that way, but the sun shone hot on our heads and we suffered with thirst. Now and then the sharp back fin of a shark could be seen cutting through the water no great ways off, but as none took a bite at us, we lost, to a certain extent, our fear of them, after a time.

But the few hours of hope and despair that I and the rest passed through was enough to answer a lifetime. Many were the regrets the 2d Mate expressed that he had not heeded my warning, and let the whale alone. Telling him that it was all right, it might have happened anyway, seemed to afford no relief to his feelings.

When we first saw the ship after the squall was over, she was on the starboard tack, heading towards us. If she kept on that course, we thought she would pass about a mile or two by us to the windward, as we were about two points on her lee bow, and some one of the many eyes on board her might see the waifs we had stuck up, one in each end of the boat; for it would be impossible for the boat, level with the water, to be seen at the distance she would pass.

With eager and longing eyes and hopeful hearts we saw her approach close-hauled on the wind, with all sail set. On, on she came, her hull fast raising above the horizon, then her white waist showing more plainly, until the upper course of her bright copper could be seen under the lee bow as she rose on a sea and, settling down, sent a sheet of foam dashing away ahead, under the dolphin striker. "She will soon see us now," we said to each other, as men could be seen on the lookout from the royal yards, topgallant and topsail yards also. The time had now arrived when every minute we expected to see her swing her head off from the wind and point for us. Our hopes were doomed to disappointment, for just then we saw the jib sheets ease off, and when they commenced to slat, we

knew she was going in stays and soon would be on the other tack and standing away from us. No one but him who has been clinging to some frail support on the wide ocean can tell of the agony of such moments.

When her headyards were braced full, and fore and main tacks boarded on the tack, so that every foot she went through the water was directly away from us, each man gazed at one another but no words were said. Every man had the same thoughts of how little chance for us was left, as in tacking ship those on board of her believed we must be somewhere to the windward; for we had been seen going that way before the squall struck. But here we were to the leeward; and they, not thinking so, would not keep so bright an outlook that way, naturally, as to the windward; and the chances were she never would come so near us again.

With hearts that seemed like they would burst, we watched her sail away, so stately and silent, until her hull had settled below the line of the horizon. But then we were gladdened to see her tack again; and although we knew that if she hugged the wind on that tack, she would pass by us some miles to the windward, still, this would be better than having her stern towards us. Besides, it showed that our Captain knew he had run off the line he ought to find us in, and that he would look to leeward, after beating across it to the windward, far enough to satisfy himself we were not in that direction.

They passed by again and stood quite a distance on before she went about. When passing us on the port tack this time, only the head of her topsails could be seen; and by the time she got ready to tack again, which she did, she could hardly be seen by us and about all our hopes of rescue were gone. Still we strained our eyes, that had now become quite painful with the spray flying into them and the heat of the sun, to catch the gleam of her white sails, so far away to the windward. I asked the 2d Mate if he could tell the time by the sun. He in a choked voice said he thought it was about 3 P.M. If so, we must have been five hours hanging on this boat and we only had about three hours more of daylight, as the sun would set at six. If we were not picked up before that time, how few of us would ever see the sun rise again?

These thoughts passing through my mind, with other thoughts of home, and how bad my poor mother and sister would feel when the loss of this boat's crew was known, caused me to lose myself partly to the surroundings that existed; and I was suddenly aroused by an exclamation from the blacksmith, who pulled our bow oar, that the ship was running off nearly before the wind.

Looking towards her, it could be seen she had come in sight more plainly, and in a short time there could be no doubt but what she was running off with the wind on her quarter and heading on a course that would carry her no great distance on the other side of us.

Up went our water-soaked spirits and never were poor devils more pleased than us, to see the rise of her full-bosomed sails, foot by foot, as she came rolling and heading nearly towards us. When within three or four miles of us, for some cause unaccounted for, she luffed two points and this carried her so far by us, to the windward, that she was farther off when she passed than she was the other time she came near. Down went our thermometers, and cold chills of despair went through our bodies which the long soaking in the water so intensified that we felt like giving up.

During the last two or three hours of our misery, not much had been said between any of us, and so indifferent had we become to our condition that a shark's fin would have to appear pretty close to us to cause much excitement or any splashing in the water with our feet to frighten them off. So, when one of the sharks caught the

"Reaching his life" with the lance.

blade of our steering oar (which was hanging in the becket at the stern, by a pin in the handle, and the blade some twenty feet away) in his teeth and gave it a heavy shake, at the same time splitting a piece off it, so deadened had we become that we hardly noticed the occurrence, or the remark made by one of the men: "Some of our legs will catch it next."

A strange fact in connection with that event is, that at the time it occurred, I had far less horror of being eaten alive by the sharks than I have had many times since, when thinking it over, or starting out of a sound sleep with perspiration streaming, by dreaming of the cold-gray look the round devilish eyes of some of those sharks had. If one of us had been bitten, short work would have been made of the rest.

Cutting in. The blubber is cut loose from the carcass in "blanket pieces" and hauled aboard.

The ship kept on her course away from us for fifteen or twenty miles longer. Then we saw her keep off before the wind. This course took her no farther from us, which encouraged us; but if she kept it up it would bring us to the windward, and if she hauled on the starboard tack, all hope of their finding us before morning, if then, would be gone.

I had been thinking for some time what we could do to attract her attention, and it now struck me she was in such a position that if our sail could be raised without the boat rolling over, the width of it could be seen a long way off, and, as we were off her beam, some eyes would catch sight of it before it tumbled down or rolled the boat over. I told my thoughts to the 2d Mate, who said the idea was good, if we could only get the sail up. The trouble of that was, the boat would roll over, bottomside up, if great care was not used; and if she did, some of us might lose the number of our

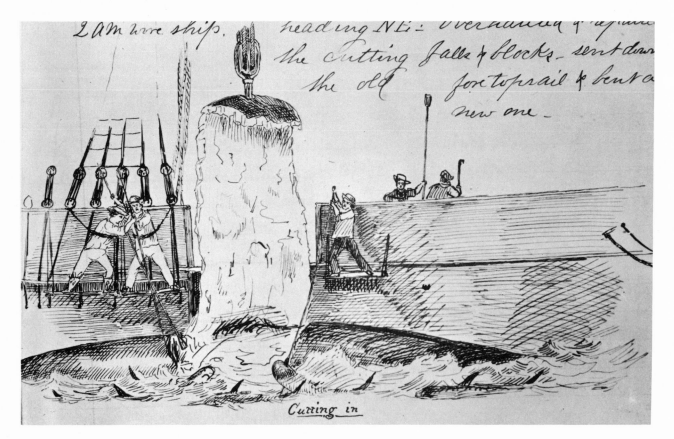

Cutting in

mess. But we would try it anyway, he said, as it might as well be ended that way as any other.

By some exertion the sail was worked out from under the after thwart where the lower part of the mast had been shoved, and was lifted on top of the oars that were lashed from side to side, the heel of the mast being over the hole in the bow thwart. Cutting a short piece of lance rope some two fathoms long, this was fastened with a clove hitch, about two feet from the end of the mast that fitted into the step on the boat's keel. The two ends of this heel rope were made fast to the midship thwart, one on each side, as near as possible where the ends of the thwart fastened to the boat's side.

The blubber is then chopped into chunks called "horse pieces."

The horse pieces, sliced thin into "Bible leaves," are "tried out," or boiled down to oil in the try-works.

The sail was unrolled. Another piece of lance warp was fastened to the top of the mast, with ends long enough to reach the sides when the mast would be upright, with one man on each side to tend these; this to answer as backstays, to keep the mast from tumbling either side. The rope that fastened the sail when rolled up was led forward, and the end of it rove through the eyebolt in the head of the boat that the hook of the tackle to hoist her with fitted into. Taking a short piece of rope with me to the head of the boat, I made with it a lashing for myself to sit in; and when in position, I had one leg each side of the boat's bows and one arm free to work with.

The end of the rope passed through the eyebolt was taken hold of by a man hanging onto the

Herman Melville very much admired these dramatic whaling views. "Taken for all in all," he wrote in Moby Dick, *"by far the finest, though in some details not the most accurate presentation of whales and whaling scenes to be anywhere found, are two large French engravings, well executed, and taken from paintings by one Garneray. Who Garneray the painter is, or was, I know not. But my life for it, he was either practically conversant with his subject, or marvelously tutored by some experienced whale-man."*

Nelson Cole Haley

harpooner's oar, and a round turn was taken with it to hold what might be gained as the mast arose. The end of the sprit pole was cut from the corner of the sail and fastened to the end of the mast; this to help lift the mast upright, as it would not do to have a man in the boat to help.

The 2d Mate and the after oarsman, holding each with one hand on the boat and using the other to shove the pole with, got as far aft on the boat as they could work, and the word was given to lift. After trying three or four times, we made out to raise the sail two-thirds upright, and although it seemed the boat must roll over, she did not. One thing in our favor was that she rode head to the sea.

During the time we were working to raise the sail, little attention had been paid to the ship. But when the sail was blowing out and showed a signal of white drilling at least fifteen by six feet, that ought to be seen plainly on the ocean eight or ten miles on a day like this, we all turned our eyes in her direction. The sail fluttered in the light gale, and the boat rolled enough at times to frighten us that our signal might tumble over before it was seen. I do not suppose ten minutes had elapsed from the time we had let our banner fly to the winds, but minutes seemed like hours; and it seemed that long, before down went her wheel and round came her noble head, with her jibboom heading straight to us.

"Sperm Whaling with Its Varieties," a remarkable view of all the features of the chase, from approaching the whale to the kill. The artist, Benjamin Russell, a New Bedford man with whaling experience, executed one panorama on this subject 1800 feet long, to be displayed in theatres by unrolling it between huge wooden cylinders.

We yelled, we shouted and laughed. Cold and sharks were nothing now to us. With blue lips and drawn faces some of the boys tried to make a joke, but it ended in a sob that was almost a fresh-water cry. When all doubt of their losing run of us had passed, we let the mast down for fear the boat might roll over and cause a tragedy.

The old ship came bowling along. Oh, how

good she looked! To me she seemed the biggest spot on earth or ocean, and to once more tread her white decks would seem bliss indeed. Soon the white foam under her forefoot could be seen rolling and tumbling as she dashed her sharp bows into the seas that attempted to stop her on her mission of mercy; she in scorn smashing them into bubbles and suds that went dancing along her sides into the wake astern, with hissing sounds that might mean regret at their impotency.

When some half-mile from us, she hauled up her mainsail and laid the main-topsail to the mast, and lowered three boats, one of which went to the whale. (It was about a half-mile from us, we had drifted apart.) The other two boats came to us. One took us into it and the other commenced

to clear the stoven boat of the oars and sail, to take it alongside the ship. The ship ran towards us as soon as they saw us leave the stoven boat, so we had but a short pull. When we arrived alongside, most of the boys had to be hauled on deck with a rope. Hot coffee was given us and we were sent below to change clothes, after which we turned in and had a rest for an hour or two, to set our blood in motion.

While we were turned in, the stoven boat was taken aboard and the whale hauled alongside, sail taken in, and all made snug for the night, as by this time it was dark. After we had our suppers, and were smoking our pipes, leaning over the bulwarks with our elbows on the rail, looking at the whale alongside, the other boat-steerers allowed that they

had given us up, and had no hopes of finding us. The Captain thought we must have been taken down by the whale; and when running off before the wind, just before they caught sight of our half-set boat sail, he had said he did not know which way to look for us now, or which tack to haul on the wind, as the ship was some way to the leeward of where the boat had last been seen. "So you see, old fellow," said one of them, "if we had not caught sight of you when we did and had run a short distance more to be leeward, we would have missed you on either tack we hauled to the wind on, and the rest of us fellows would have had a chance to have bought some of your old clothes and your chest, cheap."

"So you might," was my reply.

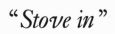

The Charles W. Morgan, under full sail.

196

Adventure 13

The Escape from Etah

from Arctic Explorations, by Elisha Kent Kane

WHAT causes, what constitutes the quality of leadership? The question may well be unanswerable. Leadership is, after all, simply the capacity to persuade others to follow, and just as men may follow because of any of several motives or compulsions, so a number of different traits may cause different men to be natural leaders.

But if personal courage, magnanimity, common sense, and—above all—a concentrated regard for the feelings and welfare of others are the elements of leadership, it is not difficult to see what made Dr. Elisha Kane the leader he was. It was certainly these qualities that enabled him to command an exhausted, half-starved band of fifteen men, making their way down the ice-ridden western coast of Greenland in three small leaky boats, and bring them to safety without losing any.

Kane's exploits place him in the front rank of arctic explorers, yet properly speaking he was not an explorer at all. He was a Philadelphia physician who was selected in 1850 to be medical officer on a government expedition led by Lieutenant Edwin DeHaven to seek for signs of Sir John Franklin, whose party had disappeared while trying to find a way to the North Pole in 1845. The first Grinnell Expedition, so called in honor of New York shipping merchant Henry Grinnell who furnished the ships, was fruitless. But Grinnell financed a second, and this time Dr. Kane was put in charge.

In the summer of 1853 Kane set out in the brig *Advance* with eighteen officers and men. There followed two years of exploration of the northwest stretches of the Greenland coast, including the discovery of a large landlocked sea fronting the enormous Humboldt Glacier. Kane modestly called it Kennedy Channel, but it was later renamed Kane Basin. Cold and privation tried the party severely, especially during the dark winters, which they were forced to spend on the frozen-in ship. During the second winter especially, there were several bad cases of scurvy and frostbite, the latter necessitating the amputation of one man's foot. Another man survived the winter only to die of pneumonia in the spring.

In the spring of 1855 it became clear that ice would prevent the *Advance* from ever leaving the Arctic, and Dr. Kane resolved to give up his quest and try to escape in the ship's boats to the Danish settlements on the southwest coast, some thirteen hundred miles from the Eskimo settlement at Etah where Kane had set up temporary camp.

Two of these were regular whaleboats, twenty-six feet long, seven feet in beam, and three feet deep, which Kane named the *Faith* and the *Hope*. These two craft were strengthened by oak beams fastened to the keel in a long "string piece," and cedar washboards were erected along the gunwales to raise their height six inches. A housing of light canvas was stretched along a "strong-back," a spar running from bow to stern, to give a little additional protection from the waves. Each boat had a single mast, stepped through a hinged piece in the forward rowing thwart, but more dependence was placed on the six oars, supplemented by poles for fending off ice. The third boat, the *Red Eric*, was smaller and not so seaworthy; it was soon relegated to store-boat.

They left the ship on Sunday, May 18, 1855. Dr. Kane conducted a short religious service before departure. He declared that the journey could only be made successfully if everyone obeyed orders and kept their faith in God's help. One order was clearly stated: Every consideration of self must be secondary to the protection of the sick and injured.

Among the most striking aspects of Kane that appear in the account of his epic open-boat voyage, aside from the qualities of character that shine through, are his acute powers of observation: in the midst of discomfort and danger he was still capable of close and detailed examination of his awesome surroundings. The result is not only a gripping narrative of adventure but a classic of objective reporting.

All illustrations come from Arctic Explorations and are engraved after Dr. Kane's own drawings.

The Advance in the far North.

"*My sturdy second officer shed tears at the prospect*"

LL hands were called to prepare for embarking. The boats were stowed, and the cargo divided between them equally; the sledges unlashed and slung outside the gunwales; and on Tuesday the 19th, at 4 P.M., with the bay as smooth as a garden-lake, I put off in the *Faith*. She was followed by the *Red Eric* on our quarter, and the *Hope* astern. In the *Faith* I had with me Mr. McGary, and Petersen, Hickey, Stephenson, and Whipple. Mr. Brooks was in the *Hope*, with Hayes, Sontag, Morton, Goodfellow, and Blake. Bonsall, Riley, and Godfrey made the crew of the *Eric*.

The wind freshened as we doubled the westernmost point of Cape Alexander, and, as we looked out on the expanse of the sound, we saw the kittiwakes and the ivory-gulls and jagers dipping their wings in the curling waves. They seemed the very same birds we had left two years before screaming and catching fish in the beautiful water. We tried to make our first rest at Sutherland Island; but we found it so barricaded by the precipitous ice-belt that it was impossible to land. I clambered myself from the boat's mast upon the platform and filled our kettles with snow, and then, after cooking our supper in the boats, we stood away for Hakluyt. It was an ugly crossing: we had a short chopping sea from the southeast; and, after a while, the Red Boat swamped. Riley and Godfrey managed to struggle to the *Faith*, and Bonsall to the *Hope;* but it was impossible to remove the cargo of our little comrade: it was as much as we could do to keep her afloat and let her tow behind us. Just at this time, too, the *Hope* made a signal of distress; and Brooks hailed us to say that she was making water faster than he could free her.

The wind was hauling round to the westward, and we could not take the sea abeam. But, as I made a rapid survey of the area round me, studded already with floating shreds of floe-ice, I saw ahead the low gray blink of the pack. I remembered well the experience of our Beechy Island trip, and knew that the margin of these large fields is almost

Elisha Kent Kane

199

always broken by inlets of open water, which give much the same sort of protection as the creeks and rivers of an adverse coast. We were fortunate in finding one of these and fastening ourselves to an old floe, alongside of which our weary men turned in to sleep without hauling up the boats.

When Petersen and myself returned from an unsuccessful hunt upon the ice, we found them still asleep, in spite of a cold and drizzling rain that might have stimulated wakefulness. I did not disturb them till eight o'clock. We then retreated from our breakwater of refuge, generally pulling along by the boat-hooks, but sometimes dragging our boats over the ice; and at last, bending to our oars as the water opened, reached the shore of Hakluyt Island.

It was hardly less repulsive than the ice-cliffs of the day before; but a spit to the southward gave us the opportunity of hauling up as the tide rose, and we finally succeeded in transferring ourselves and all our fortunes to the land-ice, and thence to the rocks beyond. It snowed hard in the night, and the work of calking went on badly, though we expended on it a prodigal share of our remaining white-lead. We rigged up, however, a tent for the sick, and reinforced our bread-dust and tallow supper by a few birds. We had shot a seal in the course of the day, but we lost him by his sinking.

In the morning of the 22d we pushed forward through the snow-storm for Northumberland Island, and succeeded in reaching it a little to the eastward of my former landing-place. Myriads of auks greeted us, and we returned their greeting by the appropriate invitation to our table. A fox also saluted us with an admirable imitation of the "Huk-huk-huk," which among the Esquimaux is the never-unheeded call of distress; but the rascal, after seducing us a mile and a half out of our way, escaped our guns.

Our boats entered a little patch of open water that conducted us to the beach, directly below one of the hanging glaciers. The interest with which these impressed me when I was turning back from my Beechy Island effort was justified very fully by what I saw of them now. It seemed as if a caldron of ice inside the coast-ridge was boiling over, and

Bidding good-by to the Eskimos at Etah.

200

throwing its crust in huge fragments from the overhanging lip into the sea below. The glacier must have been eleven hundred feet high; but even at its summit we could see the lines of viscous movement which I have endeavored to transfer to my sketch.

We crossed Murchison Channel on the 23d, and encamped for the night on the land-floe at the base of Cape Parry; a hard day's travel, partly by tracking over ice, partly through tortuous and zig-gag leads. The next day brought us to the neighbor-hood of Fitz-Clarence Rock, one of the most interesting monuments that rear themselves along this dreary coast: in a region more familiar to men, it would be a landmark to the navigator. It rises from a field of ice like an Egyptian pyramid surmounted by an obelisk.

The next day gave us admirable progress. The ice opened in leads before us, somewhat tortuous, but, on the whole, favoring, and for sixteen hours I never left the helm. We were all of us exhausted when the day's work came to a close. Our allowance had been small from the first; but the delays we seemed fated to encounter had made me reduce them to what I then thought the minimum quantity, six ounces of bread-dust and a lump of tallow the size of a walnut: a paste or broth, made of these before setting out in the morning and distributed occasionally through the day in scanty rations, was our only fare. We were all of glad when, running the boats under the lee of a berg, we were able to fill our kettles with snow and boil up for our great restorative tea. I may remark that, under the circumstances of most privation, I found no comforter so welcome to the party as this. We drank immoderately of it, and always with advantage.

While the men slept after their weary labor, McGary and myself climbed the berg for a view ahead. It was a saddening one. We had lost sight of Cary Island; but shoreward, up Wostenholme Channel, the ice seemed as if it had not yet begun to yield to the influences of summer. Every thing

The slow-flowing glacier.

showed how intense the last winter had been. We were close upon the 1st of July, and had a right to look for the North Water of the whalers where we now had solid ice or close pack, both of them almost equally unfavorable to our progress. Far off in the distance—how far I could not measure—rose the Dalrymple Rock, projecting from the lofty precipice of the island ahead; but between us and it the land-ice spread itself from the base of Saunders's Island unbroken to the Far South.

The next day's progress was of course slow and wearisome, pushing through alternate ice and water for the land-belt. We fastened at last to the great floe near the shore, making our harbor in a crack which opened with the changes of tide.

The imperfect diet of the party was showing itself more and more in the decline of their muscular power. They seemed scarcely aware of it themselves, and referred the difficulty they found in

dragging and pushing to something uncommon about the ice or sludge rather than to their own weakness. But, as we endeavored to renew our labors through the morning fog, belted in on all sides by ice-fields so distorted and rugged as to defy our efforts to cross them, the truth seemed to burst upon every one. We had lost the feeling of hunger, and were almost satisfied with our pasty broth and the large draughts of tea which accompanied it. I was anxious to send our small boat, the *Eric*, across to the lumme-hill of Appah, where I knew from the Esquimaux we should find plenty of birds; but the strength of the party was insufficient to drag her.

We were sorely disheartened, and could only wait for the fog to rise, in the hope of some smoother platform than that which was about us, or some lead that might save us the painful labor of tracking. I had climbed the iceberg; and there was nothing in view except Dalrymple Rock, with its red brassy face towering in the unknown distance. But I hardly got back to my boat, before a gale struck us from the northwest, and a floe, taking upon a tongue of ice about a mile to the north of us, began to swing upon it like a pivot and close slowly in upon our narrow resting-place.

At first our own floe also was driven before the wind; but in a little while it encountered the stationary ice at the foot of the very rock itself. On the instant the wildest imaginable ruin rose around us. The men sprang mechanically each one to his station, bearing back the boats and stores; but I gave up for the moment all hope of our escape. It was not a nip, such as is familiar to Arctic navigators; but the whole platform, where we stood and for hundreds of yards on every side of us, crumbled and crushed and piled and tossed itself madly under the pressure. I do not believe that of our little body of men, all of them disciplined in trials, able to measure danger while combating it, —I do not believe there is one who this day can explain how or why—hardly when, in fact—we found ourselves afloat. We only know that in the

midst of a clamor utterly indescribable, through which the braying of a thousand trumpets could no more have been heard than the voice of a man, we were shaken and raised and whirled and let down again in a swelling waste of broken hummocks, and, as the men grasped their boat-hooks in the stillness that followed, the boats eddied away in a tumultuous skreed of ice and snow and water.

We were borne along in this manner as long as the unbroken remnant of the in-shore floe continued revolving,—utterly powerless, and catching a glimpse every now and then of the brazen headland that looked down on us through the snowy sky. At last the floe brought up against the rocks, the looser fragments that hung round it began to separate, and we were able by oars and boat-hooks to force our battered little flotilla clear of them. To our joyful surprise, we soon found ourselves in

The narrow escape from shifting ice floes off Weary Men's Rest.

a stretch of the land-water wide enough to give us rowing-room, and with the assured promise of land close ahead.

As we neared it, we saw the same forbidding wall of belt-ice as at Sutherland and Hakluyt. We pulled along its margin, seeking in vain either an opening of access or a nook of shelter. The gale rose, and the ice began to drive again; but there was nothing to be done but get a grapnel out to the belt and hold on for the rising tide. The *Hope* stove her bottom and lost part of her weather-boarding, and all the boats were badly chafed. It was an awful storm; and it was not without constant exertion that we kept afloat, baling out the scud that broke over us, and warding off the ice with boat-hooks.

At three o'clock the tide was high enough for us to scale the ice-cliff. One by one we pulled up the boats upon a narrow shelf, the whole sixteen of us uniting at each pull. We were too much worn down to unload; but a deep and narrow gorge opened in the cliffs almost at the spot where we clambered up; and, as we pushed the boats into it on an even keel, the rocks seemed to close above our heads, until an abrupt turn in the course of the ravine placed a protecting cliff between us and the gale. We were completely encaved.

Just as we had brought in the last boat, the *Red Eric*, and were shoring her up with blocks of ice, a long-unused but familiar and unmistakable sound startled and gladdened every ear, and a flock of eiders flecking the sky for a moment passed swiftly in front of us. We knew that we must be at their breeding-grounds; and, as we turned in wet and hungry to our long-coveted sleep, it was only to dream of eggs and abundance.

203

Providence Halt.

We remained almost three days in our crystal retreat, gathering eggs at the rate of twelve hundred a day. Outside, the storm raged without intermission, and our egg-hunters found it difficult to keep their feet; but a merrier set of gourmands than were gathered within never surfeited in genial diet.

On the 3d of July the wind began to moderate, though the snow still fell heavily; and the next morning, after a patriotic egg-nog, the liquor borrowed grudgingly from our alcohol-flask, and diluted till it was worthy of temperance praise, — we lowered our boats, and bade a grateful farewell to "Weary Man's Rest." We rowed to the southeast end of Wostenholme Island; but the tide left us there, and we moved to the ice-foot.

For some days after this we kept moving slowly to the south, along the lanes that opened between the belt-ice and the floe. The weather continued dull and unfavorable for observations of any sort, and we were off a large glacier before we were aware

that further progress near the shore was impracticable. Great chains of bergs presented themselves as barriers in our way, the spaces between choked by barricades of hummocks. It was hopeless to bore. We tried for sixteen hours together without finding a possibility of egress. The whole sea was rugged and broken in the extreme.

I climbed one of the bergs to the height of about two hundred feet, and, looking well to the west, was satisfied that a lead which I saw there could be followed in the direction of Conical Rocks, and beyond toward Cape Dudley Digges. But, on conferring with Brooks and McGary, I was startled to find how much the boats had suffered in the rude encounters of the last few days. The *Hope* was in fact altogether unseaworthy: the ice had strained her bottom-timbers, and it required nearly all our wood to repair her; bit by bit we had already cut up and burned the runners and cross-bars of two sledges; the third we had to reserve as essential to our ice-crossings.

In the mean time, the birds, which had been so abundant when we left Dalrymple's Island, and which we had counted on for a continuous store, seemed to have been driven off by the storm. We were again reduced to short daily rations of bread-dust, and I was aware that the change of diet could not fail to tell upon the strength and energies of the party. I determined to keep in-shore, in spite of the barricades of ice, in the hope of renewing, to some extent at least, our supplies of game. We were fifty two hours in forcing this rugged passage: a most painful labor, which but for the disciplined endurance of the men might well have been deemed impracticable.

Once through the barrier, the leads began to open again, and on the 11th we found ourselves approaching Cape Dudley Digges, with a light breeze from the northwest. It looked for some hours as if our troubles were over, when a glacier came in sight not laid down on the charts, whose tongue of floe extended still farther out to sea than the one we had just passed with so much labor. Our first resolve was to double it at all hazards, for our crews were too much weakened to justify another tracking through the hummocks, and the soft snow which covered the land-floes was an obstacle quite insuperable. Nevertheless, we forced our way into a lead of sludge, mingled with the comminuted ice of the glacier; but the only result was a lesson of gratitude for our escape from it. Our frail and weather-worn boats were quite unequal to the duty.

I again climbed the nearest berg,—for these ice-mountains were to us like the look-out hills of men at home,—and surveyed the ice to the south far on toward Cape York. My eyes never looked on a spectacle more painful. We were in advance of the season: the floes had not broken up. There was no "western water." Here, in a *cul-de-sac*, between two barriers, both impassable to men in our condition, with stores miserably inadequate and strength broken down, we were to wait till the tardy summer should open to us a way.

Providence Cliffs.

I headed for the cliffs. Desolate and frowning as they were, it was better to reach them and halt upon the inhospitable shore than await the fruitless ventures of the sea. A narrow lead, a mere fissure at the edge of the land-ice, ended opposite a low platform: we had traced its whole extent, and it landed close under the shadow of the precipitous shore.

My sketch intended to represent this wild locality, like that of the "Weary Man's Rest," gives a very imperfect idea of the scene.

Where the cape lies directly open to the swell of the northwest winds, at the base of a lofty precipice there was left still clinging to the rock a fragment of the winter ice-belt not more than five feet wide. The tides rose over it and the waves washed against it continually, but it gave a perfectly safe perch to our little boats. Above, cliff seemed to pile over cliff, until in the high distance the rocks looked like the overlapping scales of ancient armor. They were at least eleven hundred feet high,

205

their summits generally lost in fog and mist; and all the way up we seemed to see the birds whose home is among their clefts. The nests were thickest on the shelves some fifty yards above the water; but both lumme and tridactyl gulls filled the entire air with glimmering specks, cawing and screeching with an incessant clamor.

To soften the scene, a natural bridge opened on our right hand into a little valley cove, green with mosses, and beyond and above it, cold and white, the glacier.

This glacier was about seven miles across at its "debouche"; it sloped gradually upward for some five miles back, and then, following the irregularities of its rocky sub-structure, suddenly became a steep crevassed hill, ascending in abrupt terraces. Then came two intervals of less rugged ice, from which the glacier passed into the great *mer de glace*.

On ascending a high craggy hill to the northward, I had a sublime prospect of this great frozen ocean, which seems to form the continental axis of Greenland,—a vast undulating plain of purple-tinted ice, studded with islands, and absolutely

The natural bridge.

gemming the horizon with the varied glitter of sun-tipped crystal.

The discharge of water from the lower surface of the glacier exceeded that of any of the northern glaciers except that of Humboldt and the one near Etah. One torrent on the side nearest me overran the ice-foot from two to five feet in depth, and spread itself upon the floes for several hundred yards; and another, finding its outlet near the summit of the glacier, broke over the rocks, and poured in cataracts upon the beach below.

The ranunculus, saxifrages, chickweeds, abundant mosses, and Arctic grasses, flourished near the level of the first talus of the glacier: the stone crops I found some two hundred feet higher. The thermometer was at 90° in the sun; in the shade at 38°.

I have tried to describe the natural features of the scene, but I have omitted that which was its most valued characteristic. It abounded in life. The lumme, nearly as large as canvasbacks, and, as we thought, altogether sweeter and more juicy; their eggs, well known as delicacies on the Labrador coast; the cochlearia, growing superbly on the guano-coated surface;—all of them in endless abundance:—imagine such a combination of charms for scurvy-broken, hunger-stricken men.

I could not allow the fuel for a fire; our slush and tallow was reduced to very little more than a hundred pounds. The more curious in that art which has dignified the memory of Lucullus, and may do as much for Soyer, made experiments upon the organic matters within their reach,—the dried nests of the kittiwake, the sods of poa, the heavy mosses, and the fatty skins of the birds around us. But they would none of them burn; and the most fastidious consoled himself at last with the doubt whether heat, though concentrating flavor, might not impair some other excellence. We limited ourselves to an average of a bird a-piece per meal,—of choice, not of necessity,—and renewed the zest of the table with the best salad in the world,—raw eggs and cochlearia.

Elisha Kent Kane

It was one glorious holiday, our week at Providence Halt, so full of refreshment and all-happy thoughts, that I never allowed myself to detract from it by acknowledging that it was other than premeditated. There were only two of the party who had looked out with me on the bleak ice-field ahead, and them I had pledged to silence.

It was the 18th of July before the aspects of the ice about us gave me the hope of progress. We had prepared ourselves for the new encounter with the sea and its trials by laying in a store of lumme; two hundred and fifty of which had been duly skinned, spread open, and dried on the rocks, as the *entremets* of our bread-dust and tallow.

My journal tells of disaster in its record of our setting out. In launching the *Hope* from the frail and perishing ice-wharf on which we found our first refuge from the gale, she was precipitated into the sludge below, carrying away rail and bulwark, losing overboard our best shot-gun, Bonsall's favorite, and, worst of all, that universal favorite, our kettle,—soup-kettle, paste-kettle, tea-kettle, water-kettle, in one. I may mention before I pass, that the kettle found its substitute and successor in the remains of a tin can which a good aunt of mine had filled with ginger-nuts two years before, and which had long survived the condiments that once gave it dignity. "Such are the uses of adversity."

Our descent to the coast followed the margin of the fast ice. After passing the Crimson Cliffs of Sir John Ross, it wore almost the dress of a holiday excursion,—a rude one perhaps, yet truly one in feeling. Our course, except where a protruding glacier interfered with it, was nearly parallel to the shore. The birds along it were rejoicing in the young summer, and when we halted it was upon some green-clothed cape near a stream of water from the ice-fields above. Our sportsmen would clamber up the cliffs and come back laden with little auks; great generous fires of turf, that cost nothing but the toil of gathering, blazed merrily; and our happy oarsmen, after a long day's work, made easy by the promise ahead, would stretch

Gulls.

themselves in the sunshine and dream happily away till called to the morning wash and prayers. We enjoyed it the more, for we all of us knew that it could not last.

This coast must have been a favorite region at one time with the natives,—a sort of Esquimaux Eden. We seldom encamped without finding the ruins of their habitations, for the most part overgrown with lichens, and exhibiting every mark of antiquity. One of these, in latitude 76° 20′, was once, no doubt, an extensive village. Cairns for the safe deposit of meat stood in long lines, six or eight in a group; and the huts, built of large rocks, faced each other, as if disposed on a street or avenue.

The same reasoning which deduces the subsidence of the coast from the actual base of the Temple of Serapis, proves that the depression of the Greenland coast, which I had detected as far north as Upernavik, is also going on up here. Some of these huts were washed by the sea or torn away by the ice that had descended with the tides. The turf, too, a representative of very ancient growth, was cut off even with the water's edge, giving sections two feet thick. I had not noticed before such unmistakable evidence of the depres-

An ice raft.

sion of this coast: its converse elevation I had observed to the north of Wostenholme Sound. The axis of oscillation must be somewhere in the neighborhood of latitude 77°.

We reached Cape York on the 21st, after a tortuous but romantic travel through a misty atmosphere. Here the land-leads ceased, with the exception of some small and scarcely-practicable openings near the shore, which were evidently owing to the wind that prevailed for the time. Every thing bore proof of the late development of the season. The red snow was a fortnight behind its time. A fast floe extended with numerous tongues far out to the south and east. The only question was between a new rest, for the shore-ices to open, or a desertion of the coast and a trail of the open water to the west.

208

We sent off a detachment to see whether the Esquimaux might not be passing the summer at Episok, behind the glacier of Cape Imalik, and began an inventory of our stock on hand. I give the result:—

Dried lumme	*195 birds*
Pork-slush	*112 pounds*
Flour	*50 "*
Indian meal	*50 "*
Meat-biscuit	*80 "*
Bread	*348 "*

Six hundred and forty pounds of provision, all told, exclusive of our dried birds, or some thirty-six pounds a man. Tom Hickey found a turf, something like his native peat, which we thought might help to boil our kettle; and with the aid of this our fuel-account stood thus:—

Turf, for two boilings a day	*7 days*
Two sledge-runners	6 "
Spare oars, sledges, and an empty cask	4 "

Seventeen days in all; not counting, however, the Red Boat, which would add something, and our emptied provision-bags, which might carry on the estimate of about three weeks.

The return of the party from Imalik gave us no reason to hesitate. The Esquimaux had not been there for several years. There were no birds in the neighborhood.

I climbed the rocks a second time with Mr. McGary, and took a careful survey of the ice with my glass. The "fast," as the whalers call the immovable shore-ice, could be seen in a nearly unbroken sweep, passing by Bushnell's Island, and joining the coast not far from where I stood. The outside floes were large, and had evidently been not long broken; but it cheered my heart to see that there was one well-defined lead which followed the main floe until it lost itself to seaward.

I called my officers together, explained to them the motives which governed me, and prepared to re-embark. The boats were hauled up, examined carefully, and, as far as our means permitted, repaired. The *Red Eric* was stripped of her outfit and cargo, to be broken up for fuel when the occasion should come. A large beacon-cairn was built on an eminence, open to view from the south and west; and a red flannel shirt, spared with some reluctance, was hoisted as a pennant to draw attention to the spot. Here I deposited a succinct record of our condition and purposes, and then directed our course south by west into the ice-fields.

By degrees the ice through which we were moving became more and more impacted; and it sometimes required all our ice-knowledge to determine whether a particular lead was practicable or not. The irregularities of the surface, broken by hummocks, and occasionally by larger masses, made it difficult to see far ahead; besides which, we were often embarrassed by the fogs. I was awakened

one evening from a weary sleep in my fox-skins, to discover that we had fairly lost our way. The officer at the helm of the leading boat, misled by the irregular shape of a large iceberg that crossed his track, had lost the main lead some time before, and was steering shoreward far out of the true course. The little canal in which he had locked us was hardly two boats'-lengths across, and lost itself not far off in a feeble zigzag both behind and before us: it was evidently closing, and we could not retreat.

Without apprising the men of our misadventure, I ordered the boats hauled up, and, under pretence of drying the clothing and stores, made a camp on the ice. A few hours after, the weather cleared enough for the first time to allow a view of the distance, and McGary and myself climbed a berg some three hundred feet high for the purpose. It was truly fearful: we were deep in the recesses of the bay, surrounded on all sides by stupendous icebergs and tangled floe-pieces. My sturdy second officer, not naturally impressible, and long accustomed to the vicissitudes of whaling life, shed tears at the prospect.

There was but one thing to be done: cost what it might, we must harness our sledges again and retrace our way to the westward. One sledge had been already used for firewood; the *Red Eric*, to which it had belonged, was now cut up, and her light cedar planking laid upon the floor of the other boats; and we went to work with the rue-raddies as in the olden time. It was not till the third toilsome day was well spent that we reached the berg which had bewildered our helmsman. We hauled over its tongue, and joyously embarked again upon a free lead, with a fine breeze from the north.

Our little squadron was now reduced to two boats. The land to the northward was no longer visible; and whenever I left the margin of the fast to avoid its deep sinuosities, I was obliged to trust entirely to the compass. We had at least eight days' allowance of fuel on board; but our pro-

209

visions were running very low, and we met few birds, and failed to secure any larger game. We saw several large seals upon the ice, but they were too watchful for us; and on two occasions we came upon the walrus sleeping,—once within actual lance-thrust; but the animal charged in the teeth of his assailant and made good his retreat.

On the 28th I instituted a quiet review of the state of things before us. Our draft on the stores we had laid in at Providence Halt had been limited for some days to three raw eggs and two breasts of birds a day; but we had a small ration of bread-dust besides; and when we halted, as we did regularly for meals, our fuel allowed us to indulge lavishly in the great panacea of Arctic travel, tea. The men's strength was waning under this restricted diet; but a careful reckoning up of our remaining supplies proved to me now that even this was more than we could afford ourselves without an undue reliance on the fortunes of the hunt. Our next land was to be Cape Shackleton, one of the most prolific bird-colonies of the coast, which we were all looking to, much as sailors nearing home in their boats after disaster and short allowance at sea. But, meting out our stores through the

Walrus.

number of days that must elapse before we could expect to share its hospitable welcome, I found that five ounces of bread-dust, four of tallow, and three of bird-meat, must from this time form our daily ration.

So far we had generally coasted the fast ice: it had given us an occasional resting-place and refuge, and we were able sometimes to reinforce our stores of provisions by our guns. But it made our progress tediously slow, and our stock of small-shot was so nearly exhausted that I was convinced our safety depended on an increase of speed. I determined to try the more open sea.

For the first two days the experiment was a failure. We were surrounded by heavy fogs; a southwest wind brought the outside pack upon us and obliged us to haul up on the drifting ice. We were thus carried to the northward, and lost about twenty miles. My party, much overworked, felt despondingly the want of the protection of the land-floes.

Nevertheless, I held to my purpose, steering S.S.W. as nearly as the leads would admit, and looking constantly for the thinning out of the pack that hangs around the western water.

Although the low diet and exposure to wet had again reduced our party, there was no apparent relaxation of energy; and it was not until some days later that I found their strength seriously giving way.

It is a little curious that the effect of a short allowance of food does not show itself in hunger. The first symptom is a loss of power, often so imperceptibly brought on that it becomes evident only by an accident. I well remember our look of blank amazement as, one day, the order being given to haul the *Hope* over a tongue of ice, we found that she would not budge. At first I thought it was owing to the wetness of the snow-covered surface in which her runners were; but, as there was a heavy gale blowing outside, and I was extremely anxious to get her on to a larger floe to prevent being drifted off, I lightened her cargo

Elisha Kent Kane

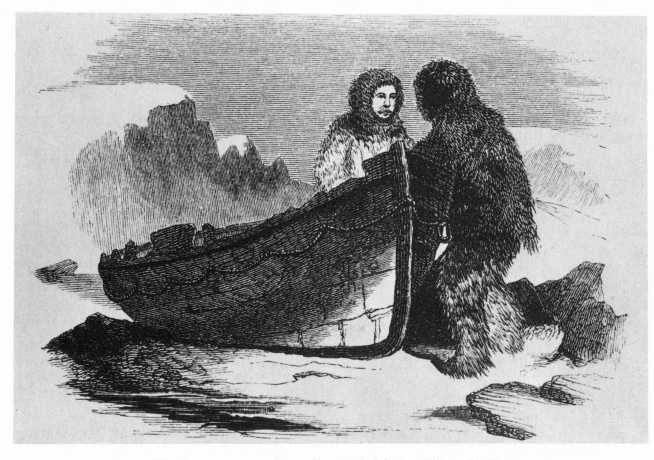

Kane's party escaped in ordinary whaleboats. This is the Hope.

and set both crews upon her. In the land of promise, off Crimson Cliffs, such a force would have trundled her like a wheelbarrow: we could almost have borne her upon our backs. Now, with incessant labor and standing-hauls, she moved at a snail's pace.

The *Faith* was left behind, and barely escaped destruction. The outside pressure cleft the floe asunder, and we saw our best boat, with all our stores, drifting rapidly away from us. The sight produced an almost hysterical impression upon our party. Two days of want of bread, I am sure, would have destroyed us; and we had now left us but eight pounds of shot in all. To launch the *Hope* again, and rescue her comrade or share her fortunes, would have been the instinct of other circumstances; but it was out of the question

now. Happily, before we had time to ponder our loss, a flat cake of ice eddied round near the floe we were upon; McGary and myself sprang to it at the moment, and succeeded in floating it across the chasm in time to secure her. The rest of the crew rejoined her by only scrambling over the crushed ice as we brought her in at the hummock-lines.

Things grew worse and worse with us: the old difficulty of breathing came back again, and our feet swelled to such an extent that we were obliged to cut open our canvas boots. But the symptom which gave me most uneasiness was our inability to sleep. A form of low fever which hung by us when at work had been kept down by the thoroughness of our daily rest: all my hopes of escape were in the refreshing influences of the halt.

It must be remembered that we were now in the open bay, in the full line of the great ice-drift to the Atlantic, and in boats so frail and unseaworthy as to require constant baling to keep them afloat.

It was at this crisis of our fortunes that we saw a large seal floating—as is the custom of these animals—on a small patch of ice, and seemingly asleep. It was an ussuk, and so large that I at first mistook it for a walrus. Signal was made for the *Hope* to follow astern, and, trembling with anxiety, we prepared to crawl down upon him.

Petersen, with the large English rifle, was stationed in the bow, and stockings were drawn over the oars as mufflers. As we neared the animal, our excitement became so intense that the men could hardly keep stroke. I had a set of signals for such occasions, which spared us the noise of the voice; and when about three hundred yards off, the oars were taken in, and we moved on in deep silence with a single scull astern.

He was not asleep, for he reared his head when we were almost within rifle-shot; and to this day I can remember the hard, careworn, almost despairing expression of the men's thin faces as they saw him move: their lives depended on his capture.

I depressed my hand nervously, as a signal for Petersen to fire. McGary hung upon his oar, and the boat, slowly but noiselessly sagging ahead, seemed to me within certain range. Looking at Petersen, I saw that the poor fellow was paralyzed by his anxiety, trying vainly to obtain a rest for his gun against the cut-water of the boat. The seal rose on his fore-flippers, gazed at us for a moment with frightened curiosity, and coiled himself for a plunge. At that instant, simultaneously with the crack of our rifle, he relaxed his long length on the ice, and, at the very brink of the water, his head fell helpless to one side.

I would have ordered another shot, but no discipline could have controlled the men. With a wild yell, each vociferating according to his own impulse, they urged both boats upon the floes. A crowd of hands seized the seal and bore him up to safer ice. The men seemed half crazy: I had not realized how much we were reduced by absolute famine. They ran over the floe, crying and laughing and brandishing their knives. It was not five minutes before every man was sucking his bloody fingers or mouthing long strips of raw blubber.

Not an ounce of this seal was lost. The intestines found their way into the soup-kettles without any observance of the preliminary home-processes. The cartilaginous parts of the fore-flippers were cut off in the *melee*, and passed round to be chewed upon; and even the liver, warm and raw as it was, bade fair to be eaten before it had seen the pot. That night, on the large halting-floe, to which, in contempt of the dangers of drifting, we happy men had hauled our boats, two entire planks of the *Red Eric* were devoted to a grand cooking-fire, and we enjoyed a rare and savage feast.

This was our last experience of the disagreeable effects of hunger. In the words of George Stephenson, "The charm was broken, and the dogs were safe." The dogs I have said little about, for none of us liked to think of them. The poor creatures Toodla and Whitey had been taken with us as last resources against starvation. They were, as McGary worded it, "meat on the hoof," and "able to carry their own fat over the floes." Once, near Weary Man's Rest, I had been on the point of killing them; but they had been the leaders of our winter's team, and we could not bear the sacrifice.

I need not detail our journey any farther. Within a day or two we shot another seal, and from that time forward had a full supply of food.

On the 1st of August we sighted the Devil's Thumb, and were again among the familiar localities of the whalers' battling-ground. The bay was quite open, and we had been making easting for two days before. We were soon among the Duck Islands, and, passing to the south of Cape Shackleton, prepared to land.

"Terra firma! Terra firma!" How very pleasant it was to look upon, and with what a tingle of excited thankfulness we drew near it! A little time to

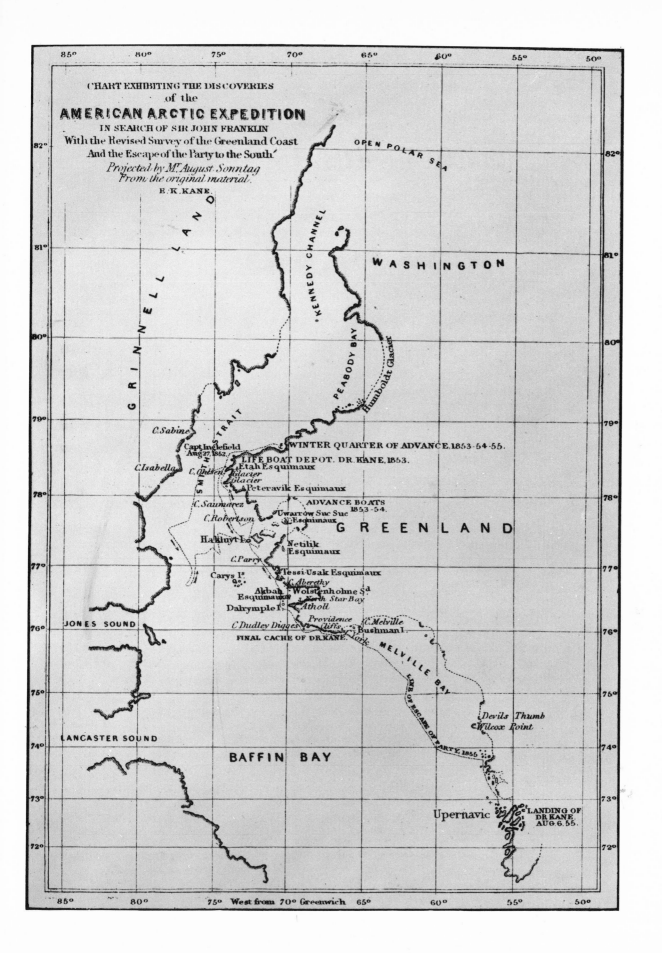

seek a cove among the wrinkled hills, a little time to exchange congratulations, and then our battered boats were hauled high and dry upon the rocks, and our party, with hearts full of our deliverance, lay down to rest.

And now, with the apparent certainty of reaching our homes, came that nervous apprehension which follows upon hope long deferred. I could not trust myself to take the outside passage, but timidly sought the quiet-water channels running deep into the archipelago which forms a sort of labyrinth along the coast.

Thus it was that at one of our sleeping-halts upon the rocks—for we still adhered to the old routine—Petersen awoke me with a story. He had just seen and recognised a native, who, in his frail kayak, was evidently seeking eider-down among the islands. The man had once been an intimate of his family. "Paul Zacharias, don't you know me? I'm Carl Petersen!" "No," said the man; "his wife says he's dead"; and, with a stolid expression of wonder, he stared for a moment at the long beard that loomed at him through the fog, and paddled away with all the energy of fright.

Adventure 14

Navigating the Strait of Magellan
from Sailing Alone around the World, by Joshua Slocum

CHOOSING to face the sea alone in a small boat requires enormous courage, the ingenuity of an inventor, an optimistic disposition, and complete mastery of seamanship. All these capacities were possessed by the first and in many respects the greatest of the famous "single-sailers," Captain Joshua Slocum, who made history when he landed alone in his thirty-six-foot yawl *Spray* at Newport, June 27, 1898, after having spent more than three years retracing Magellan's route around the world.

It would be hard to imagine someone better suited to such a Herculean task than this "naturalized Yankee," born of seafaring folk near the Bay of Fundy in Nova Scotia, who had spent almost his whole life on the water. For most of his life he was a captain of clippers and other merchant vessels. Then a 5000-mile voyage from Brazil, with only his family aboard, in a strange canoe called the *Liberdade*, turned his interest to small boats and to solo navigation.

His boat, the doughty *Spray*, started life as Massachusetts oystering sloop, but Slocum completely rebuilt it. With a heavy keel and frames of oak and an inch and a half of pine planking she was, whaling masters assured him, "fit to smash ice." After his first trip across the Atlantic he added an extra mast aft for greater stability and ease of handling, thus converting the sloop to a yawl. Later he further strengthened and simplified her rig by shortening his mainmast seven feet and his bowsprit five.

The *Spray* was a stout ship, but a very small and shallow one, and it is doubtful that any seaman less skillful than Slocum could have sailed her successfully out of Massachusetts Bay, much less around the world. As it was, he faced many a danger, from storms and fogs to attacks by pirates. Upon his return he revealed a talent for expression equal to his talents for sailing and shipbuilding in his vivid and zestful account of his numerous exploits, *Sailing Alone around the World.*

Slocum never tired of adventure. In 1909, at the age of sixty-five, he again took to the sea in the *Spray*, as usual alone. He disappeared off the coast of South America; apparently the *Spray* ran into one storm that was too much for her. But Slocum and his ship are forever immortalized in the justly celebrated *Sailing Alone around the World.*

"The Hand that held these held also the Spray"

THE scene was again gloomy; the wind, northeast, and blowing a gale, sent feather-white spume along the coast; such a sea ran as would swamp an ill-appointed ship. As the sloop neared the entrance to the strait I observed that two great tide-races made ahead, one very close to the point of the land and one farther offshore. Between the two, in a sort of channel, through combers, went the *Spray* with close-reefed sails. But a rolling sea followed her a long way in, and a fierce current swept around the cape against her; but this she stemmed, and was soon chirruping under the lee of Cape Virgins and running every minute into smoother water. However, long trailing kelp from sunken rocks waved forebodingly under her keel, and the wreck of a great steamship smashed on the beach abreast gave a gloomy aspect to the scene.

I was not to be let off easy. The Virgins would collect tribute even from the *Spray* passing their promontory. Fitful rain-squalls from the northwest followed the northeast gale. I reefed the sloop's sails, and sitting in the cabin to rest my eyes, I was so strongly impressed with what in all nature I might expect that as I dozed the very air I breathed seemed to warn me of danger. My senses heard "*Spray* ahoy!" shouted in warning. I sprang to the deck, wondering who could be there that knew the *Spray* so well as to call out her name passing in the dark; for it was now the blackest of nights all around, except away in the southwest where rose the old familiar white arch, the terror of Cape Horn, rapidly pushed up by a southwest gale. I had only a moment to douse sail and lash all solid when it struck like a shot from a cannon, and for the first half-hour it was something to be remembered by way of a gale. For thirty hours it kept on blowing hard. The sloop could carry no more than a three-reefed mainsail and forestaysail; with these she held on stoutly and was not blown out of the strait. In the height of the squalls in this gale she doused all sail, and this occurred often enough.

After this gale followed only a smart breeze, and the *Spray*, passing through the narrows without mishap, cast anchor at Sandy Point on February 14, 1896.

Sandy Point (Punta Arenas) is a Chilean coaling-station, and boasts about two thousand inhabitants, of mixed nationality, but mostly Chileans. What with sheep-farming, gold-mining, and hunting, the settlers in this dreary land seemed not the worst off in the world. But the natives, Patagonian and Fuegian, on the other hand, were as squalid as contact with unscrupulous traders could make them. A large percentage of the business there was traffic in "fire-water." If there was a law against selling the poisonous stuff to the natives, it was not enforced. Fine specimens of the Patagonian race, looking smart in the morning when they came into town, had repented before night of ever having seen a white man, so beastly drunk were they, to say nothing about the peltry of which they had been robbed.

The port at that time was free, but a custom-

217

*Just before reaching the Strait, the Spray was hit by an enormous wave, and Slocum
was forced to climb up the rigging to escape being swept overboard.*

house was in course of construction, and when it is finished, port and tariff dues are to be collected. A soldier police guarded the place, and a sort of vigilante force besides took down its guns now and then; but as a general thing, to my mind, whenever an execution was made they killed the wrong man. Just previous to my arrival the governor, himself of a jovial turn of mind, had sent a party of young bloods to foray a Fuegian settlement and wipe out what they could of it on account of the recent massacre of a schooner's crew somewhere else. Altogether the place was quite newsy and supported two papers—dailies, I think. The port captain, a Chilean naval officer, advised me to ship hands to fight Indians in the strait farther west, and spoke of my stopping until a gunboat should be going through, which would give me a tow. After canvassing the place, however, I found only one man willing to embark, and he on condition that I should ship another "mon and a doog." But as no one else was willing to come along, and as I drew the line at dogs, I said no more about the matter, but simply

loaded my guns. At this point in my dilemma Captain Pedro Samblich, a good Austrian of large experience, coming along, gave me a bag of carpet-tacks, worth more than all the fighting men and dogs of Tierra del Fuego. I protested that I had no use for carpet-tacks on board. Samblich smiled at my want of experience, and maintained stoutly that I would have use for them. "You must use them with discretion," he said; "that is to say, don't step on them yourself." With this remote hint about the use of the tacks I got on all right, and saw the way to maintain clear decks at night without the care of watching.

Samblich was greatly interested in my voyage, and after giving me the tacks he put on board bags of biscuits and a large quantity of smoked venison. He declared that my bread, which was ordinary sea-biscuits and easily broken, was not nutritious as his, which was so hard that I could break it only with a stout blow from a maul. Then he gave me, from his own sloop, a compass which was certainly better than mine, and offered to unbend her main-

218

sail for me if I would accept it. Last of all, this large-hearted man brought out a bottle of Fuegian gold-dust from a place where it had been *cached* and begged me to help myself from it, for use farther along the voyage. But I felt sure of success without this draft on a friend, and I was right. Samblich's tacks, as it turned out, were of more value than gold.

The port captain finding that I was resolved to go, even alone, since there was no help for it, set up no further objections, but advised me, in case the savages tried to surround me with their canoes, to shoot straight, and begin to do it in time, but to avoid killing them if possible, which I heartily agreed to do. With these simple injunctions the officer gave me my port clearance free of charge, and I sailed on the same day, February 19, 1896. It was not without thoughts of strange and stirring adventure beyond all I had yet encountered that I now sailed into the country and very core of the savage Fuegians.

A fair wind from Sandy Point brought me on the first day to St. Nicholas Bay, where, so I was told, I might expect to meet savages; but seeing no signs of life, I came to anchor in eight fathoms of water, where I lay all night under a high mountain. Here I had my first experience with the terrific squalls, called williwaws, which extended from this point on through the strait to the Pacific. They were compressed gales of wind that Boreas handed down over the hills in chunks. A full-blown williwaw will throw a ship, even without sail on, over on her beam ends; but, like other gales, they cease now and then, if only for a short time.

February 20 was my birthday, and I found myself alone, with hardly so much as a bird in sight, off Cape Froward, the southernmost point of the continent of America. By daylight in the morning I was getting my ship under way for the bout ahead.

The sloop held the wind fair while she ran thirty miles farther on her course, which brought her to Fortescue Bay, and at once among the natives' signal-fires, which blazed up now on all sides. Clouds flew over the mountain from the west all day; at night my good east wind failed, and in its stead a gale from the west soon came on. I gained anchorage at twelve o'clock that night, under the lee of a little island, and then prepared myself a cup of coffee, of which I was sorely in need; for, to tell the truth, hard beating in the heavy squalls and against the current had told on my strength. Finding that the anchor held, I drank my beverage, and named the place Coffee Island. It lies to the south of Charles Island, with only a narrow channel between.

By daylight the next morning the *Spray* was again under way, beating hard; but she came to in a cove in Charles Island, two and a half miles along on her course. Here she remained undisturbed two days, with both anchors down in a bed of kelp. Indeed, she might have remained undisturbed indefinitely had not the wind moderated; for during these two days it blew so hard that no boat could venture out on the strait, and the natives being away to other hunting-grounds, the island anchorage was safe. But at the end of the fierce wind-storm fair weather came; then I got my anchors, and again sailed out upon the strait.

Entrance to the Strait of Magellan.

Canoes manned by savages from Fortescue now came in pursuit. The wind falling light they gained on me rapidly till coming within hail, when they ceased paddling, and a bow-legged savage stood up and called to me, "Yammerschooner! yammerschooner!" which is their begging term. I said, "No!" Now, I was not for letting on that I was alone, and so I stepped into the cabin, and, passing through the hold, came out at the fore-scuttle, changing my clothes as I went along. That made two men. Then the piece of bowsprit which I had sawed off at Buenos Aires, and which I had still on board, I arranged forward on the outlook, dressed as a seaman, attaching a line by which I could pull it into motion. That made three of us, and we didn't want to "yammerschooner"; but for all that the savages came on faster than before. I saw that besides four at the paddles in the canoe nearest to me, there were others in the bottom, and that they were shifting hands often. At eighty yards I fired a shot across the bows of the nearest canoe, at which they all stopped, but only for a moment. Seeing that they persisted in coming nearer, I fired the second shot so close to the chap who wanted to "yammerschooner" that he changed his mind quickly enough

and bellowed with fear, "Bueno jo via Isla," and sitting down in his canoe, he rubbed his starboard cat-head for some time. I was thinking of the good port captain's advice when I pulled the trigger, and must have aimed pretty straight; however, a miss was as good as a mile for Mr. "Black Pedro," as he it was, and no other, a leader in several bloody massacres. He made for the island now, and the others followed him. I knew by his Spanish lingo and by his full beard that he was the villain I had named, a renegade mongrel, and the worst murderer in Tierra del Fuego. The authorities had been in search of him for two years. The Fuegians are not bearded.

So much for the first day among the savages. I came to anchor at midnight in Three Island Cove, about twenty miles along from Fortescue Bay. I saw on the opposite side of the strait signal-fires, and heard the barking of dogs, but where I lay it was quite deserted by natives. I have always taken it as a sign that where I found birds sitting about, or seals on the rocks, I should not find savage Indians. Seals are never plentiful in these waters, but in Three Island Cove I saw one on the rocks, and other signs of the absence of savage men.

On the next day the wind was again blowing a

The notorious "Black Pedro," hailing the Spray.

Joshua Slocum

Slocum firing across the bows of the Fuegian canoes.

gale, and although she was in the lee of the land, the sloop dragged her anchors, so that I had to get her under way and beat farther into the cove, where I came to in a landlocked pool. At another time or place this would have been a rash thing to do, and it was safe now only from the fact that the gale which drove me to shelter would keep the Indians from crossing the strait. Seeing this was the case, I went ashore with gun and axe on an island, where I could not in any event be surprised, and there felled trees and split about a cord of fire-wood, which loaded my small boat several times.

While I carried the wood, though I was morally sure there were no savages near, I never once went to or from the skiff without my gun. While I had that and a clear field of over eighty yards about me I felt safe.

The trees on the island, very scattering, were a sort of beech and a stunted cedar, both of which made good fuel. Even the green limbs of the beech, which seemed to possess a resinous quality, burned

readily in my great drum-stove. I have described my method of wooding up in detail, that the reader may see that in this, as in all other particulars of my voyage, I took great care against all kinds of surprises, whether by animals or by the elements. In the Strait of Magellan the greatest vigilance was necessary. In this instance I reasoned that I had all about me the greatest danger of the whole voyage—the treachery of cunning savages, for which I must be particularly on the alert.

The *Spray* sailed from Three Island Cove in the morning after the gale went down, but was glad to return for shelter from another sudden gale. Sailing again on the following day, she fetched Borgia Bay, a few miles on her course, where vessels had anchored from time to time and had nailed boards on the trees ashore with name and date of harboring carved or painted. Nothing else could I see to indicate that civilized man had ever been there. I had taken a survey of the gloomy place with my spyglass, and was getting my boat out to land and take

221

notes, when the Chilean gunboat *Huemel* came in, and officers, coming on board, advised me to leave the place at once, a thing that required little eloquence to persuade me to do. I accepted the captain's kind offer of a tow to the next anchorage, at the place called Notch Cove, eight miles farther along, where I should be clear of the worst of the Fuegians.

We made anchorage at the cove about dark that night, while the wind came down in fierce williwaws from the mountains. An instance of Magellan weather was afforded when the *Huemel*, a well-appointed gunboat of great power, after attempting on the following day to proceed on her voyage, was obliged by sheer force of the wind to return and take up anchorage again and remain till the gale abated; and lucky she was to get back!

Meeting this vessel was a little godsend. She was commanded and officered by high-class sailors and educated gentlemen. An entertainment that was gotten up on her, impromptu, at the Notch would be hard to beat anywhere. One of her midshipmen sang popular songs in French, German, and Spanish, and one (so he said) in Russian. If the audience did not know the lingo of one song from another, it was no drawback to the merriment.

I was left alone the next day, for then the *Huemel* put out on her voyage, the gale having abated. I spent a day taking in wood and water; by the end of that time the weather was fine. Then I sailed from the desolate place.

There is little more to be said concerning the *Spray*'s first passage through the strait that would differ from what I have already recorded. She anchored and weighed many times, and beat many days against the current, with now and then a "slant" for a few miles, till finally she gained anchorage and shelter for the night at Port Tamar, with Cape Pillar in sight to the west. Here I felt the throb of the great ocean that lay before me. I knew now that I had put a world behind me, and that I was opening out another world ahead. I had passed the haunts of savages. Great piles of granite mountains of bleak and lifeless aspect were now astern; on some of them not even a speck of moss had ever grown. There was an unfinished newness all about the land. On the hill back of Port Tamar a small beacon had been thrown up, showing that some man had been there. But how could one tell but that he had died of loneliness and grief? In a bleak land is not the place to enjoy solitude.

Looking west from Fortescue Bay.

Joshua Slocum

Throughout the whole of the strait west of Cape Froward I saw no animals except dogs owned by savages. These I saw often enough, and heard them yelping night and day. Birds were not plentiful. The scream of a wild fowl, which I took for a loon, sometimes startled me with its piercing cry. The steamboat duck, so called because it propels itself over the sea with its wings, and resembles a miniature side-wheel steamer in its motion, was sometimes seen scurrying on out of danger. It never flies, but, hitting the water instead of the air with its wings, it moves faster than a rowboat or a canoe. The few fur-seals I saw were very shy; and of fishes I saw next to none at all. I did not catch one; indeed, I seldom or never put a hook over during the whole voyage. Here in the strait I found great abundance of mussels of an excellent quality. I fared sumptuously on them. There was a sort of swan, smaller than a Muscovy duck, which might have been brought down with the gun, but in the loneliness of life about the dreary country I found myself in no mood to make one life less, except in self-defense.

It was the 3rd of March when the *Spray* sailed from Port Tamar direct for Cape Pillar, with the wind from the northeast, which I fervently hoped might hold till she cleared the land; but there was no such good luck in store. It soon began to rain and thicken in the northwest, boding no good. The *Spray* neared Cape Pillar rapidly, and, nothing loath, plunged into the Pacific Ocean at once, taking her first bath of it in the gathering storm. There was no turning back even had I wished to do so, for the land was now shut out by the darkness of night. The wind freshened, and I took in a third reef. The sea was confused and treacherous. In such a time as this the old fisherman prayed, "Remember Lord, my ship is so small and thy sea is so wide!" I saw now only the gleaming crests of waves. They showed white teeth while the sloop balanced over them. "Everything for an offing," I cried, and to this end I carried on all the sail she would bear. She ran all night with a free sheet, but on the morning of March 4 the wind shifted to southwest, then back suddenly to northwest, and blew with terrific force. The *Spray*, stripped of her sails, then bore off under bare poles. No ship in the world could have stood up against so violent a gale. Knowing that this storm might continue for many days, and that it would be impossible to work back to the westward along the coast outside of Tierra del Fuego, there seemed nothing to do but to keep on and go east about, after all. Anyhow, for my present safety the only course lay in keeping her before the wind. And so she drove southeast, as though about to round the Horn, while the waves rose and fell and bellowed their never-ending story of the sea; but the Hand that held these held also the *Spray*. She was running now with a reefed forestaysail, the sheets flat amidship. I paid out two long ropes to steady her course and to break combing seas astern, and I lashed the helm amidship. In this trim she ran before it, shipping never a sea. Even while the storm raged at its worst, my ship was wholesome and noble. My mind as to her seaworthiness was put to ease for aye.

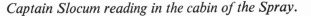

Captain Slocum reading in the cabin of the Spray.

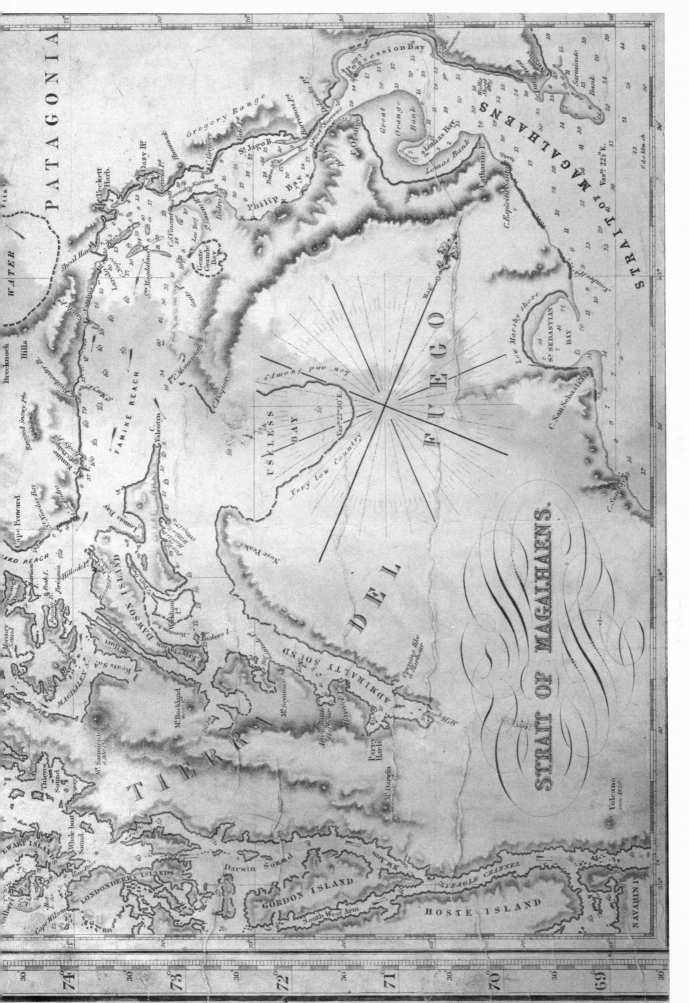

A British Admiralty Chart of the nineteenth century, of the kind Slocum might have used, showing the places mentioned in his narrative.

When all had been done that I could do for the safety of the vessel, I got to the fore-scuttle, between seas, and prepared a pot of coffee over a wood fire, and made a good Irish stew. Then, as before and afterward on the *Spray*, I insisted on warm meals. In the tide-race off Cape Pillar, however, where the sea was marvelously high, uneven, and crooked, my appetite was slim, and for a time I postponed cooking. (Confidentially, I was seasick!)

Cape Pillar.

The first day of the storm gave the *Spray* her actual test in the worst sea that Cape Horn or its wild regions could afford, and in no part of the world could a rougher sea be found than at this particular point, namely, off Cape Pillar, the grim sentinel of the Horn.

Farther offshore, while the sea was majestic, there was less apprehension of danger. There the *Spray* rode, now like a bird on the crest of a wave, and now like a waif deep down in the hollow between seas; and so she drove on. Whole days passed, counted as other days, but with always a thrill—yes, of delight.

On the fourth day of the gale, rapidly nearing the pitch of Cape Horn, I inspected my chart and pricked off the course and distance to Port Stanley, in the Falkland Islands, where I might find my way and refit, when I saw through a rift in the clouds a high mountain, about seven leagues away on the port beam. The fierce edge of the gale by this time had blown off, and I had already bent a squaresail on the boom in place of the mainsail, which was torn to rags. I hauled in the trailing ropes, hoisted

this awkward sail reefed, the forestaysail being already set, and under this sail brought her at once on the wind heading for the land, which appeared as an island in the sea. So it turned out to be, though not the one I had supposed.

I was exultant over the prospect of once more entering the Strait of Magellan and beating through again into the Pacific, for it was more than rough on the outside coast of Tierra del Fuego. It was indeed a mountainous sea. When the sloop was in the fiercest squalls, with only the reefed forestaysail set, even that small sail shook her from keelson to truck when it shivered by the leech. Had I harbored the shadow of a doubt for her safety, it would have been that she might spring a leak in the garboard at the heel of the mast; but she never called me once to the pump. Under pressure of the smallest sail I could set she made for the land like a racehorse, and steering her over the crests of the waves so that she might not trip was nice work. I stood at the helm now and made the most of it.

Night closed in before the sloop reached the land, leaving her feeling the way in pitchy darkness. I saw breakers ahead before long. At this I wore ship and stood offshore, but was immediately startled by the tremendous roaring of breakers again ahead and on the lee bow. This puzzled me, for there should have been no broken water where I supposed myself to be. I kept off a good bit, then wore round, but finding broken water also there, threw her head again offshore. In this way, among dangers, I spent the rest of the night. Hail and sleet in the fierce squalls cut my flesh till the blood trickled over my face; but what of that? It was daylight, and the sloop was in the midst of the Milky Way of the sea, which is northwest of Cape Horn, and it was the white breakers of a huge sea over sunken rocks which had threatened to engulf her through the night. It was Fury Island I had sighted and steered for, and what a panorama was before me now, and all around! It was not the time to complain of a broken skin. What could I do but fill away among the breakers and find a channel between them, now that it was day? Since she had escaped the rocks through the night, surely she would find her way by daylight. This was the greatest sea adventure of my life. God knows how my vessel escaped.

The sloop at last reached inside of small islands that sheltered her in smooth water. Then I climbed the mast to survey the wild scene astern. The great naturalist Darwin looked over this seascape from the deck of the *Beagle*, and wrote in his journal, "Any landsman seeing the Milky Way would have nightmare for a week." He might have added, "or seaman" as well.

The *Spray*'s good luck followed fast. I discovered, as she sailed along through a labyrinth of islands, that she was in the Cockburn Channel, which leads into the Strait of Magellan at a point opposite Cape Froward, and that she was already passing Thieves' Bay, suggestively named. And at night, March 8, behold, she was at anchor in a snug cove at the Turn! Every heart-beat on the *Spray* now counted thanks.

Here I pondered on the events of the last few days, and, strangely enough, instead of feeling rested from sitting or lying down, I now began to feel jaded and worn; but a hot meal of venison stew soon put me right, so that I could sleep. As drowsiness came on I sprinkled the deck with tacks, and then I turned in, bearing in mind the advice of my old friend Samblich that I was not to step on them myself. I saw to it that not a few of them stood "business end" up; for when the *Spray* passed Thieves' Bay two canoes had put out and followed in her wake, and there was no disguising the fact any longer that I was alone.

Now, it is well known that one cannot step on a tack without saying something about it. A pretty good Christian will whistle when he steps on the "commercial end" of a carpet-tack; a savage will howl and claw the air, and that was just what happened that night about twelve o'clock, while I was asleep in the cabin, where the savages thought they "had me," sloop and all, but changed their minds when they stepped on deck, for then they thought that I or somebody else had them. I had no need of a dog; they howled like a pack of hounds. I had hardly use for a gun. They jumped pell-mell, some into their canoes and some into the sea, to cool off,

Fuegian savages repelled by carpet tacks.

I suppose, and there was a deal of free language over it as they went. I fired several guns when I came on deck, to let the rascals know that I was home, and then I turned in again, feeling sure I should not be disturbed any more by people who left in so great a hurry.

The Fuegians, being cruel, are naturally cowards; they regard a rifle with superstitious fear. The only real danger one could see that might come from their quarter would be from allowing them to surround one within bow-shot, or to anchor within range where they might lie in ambush. As for their coming on deck at night, even had I not put tacks about, I could have cleared them off by shots from the cabin and hold. I always kept a quantity of ammunition within reach in the hold and in the cabin and in the forepeak, so that retreating to any of these places I could "hold the fort" simply by shooting up through the deck.

The Spray, under sail.

228

Perhaps the greatest danger to be apprehended was from the use of fire. Every canoe carries fire; nothing is thought of that, for it is their custom to communicate by smoke-signals. The harmless brand that lies smouldering in the bottom of one of their canoes might be ablaze in one's cabin if he were not on the alert. The port captain of Sandy Point warned me particularly of this danger. Only a short time before they had fired a Chilean gunboat by throwing brands in through the stern windows of the cabin. The *Spray* had no openings in the cabin or deck, except two scuttles, and these were guarded by fastenings which could not be undone without waking me if I were asleep.

On the morning of the 9th, after a refreshing rest and a warm breakfast, and after I had swept the deck of tacks, I got out what spare canvas there was on board, and began to sew the pieces together in the shape of a peak for my square-mainsail, the tarpaulin. The day to all appearances promised fine weather and light winds, but appearances in Tierra del Fuego do not always count. While I was wondering why no trees grew on the slope abreast of the anchorage, half minded to lay by the sail-making and land with my gun for some game and to inspect a white boulder on the beach, near the brook, a williwaw came down with such terrific force as to carry the *Spray*, with two anchors down, like a feather out of the cove and away into deep water. No wonder trees did not grow on the side of that hill! Great Boreas! a tree would need to be all roots to hold on against such a furious wind.

From the cove to the nearest land to leeward was a long drift, however, and I had ample time to weigh both anchors before the sloop came near any danger, and so no harm came of it. I saw no more savages that day or the next; they probably had some sign by which they knew of the coming williwaws; at least, they were wise in not being afloat even on the second day, for I had no sooner gotten to work at sail-making again, after the anchor was down, than the wind, as on the day before, picked the sloop up and flung her seaward with a vengeance, anchor and all, as before. This fierce wind, usual to the Magellan country, continued on through the day, and swept the sloop by several miles of steep bluffs and precipices overhanging a bold shore of wild and uninviting appearance. I was not sorry to get away from it, though in doing so it was no Elysian shore to which I shaped my course. I kept on sailing in hope, since I had no choice but to go on, heading across for St. Nicholas Bay, where I had cast anchor February 19. It was now the 10th of March! Upon reaching the bay the second time I had circumnavigated the wildest part of desolate Tierra del Fuego. But the *Spray* had not yet arrived at St. Nicholas, and by the merest accident her bones were saved from resting there when she did arrive. The parting of a staysail-sheet in a williwaw, when the sea was tur-

bulent and she was plunging into the storm, brought me forward to see instantly a dark cliff ahead and breakers so close under the bows that I felt surely lost, and in my thoughts cried, "Is the hand of fate against me, after all, leading me in the end to this dark spot?" I sprang aft again, unheeding the flapping sail, and threw the wheel over, expecting, as the sloop came down into the hollow of a wave, to feel her timbers smash under me on the rocks. But at the touch of her helm she swung clear of the danger, and in the next moment she was in the lee of the land.

The sail plan of the Spray. The original sloop rig, represented in solid lines, was altered by shortening the boom and bowsprit and adding a mizzenmast. A flying jib was occasionally set to a bamboo stick that was in turn attached to the bowsprit.

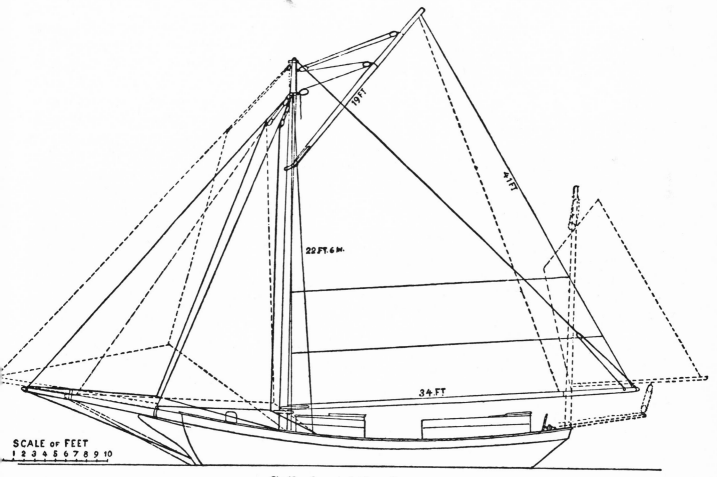

SCALE OF FEET
1 2 3 4 5 6 7 8 9 10

Sail-plan of the *Spray*.

The solid lines represent the sail-plan of the *Spray* on starting for the long voyage. With it she crossed the Atlantic to Gibraltar, and then crossed ∂in southwest to Brazil. In South American waters the bowsprit and boom were shortened and the jigger-sail added to form the yawl-rig with ⅎch the rest of the trip was made, the sail-plan of which is indicated by the dotted lines The extreme sail forward is a flying jib occasionally used, to a bamboo stick fastened to the bowsprit. The manner of setting and bracing the jigger-mast is not indicated in this drawing, but may be ⅎtly observed in the plans on pages 237 and 289.

It was the small island in the middle of the bay for which the sloop had been steering, and which she made with such unerring aim as nearly to run it down. Farther along in the bay was the anchorage, which I managed to reach, but before I could get the anchor down another squall caught the sloop and whirled her round like a top and carried her away, altogether to leeward of the bay. Still farther to leeward was a great headland, and I bore off for that. This was retracing my course toward Sandy Point, for the gale was from the southwest.

I had the sloop soon under good control, however, and in a short time rounded to under the lee of a mountain, where the sea was as smooth as a millpond, and the sails flapped and hung limp while she carried her way close in. Here I thought I would anchor and rest till morning, the depth being eight fathoms very close to the shore. But it was interesting to see, as I let go the anchor, that it did not reach the bottom before another williwaw struck down from this mountain and carried the sloop off faster than I could pay out cable. Therefore, instead of resting, I had to "man the windlass"

and heave up the anchor with fifty fathoms of cable hanging up and down in deep water. This was in that part of the strait called Famine Reach. Dismal Famine Reach! On the sloop's crab-windlass I worked the rest of the night, thinking how much easier it was for me when I could say, "Do that thing or the other," than now doing all myself. But I hove away and sang the old chants that I sang when I was a sailor. Within the last few days I had passed through much and was now thankful that my state was no worse.

It was daybreak when the anchor was at the hawse. By this time the wind had gone down, and cat's-paws took the place of williwaws, while the sloop drifted slowly toward Sandy Point. She came within sight of ships at anchor in the roads, and I was more than half minded to put in for new sails, but the wind coming out from the northeast, which was fair for the other direction, I turned the prow of the *Spray* westward once more for the Pacific, to traverse a second time the second half of my first course through the strait.

Adventure 15

A Descent into Perpetual Night

from Half Mile Down, by William Beebe

UNTIL the present century, man, while having reached nearly every navigable part of the sea, had achieved little in attempts to penetrate the even greater unknown beneath the sea. Pearl and sponge divers with no other resources than their lungs had been able to reach only a few feet below the surface; and diving bells, in existence since the end of the sixteenth century, enabled men to remain underwater for longer periods but not to reach great depths. Neither did the diving suits or submarines developed in the late nineteenth and early twentieth centuries. It lay to William Beebe and his associates, in the famous bathysphere, to give the world its first vicarious glimpse of the great ocean depths where the light of the sun never reaches.

Like many great inventions, the bathysphere was essentially a very simple device. The round shape of its hull, formed of thick cast steel, was devised as the most efficient to distribute and withstand the enormous pressure of water far beneath the surface. Its single entrance was a steel hatch, bolted to the hull; its windows two thick, round panes of fused quartz. Simple chemical absorbents helped purify and dehumidify the air within; oxygen was supplied compressed in tanks, and was slowly released at the rate of ordinary consumption. The principal and essential difference between the bathysphere and the suits and bells ordinarily used for diving work was that no effort was made to resist the pressure of the water with a counter-pressure of air within the vessel. The bathysphere itself was built strongly enough to resist the pressure of the depths, and the air pressure within was only a little more than at the surface.

Since Dr. Beebe's historic dives in the early 1930s many scientists, using much more refined equipment, have gone much deeper into the sea. But these triumphs cannot detract from the glory of Dr. Beebe, who first pioneered in the dark world a half-mile down and described it so unforgettably to the world above.

Dr. Beebe, left, and Otis Barton standing by the bathysphere following the dive recorded in this narrative. Mr. Barton was chiefly responsible for the development of the bathysphere. The secondary cable contained electrical and telephone lines. Only two of the three windows were in use; the third was sealed with a steel plug.

⚞[1934]⚟

"*The only other place comparable to these marvellous nether regions must surely be naked space itself*"

AY after day my weather held good and Wednesday, August fifteenth, was no exception. At 6:45 in early morning we were arranging to leave St. Georges anchorage, the barge *Ready* with the bathysphere and ourselves, and the tug *Gladisfen* towing. Three hours later Mr. Barton and I were dropped overboard far out at sea. As well as we could determine from sights on the lighthouses we submerged at the identical spot into which we had splashed four days before.

The same spot, but far from the same visible life. Surprises came at every few feet and again the mass of life was totally unexpected, the sum total of creatures seen unbelievable. At 1000 feet I distinctly saw a shrimp outlined and distinguished several of its pale greenish lights. Although I delayed very little at the hundred foot stops, when the rope guys were attached, yet I dictated page after page of observations. I used the light as little as possible and carefully shielded my eyes, so that very soon they became dark adapted. I was watching for two or three things which I wanted to solve. Large Mellanostomiatid dragon-fish with their glowing porthole lights showed themselves now and then, by which I mean on three separate occasions; and more than elsewhere, in our electric light, we had frequent glimpses of small opalescent copepods, appropriately called *Sapphirina*, which renewed for us all the spectrum of the sunlight.

I have spoken of the three outstanding moments in the mind of a bathysphere diver, the first flash of animal light, the level of eternal darkness, and the discovery and description of a new species of fish. There is a fourth, lacking definite level of anticipation, a roving moment which might very possibly occur near the surface or at the greatest depth, or even as one lies awake, days after the dive, thinking over and reliving it. It is, to my mind, the most important of all, far more so than the discovery of new species. It is the explanation of some mysterious occurrence, of the display of some inexplicable habit which has taken place before our eyes, but which, like a sublimated trick of some master fakir, evades understanding.

This came to me on this last deep dive at 1680 feet, and it explained much that had been a complete puzzle. I saw some creature, several inches long, dart toward the window, turn sideways and — explode. This time my eyes were focused and my mind ready, and at the flash, which was so strong that it illumined my face and the inner sill of the window, I saw the great red shrimp and the outpouring fluid of flame. This was a real Fourth Moment, for many "dim gray fish" as I had reported them, now resolved into distant clouds of light, and all the previous "explosions" against the glass became intelligible. At the next occurrence the shrimp showed plainly before and during the phenomenon, illustrating the value in observa-

233

tion of knowing what to look for. The fact that a number of the deep-sea shrimps had this power of defense is well known, and I have had an aquarium aglow with the emanation. It is the abyssal complement of the sepia smoke screen of a squid at the surface.

Before this dive was completed, I had made a still greater refinement in discernment, perceiving that there were two very distinct types of defense clouds emitted, one which instantly diffused into a glowing mist or cloud, and the other which exploded in a burst of individual sparks, for all the world like a diminutive roman candle. Both occurred at the window or near it a number of times, but it was the latter which was the more startling.

At 1800 I saw a small fish with illumined teeth, lighted from below, with distinct black interspaces; and ten feet below this my favorite sea-dragons, *Lamprotoxus*, appeared, they of the shining green bow. Only sixteen of these fish have ever been taken, seven of which came up in our own nets. The record size is about eight inches, while here before me were four individuals all more than twice that length, and very probably representing a new species. The green side line glowed but the long chin tentacle was quite invisible, certainly giving out no

All of the water-color drawings that follow were made by Else Bostelmann and Helen Tee-Van from specimens which were gathered during Dr. Beebe's oceanographic expeditions, and suggest the variety of species observed from the bathysphere.

Echiostoma barbatum, of the family Melanostomiatidae, or dragon-fish.

light. At 2100 feet two large fish, quite three feet all over, lighted up and then became one with the darkness about them, a tantalizing glimpse which made me, more than ever, long for bigger and better nets.

At 2450 a very large, dim, but not indistinct outline came into view for a fraction of a second, and at 2500 a delicately illumined ctenophore jelly throbbed past. Without warning, the large fish returned and this time I saw its complete, shadow-like contour as it passed through the farthest end of the beam. Twenty feet is the least possible estimate I can give to its full length, and it was deep in proportion. The whole fish was monochrome, and I could not see even an eye or a fin. For the majority of the "size-conscious" human race this MARINE MONSTER would, I suppose, be the supreme sight of the expedition. In shape it was a deep oval, it swam without evident effort, and it did not return. That is all I can contribute, and while its unusual size so excited me that for several hundred feet I kept keenly on the lookout for hints of the same or other large fish, I soon forgot it in the (very literal) light of smaller, but more distinct and interesting organisms.

What this great creature was I cannot say. A first, and most reasonable guess would be a small whale or blackfish. We know that whales have a special chemical adjustment of the blood which makes it possible for them to dive a mile or more, and come up without getting the "bends." So this paltry depth of 2450 feet would be nothing for any similarly equipped cetacean. Or, less likely, it may have been a whale shark, which is known to reach a length of forty feet. Whatever it was, it appeared and vanished so unexpectedly and showed so dimly that it was quite unidentifiable except as a large, living creature.

Alexander the Great still holds the record for size of a deep-sea fish, when, in the Ethiopic version of Pseudo-Callisthenes, we are told that he looked out of his glass cage, and was shown by an angel of the Lord a monster which, swimming

A legendary prototype of the bathysphere. Alexander the Great was said to have been lowered to the bottom of the sea in a glass cage, and to have seen, among other wonders, a sea monster that took three days and nights to swim past him.

rapidly, took three days and three nights to pass before him! Nevertheless, my creature is a good beginning. Seriously, it shows what still remains for the pioneer explorer of the depths of the sea.

Anyone who, from an airplane high above the earth, has tried to spot another plane somewhere near, in full view, will appreciate the even greater difficulty of focusing in this three-dimensional, stygian blackness, upon some creature, suddenly appearing six inches from our faces, or forty-five feet away. Again and again before the eye can refocus, the flash and its owner have vanished.

235

Mr. Barton saw no trace of the large creature I have mentioned, although I called out to him and got him at the window immediately. Soon after, when we were both looking out, he saw the first living *Stylophthalmus* ever seen by man, which completely escaped me, although it must have been within a foot of the windows. This is one of the most remarkable of deep-sea fish, with the eyes on the ends of long, periscope stalks, almost one-third as long as the entire body. My missing the fish was all the more disappointing because I had recently been thoroughly studying these strange beings, and in fact had abolished their entire family, after proving that they were the larvae of the golden-tailed serpent-dragons, *Idiacanthus*.

The next fish of unusual size was seen at 2900 feet. It was less than three feet long, rather slender, with many small luminous spots on the body, and a relatively large, pale green, crescent-shaped light under the eye. Near it were five lanternfish, unlike all others I had seen. They swam so slowly that I made certain before they disappeared that they were of the genus *Lampadena*.

At 11:12 A.M. we came to rest gently at 3000 feet, and I knew that this was my ultimate floor; the cable on the winch was very near its end. A few days ago the water had appeared blacker at 2500 feet than could be imagined, yet now to this same imagination it seemed to show as blacker than black. It seemed as if all future nights in the upper world must be considered only relative degrees of twilight. I could never again use the word BLACK with any conviction.

I looked out and watched an occasional passing light and for the first time I realized how completely lacking was the so-called phosphorescence with which we are familiar at the surface. There, whenever an ordinary fish passes, it becomes luminous by reflection from the lights of the myriads of the minute animals and plants floating in the water. Here each light is an individual thing, often under direct control of the owner. A gigantic fish could tear past the window, and if unillumined might never be seen.

My eyes became so dark adapted at these depths that there was no possibility of error; the jet blackness of the water was broken only by sparks and flashes and steadily glowing lamps of appreciable diameter, varied in color and of infinite variety as regards size and juxtaposition. But they were never dimmed or seen beyond or through any lesser mist or milky-way of organisms. The occasional, evanescent, defense clouds of shrimps hence stand out all the more strongly as unusual phenomena, and are quite apart from the present theme. If the surface light is emitted chiefly by

Stylophthalmus, the larva of Idiacanthus, with its eyes on long stalks.

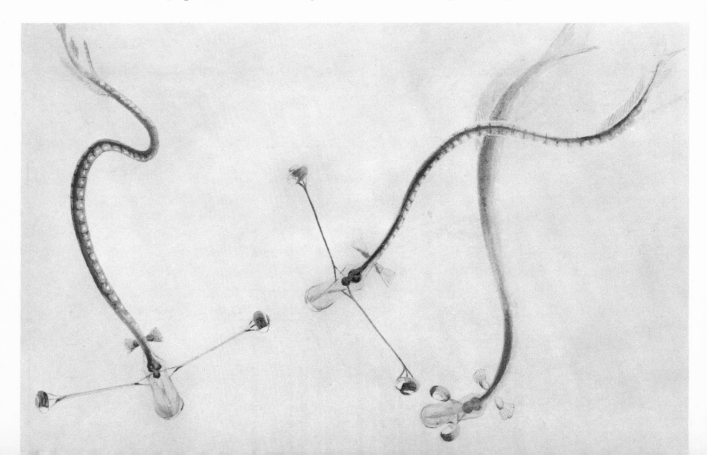

*Cyclothones, or round-mouths (Cyclothone microdon), "by far,"
Dr. Beebe wrote, "the most numerous deep-sea fish in this area."*

The bathysphere emerging from a dive.

Noctiluca and single-celled plants, the explanation of its abyssal absence is easy, for all surface forms of these groups have died out hundreds of feet overhead.

A second thing which occurred to me as I sat coiled in the bathysphere, *more* than half a mile down, was the failure of our powerful beam of light to attract organisms of any kind. Some fled at its appearance, others seemed wholly unconcerned, but not a single copepod or worm or fish gathered along its length or collected against the starboard window from which it poured. We sometimes kept the lesser beam on for three minutes at a time, so there was abundance of time for the plankton, which abounded in all parts of the path of light, to feel and react to its influence. The reason for this

238

William Beebe

demands far more study than I have been able to give it. One factor is doubtless not only lack of the rhythm of day and night, but the eternal absence of all except animal light.

Even in this extremity of blackness I sensed the purity of the water, its freedom from sediment and roiling; six miles from shore and a full mile from the bottom insured this. So there was no diffusion of light, no trails, no refraction. When sparks or larger lights moved they were as distinct as when they were motionless. But reflection was noticeable, as upon the eye or skin from a sub-ocular or a lateral photophore, or upon my face when a shrimp exploded close in front.

Now and then I felt a slight vibration and an apparent slacking off of the cable. Word came that a cross swell had arisen, and when the full weight of bathysphere and cable came upon the winch, Captain Sylvester let out a few inches to ease the strain. There were only about a dozen turns of cable left upon the reel, and a full half of the drum showed its naked, wooden core. We were swinging at 3028 feet, and, Would we come up? We would.

Whatever I thought about the relative value of intensive observation as compared with record-breaking, I had to admit that this ultimate depth which we had attained showed a decided increase in the number of large fish—more than a dozen from three to twenty feet having been seen—and a corresponding greater number of lights, though not in actual size of their diameters.

Now and then, when lights were thickest, and the watery space before me seemed teeming with life, my eyes peered into the distance beyond them, and I thought of the lightless creatures forever invisible to me, those with eyes which depended for guidance through life upon the glow from the lamps of other organisms, and, strangest of all the inhabitants of the deeper parts of the ocean, those blind from birth to death, whose sole assistants, to food, to mates and from enemies, were cunning sense organs in the skin, or long, tendril-like rays of their fins.

Anoplogaster cornutus.

Opisthoproctus soleatus Vaill.

Melanocetus murrayi.

239

Before we began to ascend, I had to stop making notes of my own, so numb were my fingers from the cold steel of the window sill, and to change from my cushion to the metal floor, was like shifting to a cake of ice. Of the blackness of the outside water I have already written too much. As to pressure, there seemed no reason why we should not be outside in a diving helmet as well as in. I thought of a gondola 60,000 feet up in the stratosphere with a pressure of one pound to the square inch. And then through the telephone we learned that at this moment we were under a pressure of 1360 pounds to each square inch, or well over half a ton. Each window held back over nineteen tons of water, while a total of 7016 tons were piled up in all directions upon the bathysphere itself. Yes, we had heard clearly, we were ready to be pulled up at once!

At 2929 feet I heard a metallic twang through the phone, asked what it was, and got some noncommittal answer. I found out later that one of the guy ropes used in spooling the incoming cable on the drum had suddenly given way with a terrific report—a ghastly shock to everyone on deck until they realized it was a rope and not the cable. Truly, we in the bathysphere had the best of it at all times.

Whenever I sink below the last rays of light, similes pour in upon me. Throughout all this account I have consciously rejected the scores of "as ifs" which sprang to mind. The stranger the situation the more does it seem imperative to use comparisons. The eternal one, the one most worthy and which will not pass from mind, the only other place comparable to these marvelous nether regions, must surely be naked space itself, out far beyond atmosphere, between the stars, where sunlight has no grip upon the dust and rubbish of planetary air, where the blackness of space, the shining planets, comets, suns, and stars must really be closely akin to the world of life as it appears to the eyes of an awed human being, in the open ocean, one half mile down.

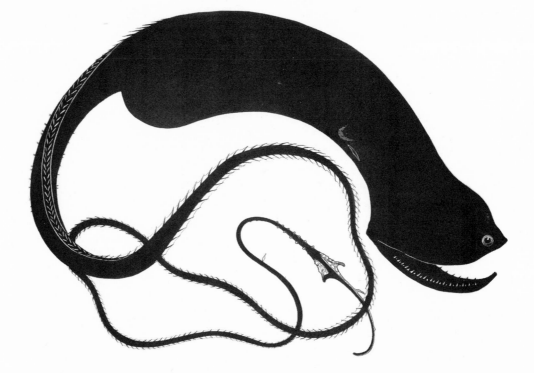

Saccopharynx harrisoni.

240

Adventure 16

The Torpedoing of the Assyrian

by William H. Venables, from Touching the Adventures
of Merchantmen in the Second World War

IN the early years of World War II, before the United States entered the conflict on the side of the Allies, the German U-boats had Great Britain close to defeat. It was absolutely necessary to maintain the convoys which crossed the Atlantic if Britain was not to be starved into submission. How this was done is best appreciated through the accounts of those who braved the dangers of these convoys, in complete knowledge of the tremendous odds against them.

The escort ship *Assyrian* on which William Venables served was a tired old veteran of World War I—a captured prize of the Germans, the former *Fritz*. She was 150 feet long, a twin-screw craft, capable of 18 knots at the top of her steam engines' capacity. Lightly armed, she had long since ceased to be an effective naval craft, and only the desperation of Britain's emergency had pressed her into service. When she set out from Cape Breton, the eastern extremity of Nova Scotia, late in the fall of 1940, she led a convoy composed of slow, obsolete craft, the rusty remnants of a ship graveyard. Putting to sea with such a convoy was a problem in itself—to face the German submarines was simply foolhardy.

What makes Venables' story memorable is the detached, unemotional manner of its telling. The understatement of his narrative is no deliberate attempt to discount his own role, but typical of the British mariners' quiet determination against desperate odds. The destruction of the *Assyrian*, her three naval escort companions, and her convoy—an early demonstration of the effectiveness of the German "wolf-pack" technique—was only one of many such episodes.

To read this record of heroism is not only to share an unforgettable experience with a man of rare courage but also to recall this period when the human spirit was as much a part of the arsenal of war as guns, bombs, and torpedoes.

A sinking British transport.

⸙❲ 1 9 4 0 ❳⸙

"I wanted to see the dawn of a new day, then I would die"

EARLY in October 1940 the *Assyrian* steamed out of Sydney, Cape Breton, at the head of a convoy of thirty-five ships. She was commodore ship — an honour which was the more pointed because of her German origin. Originally the *Fritz*, the *Assyrian* had been taken from Germany after the First World War, and now, in World War II she was leading a convoy across the U-boat tracks to England. True her convoy was not the fine cavalcade one likes to imagine. It was a quaint fleet of square-nosed tramps and old tankers — cast-offs from the faster convoys. Three lake-boats crept doggedly in the tail of the convoy, reducing its maximum speed to six knots. Though not impressive, it was a convoy of ships deep-laden with the food of war. The *Assyrian* was its leader. The weather was good and the voyage uneventful until October 18th, when recent wreckage floating on the quiet swell told an ominous tale of U-boat activity.

At four the following morning I was going on watch when I saw the stern of the ship abeam of us suddenly flash into flame. There was a thunderous explosion, and a blast which nearly made me drop the mug of cocoa I was stirring. As the torpedoed ship dropped astern to sink in the darkness there came a second flash and a rumble from one of the outer columns. The U-boats had found us. I went below wondering if we were next.

At seven that evening, when we were about four hundred miles nor'-west of Scotland, a wolf-pack

of U-boats under Commander Prien — so the German radio claimed — began its attack. I think this was the first time the Germans had used the wolf-pack technique. Despite gallant efforts, our inadequate escort of three slow sloops was powerless to save us. The torpedoes found ship after ship, and each sank according to its cargo; the ammunition ship blew up, the tanker blazed, the ore ship sank like a stone.

The moonlight night was bright with starshells and the blaze of burning ships. We saw no submarines on the surface because our convoy was so slow that the U-boats could deal with us while submerged.

From the bridge Captain Kearon and Admiral McKinnon (the commodore) saw the periscope of a submarine ahead of us. They asked for all possible speed for an attempt to ram the U-boat. I spoke to the three firemen in the stokehold, and they grinned at the thought of the old *Assyrian* ramming a U-boat. They fired her boilers as they had never been fired before; even with both engines full out her steam was on the feather. It was a great effort on their part. I regret to say that all three were killed shortly after.

With everything she had in her the *Assyrian* pounded after the U-boat's periscope. Every second we hoped to feel her shudder as her bow ripped the enemy's stern. But the *Assyrian*'s best was not enough; we neither gained nor lost in the race. I understood from Captain Kearon that for nearly

243

an hour we were so hot on the U-boat's trail that it dared not try to turn away from us. Then a cloud momentarily obscured the moon, and the U-boat slipped to one side.

Coming out of the engine-room, I was startled by a flash and an explosion. I thought we had been torpedoed, but it was our four-inch gun firing at the U-boat. Unfortunately the light was poor, and our target vanished without being hit.

On the commodore's orders our gunners set off some of our smoke floats. At first they flamed, making us an ideal target, then a dense pall of smoke trailed from our stern—it was as if an old hen had spread her wings to protect her chicks from a horde of rats—and the gesture was just as hopeless. The U-boats seemed to be everywhere. Every twenty minutes or so a German torpedo was aimed at a ship's engine-room, and its war-head exploded on or near its target.

We on the *Assyrian* knew that for her temerity in attacking, the U-boats would make a special target of us. Only the sheerest luck could save us. Men who had no duty posts stood listlessly outside the engine-room doors to keep warm. Some stood on the boat-deck at their lifeboat stations. Now and again someone would crack a joke which, no matter how flimsy, was greeted with chuckles of nervous laughter.

As the assistant stewards formed part of the gun-crew, and Daley, the chief steward, had no one to assist him, I took a jug of tea to the gun-crew. They had been standing for three hours in a cold wind, waiting for a chance to fire at a U-boat. They were glad of the hot tea. They told me that they had

A torpedoed tanker, breaking in half.

seen the wake of two torpedoes just skim our stern. Two others barely missed our bow.

Just before midnight I was speaking to the three firemen in the stokehold. They were disappointed at not having rammed the U-boat. Both engines were working beautifully, despite the strain of the chase.

When I came on deck I found that the twelve-to-four firemen had already gone towards the fiddley. I went after them to warn them about smoky fires. I was just stepping into the port fiddley when a torpedo struck near the stokehold on the starboard side, right opposite me. I was flung heavily to the deck. The three firemen in the stokehold were killed instantly. Some of the men standing on the boat-deck beside the starboard lifeboat were blown into the sea.

Thinking I had picked myself up immediately, I ran to the engine-room. The ship was in total darkness, and I had lost my torch. I was not sure where we had been struck, and thought perhaps the fuses had been jerked from their holders. I could see nothing as I started to go down the engine-room ladder. Everything was deathly still, and there was a strong smell of steam. As I called out to see if the fourth engineer was safe I slipped on the ladder and fell into oily water which had risen many feet above the cylinder tops. From the quantity of water in the engine-room I knew that I must have lain unconscious on the deck for many minutes. It was only now that I realized that my head was bleeding and that I had lost my glasses.

I got another torch and searched the water in the engine-room, trying to find the fourth engineer. As I could not see him I thought he had been killed and his body trapped beneath the gratings.

Finding that I could do nothing in the engine-room, I went to the boat-deck. Men were swarming down ropes and ladders into the port lifeboat. I was glad to see the fourth engineer and his greaser sitting in the boat.

Hearing shouts, I went to the fiddley top and found Captain Kearon trying to lift up the grating. The three firemen who had been going below when the torpedo struck had been startled by the explosion and had climbed too high up the stokehold ladder. The fiddley hurricane-lamp had been smashed by the detonation and the men could not see. Feeling the fiddley grating above them, they thought they were trapped. As I knew which was the loose part of the grating, we soon released them.

Captain Kearon and I then went to the ship's side to look at the lifeboat. The boat had been swamped, and we could see men sitting on the gunwale, but no boat. The captain then told the third mate, who was in charge, to row away from the ship's side in case she suddenly plunged.

There were about a dozen of us left on board the sinking ship, including the commodore and three of his staff. I was the only engineer left on board and I was glad I was left because I had been seven years second engineer of the *Assyrian* and did not want to leave her while she still floated.

While we were launching the small rafts another torpedoed ship drifted across our bow. She swung away and deliberately stood on end. Her bow reared vertically above the sea and she whined as she slid below the water. She carried thousands of pit-props, and these burst from her holds as she sank.

I was sitting on one of the small rafts with one of the naval ratings when the pit-props from the sunken ship began to hit our raft and break it up. The rating scrambled back on board the *Assyrian*. I made a jump for it, but my hands were cold and I missed. I fell into the water beneath the pit-props. I forced my way back to the raft and made a second attempt. Fortunately, the commodore managed to grip my hand and pull me on board.

Those of us left on board the *Assyrian* were now in sorry plight. We had neither boat nor raft. The ship's bow was submerged and she had a list to port. The water made a mournful sound which turned one's stomach as it soughed up and down the alleyways.

With my torch I looked into the engine-room. As I could see no gain in the water I began to have hopes that the ship might yet be towed to port. I looked in the fiddley and saw a fireman sitting there. He had a broken arm and jaw. He was dazed. Daley, the chief steward, gave him first aid and we then placed him on a raft which we found floating alongside. The raft was in fair condition, and we hoped that it would float him until daylight. We heard later that one of the rescuing ships had found the fireman dead on the raft.

Under the captain's direction we all gathered under the poop and made a big raft out of painting-planks and hatch-boards. We were all soaking wet, and our hands so cold that we could hardly tie the knots which bound our raft. We joked while the carpenter sawed the wood.

By a natural process of selection the men left on board were the pick of the crew. They all showed courage and opened up remarkable funds of humour. I hid my own nervousness by laughing and joking with the rest, but at the back of my mind I was wondering what it was like to die.

By the time our raft was ready the sea for hundreds of yards about us was covered with a floor of pit-props. While going to the top of the engine-room to see if the water was gaining, I heard a voice calling my name from the sea. After getting my spare pair of glasses from my cabin I could see across the sea of pit-props. The moonlight was clear and I saw Mr. King, the mate, waving to me.

He was hemmed in by pit-props, twenty yards from the ship's side. He wanted me to get a rope and pull him on board. While I was getting the rope the wind and sea shifted the pit-props so that Mr. King was able to make the ship's side and clamber on board. I was surprised to see him and we laughed at his adventure. To us the deck of a sinking ship was perfect safety. Unfortunately Mr. King died later from exposure.

On looking over the side I saw Keoghan, the third engineer, hanging on to a rope in the water. He had been in the lifeboat, but had tried to get back on board when he thought the lifeboat was sinking. With the bos'n's assistance I got him on board. He went to his cabin and changed into dry clothing. Later, I again found him in the water, clinging to the same rope. The ship had by now sunk a little lower in the water and I was able to lower myself quite easily alongside Keoghan. I could not unclasp his hands from the rope. I think he was dead.

When I got back on board I heard a voice calling from the fiddley. I went there, and my torch showed me the head of one of the trimmers. His forehead was badly cut and he was hanging on to the grating. Where he had come from I do not know. I had previously made sure that no one was in the fiddley, and it was now more than an hour since the torpedo had hit us. I could not get the trimmer out of the fiddley until I got the assistance of Daley and a greaser, Bishop.

Together we carried the trimmer out on deck. He was terribly injured. His legs were almost off at the thigh and his stomach was torn. We wrapped him in blankets and gave him water. One of us stayed with him most of the time, giving him water and trying to make him comfortable. We could do no more.

While we were waiting for the ship to sink we hailed the occasional lifeboat which we saw rowing about in the distance. Always the reply was the same: "We are full up, mates," or, "Sorry, we're sinking ourselves." The remnants of the convoy had gone on, still under attack.

In order to keep ourselves occupied we flung everything floatable into the water. We cut the fall of the damaged lifeboat. It fell in the water, upside down. Bishop jumped on to it, and we made it fast to the bulwark. A sailor and a fireman sat on the capsized lifeboat with Bishop. Thinking that the ship might yet float until daylight, and give us a chance to be picked up, we decided to keep the capsized lifeboat alongside. The three men sat on it, waiting.

Suddenly, a tremor ran through the ship and we knew that she was going. Captain Kearon ordered abandon ship and told us the time—two-twenty.

William H. Venables

We began to push the huge raft over the stern. But it was already breaking up. Our hands had been cold when we tied its knots. Already the stern was rising quickly out of the water. Men were jumping from the rail after the raft. I believe Bellas, the second mate, climbed down to the propeller boss before jumping.

As I know the raft would not hold all the survivors, I ran amidships and jumped for the capsized lifeboat. Bishop caught me as I nearly fell into the water. We then called as loud as we could so that if anyone could not make the raft they would know there was plenty of room on the keel of our boat.

When we found that no one else was coming we tried to push the boat away from the ship's side. We could not. The suction of the sinking ship was holding us alongside her. It was a strangely helpless feeling. I sat down on the keel and wondered how we could manage to push away. Suddenly, the ship's side seemed to jump at us. The boat-davit swooped through the air and cut clean through the boat between Bishop and me. We found ourselves strug-

Survivors from a torpedoed freighter.

gling beneath the water. Something like a huge hand seemed to be pressing my back, and ropes twined themselves about me.

Somehow, I came to the surface. I distinctly remember holding my glasses to my eyes as I bobbed up and saw the after part of the *Assyrian* rear slowly above the sea. In the clear moonlight I could see every plate of her, the sea-grass vivid on her side, and every detail of her two propellers. Just before me was the gaping black hole where the torpedo had ripped her side. I swam on my back away from it. I was afraid of being sucked inside.

Quite impersonally, as if viewing it on a cinema screen, I pictured myself being sucked to the bottom of the sea behind the ship. I could not turn on my breast and swim faster because I could not take my eyes from the ship. I saw her poise for a moment above the water, and heard a crashing inside her as her boilers broke adrift from their cradles. As she slid beneath the sea, the air escaping from her holds droned from the ventilators like a great organ.

With startling suddenness nothing was left on the surface of the sea but a patch of frothing water. Then I saw bales of cargo bobbling in the white foam as it burst from her holds. Wondering why I had not been sucked down, I swam away.

I was glad to find that the three men who had been on the capsized lifeboat with me had so far escaped. They could not swim, but as they wore life-jackets they could keep afloat easily. I swam to the pit-props and pushed some in their direction. The pit-props gave us added confidence. We joked a bit, and I told them to keep their legs moving even if they could not swim. The water was cold, and we had to keep our blood circulating.

The raft was somewhere in the vicinity, but I could not see it because of the debris which littered the sea. I heard Bellas call to see if I was safe. I replied and told him the names of the men who were with me. With Bellas on the raft were the captain, commodore, mate, chief steward, bos'n, and carpenter, and a few others.

We four soon lost contact with the raft. We swam aimlessly about, trying to keep together for company. Soon I found I was alone. I was fully dressed, complete with Merchant Navy muffler. I was rigged for a night in a boat or on a raft, not for swimming the Atlantic. I tried to take my shoes off, but the water had tightened the laces and my hands were cold.

I found that my wrist-watch was still going, despite its immersion and the fact that its glass had been cracked by the torpedo. For over an hour I swam with a pit-prop beneath each arm, swimming with very methodical strokes of my legs, trying to get the best out of them, anything to keep my mind from the great loneliness of the ocean.

At times I came across dead men floating face down in their life-jackets. I turned some of them over to see if I knew them. They were all from other ships. I hear some one in the distance singing "Roll out the Barrel" in a very discordant voice—I found later that it was our mess-room steward. I felt so fine at not being afraid that I wanted to burst into song myself. I tried one or two songs, but my voice was even more croakly than the steward's. I contented myself with merely humming.

Although I was swimming in the North Atlantic in the middle of October, the water did not feel as cold as I would have imagined. But my hands had lost all feeling, and my stomach felt as if it were full of ice. I feared that even if I were eventually picked up I would be a physical wreck.

Huge packing cases from the sunken ships floated past me. I swam to some of them and tried to climb on top. But the packing cases rolled on top of me and pushed me beneath the water. I decided to rely on my pit-props.

After two hours in the water I saw a submarine's periscope skimming through the moonlight. Her conning-tower was almost awash, and I thought she was going to surface. I hid behind a floating bale, not wanting to be taken prisoner. The U boat passed on, not noticing me.

When I had been nearly three hours in the water

William H. Venables

I had given up all hope of being saved. The icy feeling in my stomach was creeping higher, and I knew that when it reached my heart I would die. I never felt fitter in my life.

The moon was lowering behind the scudding clouds, and I was afraid it would go, leaving me in darkness. I seemed to be the only thing that lived on the face of the sea. I thought of the fine ships lying far beneath me on the ocean bed, and of the men still in them. The solitude awed me so that I swam quietly, just as I would tiptoe into church.

In my mind's eye I could picture myself sitting with the folks at home beside the fire, I knew that was worth fighting for, and swam on. My hands ached with the cold, but I kept them clasped about my chest so that the pit-props hugged beneath my armpits formed a V about me, my head being at the apex. I did not know then that V was for Victory. I swam on and on, waiting for the daylight. I wanted to see the dawn of a new day, then I would die.

When I saw the dark shape of a sloop ahead of me I could hardly believe my eyes. Silhouetted as she was, she seemed to have come out of the moon. I cried out, "Sloop, ahoy," and a voice answered me. Again I called, and a voice replied: "Keep calling! Keep calling!"

The captain of the sloop could not see me, but my voice told him my direction. I understand that a torpedo passed beneath the sloop—H.M.S. *Leith* —while she was maneuvering to pick me up. When she got nearer I abandoned my pit-props and swam like a madman towards her. Men lined her bulwarks and clung to boarding nets on her side as they urged me on. I saw a life-belt drop in the water beside me. Thankfully I put it over my head.

I remembered nothing more until I woke up, wrapped in a blanket, on the mess-deck of the sloop the following morning. A Greek sailor lying beside me was trying to put a cigarette in my mouth.

Survivors on life rafts.

I believe that when I was taken on board the *Leith* my clothes were badly torn, my life-jacket in shreds—probably due to my struggle when the *Assyrian* rolled on top of me. The sloop's petty officers took me to the galley and massaged me for an hour before I showed signs of life. Then it took two of them to hold me as I struggled to get at the galley fire. I drank a mug of cocoa which scalded my throat. But of these things I knew nothing. Only my scalded throat remained.

I was glad to find several of the *Assyrian*'s survivors among the two hundred on the *Leith*. Two of the *Assyrian*'s men died later and were buried with full naval honours. It was an impressive ceremony, particularly to those of us who had just been through the battle of the *Assyrian* with the men whose canvas-wrapped bodies lay so still beneath the Red Ensign.

That is the story of the *Assyrian*'s convoy as I saw it. It contains no examples of outstanding heroism. It is simply a tale of men facing death calmly, doing their duty as they saw it, helping each other. Lives were saved, only to be lost again. It is a typical tale of British seamen fighting the U-boats while their womenfolk were defying the Nazi bombers at home. It is, in short, a tale of Britishers.

A rescued survivor on a Coast Guard ship.

Adventure 17

Rapture of the Depths

from The Silent World, by Jacques-Yves Cousteau

IN 1943, a small group of French diving enthusiasts took to the Mediterranean to test a new and untried piece of equipment, the result of numerous unsuccessful efforts to invent means of breathing under water that would not require an air line to the surface. This particular device consisted of tanks of compressed natural air strapped to the diver's back. A short length of hose ran from the tanks to a mouthpiece. The mouthpiece contained a valve that drew in air from the tanks when the diver inhaled but released his exhaled breath into the water. The apparatus was called the aqualung.

The leader of what was an astonishingly successful experiment was a French naval officer enjoying enforced leisure during the German occupation, Jacques-Ives Cousteau. It was he who in his enormously successful book and motion picture, *The Silent World*, communicated not only the importance of a great scientific triumph, but—importance of a great scientific triumph, but—

perhaps more important—the new dimensions of human experience it created.

The aqualung did not merely render underwater diving easier and more practicable; it gave the diver an exhilarating and unique freedom, the freedom to maneuver weightlessly and almost effortlessly in the alien element of the sea. It is hardly surprising that its major chronicler should be Cousteau, a sensitive and philosophic man with the concentrated curiosity of a scientist and the imagination and expressive powers of a poet.

These pioneers in the use of the aqualung had to encounter certain special dangers, dangers made all the more menacing because they were unknown and unforeseeable. One of the greatest of these is described here. It is typical of Cousteau and his dedicated companions that they systematically investigated these dangers with the cool determination of the true explorers they were.

Philippe Tailliez swimming with the aqualung.

⌈ 1943 & 47 ⌉

"I sank slowly through a period of intense visions"

N an October afternoon in 1943 we arrived in a Mediterranean fishing village to rendezvous with persons involved in the test. A hundred-meter length of knotted rope lying along the jetty was under examination by Monsieur Methieu, the harbor engineer, and Maitre Gaudry, *huissier*. This French functionary is licensed by the Republic as a bailiff, unimpeachable witness and investigator. His testimony is accepted without challenge in any court of law. The engineer and the *huissier* methodically counted and measured the metric knots in the rope along which Frédéric Dumas was to descend into the sea.

Two launches, full of witnesses, accompanied the condemned man to sea. The first launch towed the second, in which were Didi and I, embarrassed by the attentions of the crowd. We had talked over all conceivable problems of the dive, and Didi had himself weighed, catalogued everything that could happen and was ready for it. The plunge was well planned. He would submerge in the clear calm water, wearing a factory-new aqualung and a heavily weighted belt, and descend feet first without undue exertion along the knotted rope to the greatest depth he could reach. There he would remove his weights, tie them on the rope, and speed to the surface. When the line was brought up it would show what depth he had attained. After the terrors of thinking about it, Didi considered the plunge a formality.

The towboat anchored in two hundred and forty feet of water. The sky was clouded and an early autumn wind drove a muddy white-crowned chop past our gunwales. The air was raw. As Dumas's safety man, I entered the water first and was swept away from the launch. I swam hard to get back to the ladder and had to struggle to stay alongside. Didi came into the water. The launch skipper was distressed at the sight of men abandoning a vessel in such a sea and ran around, hurling lines to us. Dumas saluted his gallantry and sank. He did so unwillingly, as he was overweighted. Underwater he discovered that when he turned his head to the left it pinched off his air intake hose. I swam to catch the knotted rope as it was thrown overboard. I clutched the rope, out of breath, with the big dive not yet started. Dumas went under again.

I looked down and saw Didi sinking under his weights and swimming with both arms and legs against the sweep of current to gain the shot-line. When he caught it a flume of air came out of his regulator, a sign of exhaustion. He rested on the rope for a moment and then lowered himself rapidly hand under hand into the turbid, racing sea.

Still panting from the fight on the surface, I followed him toward my sentry post a hundred feet down. My brain was reeling. Didi did not look up. I saw his fists and head melting into the dun water.

253

Exploring sunken ships. Above: A diver swims through the torpedo hole in a ship sunk in World War II. Opposite: Frédéric Dumas stares through a porthole in another wreck.

Here is how he described the record dive:

"The light does not change color as it usually does underneath a turbid surface. I cannot see clearly. Either the sun is going down quickly or my eyes are weak. I reach the hundred-foot knot. My body doesn't feel weak but I keep panting. The damned rope doesn't hang straight. It slants off into the yellow soup. It slants more and more. I am anxious about that line, but I really feel wonderful. I have a queer feeling of beatitude. I am drunk and carefree. My ears buzz and my mouth tastes bitter. The current staggers me as though I had had too many drinks.

"I have forgotten Jacques and the people in the boats. My eyes are tired. I lower on down, trying to think about the bottom, but I can't. I am going to sleep, but I can't fall asleep in such dizziness. There is a little light around me. I reach for the next knot and miss it. I reach again and tie my belt on it.

"Coming up is merry as a bubble. Liberated from weights I pull on the rope and bound. The drunken sensation vanishes. I am sober and infuriated to have missed my goal. I pass Jacques and hurry on up. I am told I was down seven minutes."

Didi's belt was tied off two hundred and ten feet down. The *huissier* attested it. No independent diver had been deeper. Yet Dumas's subjective impression was that he had been slightly under one hundred feet.

Jacques-Ives Cousteau

Didi's drunkenness was nitrogen narcosis, a factor of diving physiology which had been studied by Captain A. R. Behnke, U.S.N., several years before. In occupied France we knew nothing of his work. We called the seizure *l'ivresse des grandes profondeurs* (rapture, or "intoxication," of the great depths).

The first stage is a mild anesthesia, after which the diver becomes a god. If a passing fish seems to require air, the crazed diver may tear out his air pipe or mouth grip as a sublime gift. The process is complex and still an issue among diving physiologists. It may derive from nitrogen oversaturation, according to Captain Behnke. It has no relation to the bends. It is a gaseous attack on the central nervous system. Recent laboratory studies attribute "rapture of the great depths" to residual carbon dioxide retained in the viscosity of nerve tissues.

I am personally quite receptive to nitrogen rapture. I like it and fear it like doom. It destroys the instinct of life. Tough individuals are not overcome as soon as neurasthenic persons like me, but they have difficulty extricating themselves. Intellectuals get drunk early and suffer acute attacks on all the senses, which demand hard fighting to overcome. When they have beaten the foe, they recover quickly. The agreeable glow of depth rapture resembles the giggle-party jags of the nineteen-twenties when flappers and sheiks convened to sniff nitrogen peroxide.

L'ivresse des grandes profondeurs has one salient advantage over alcohol—no hangover. If one is able to escape from its zone, the brain clears instantly and there are no horrors in the morning. I cannot read accounts of a record dive without wanting to ask the champion how drunk he was.

Caves beneath the sea.   Dumas adjusts his eyes to the darkness before entering a cave
one hundred feet down.   Opposite: Tailliez discovers a cave in the reefs off Cassis.

WE continued to be puzzled with the rapture of the depths and felt that we were challenged to go deeper. Didi's deep dive made us aware of the problem, and the Group had assembled detailed reports on its deep dives. But we had only a literary knowledge of the full effects of *l'ivresse des grandes profondeurs* as it must strike lower down. In the summer of 1947 we set out to make a series of deeper penetrations.

Here I must say that we were not trying for record descents, although the dives did set new world marks. We have always placed a reasonable premium on returning alive. Even Didi, the boldest

among us, is not a stunt man. We went lower because that was the only way to learn more about the drunken effect, and to sample individual reactions on what aqualung work could be done in severe depths. The attempts were surrounded with careful preparations and controls, in order to obtain clear data. The objective range we set was three hundred feet or fifty fathoms. No independent diver had yet been deeper than Dumas's two hundred and ten feet.

The dives were measured by a heavy shotline hanging from the *Élie Monnier*. On the line at sixteen-and-one-half-foot intervals (five meters) there were white boards. The divers carried indelible pencils to sign their names on the deepest board they could reach, and to write a sentence describing their sensations.

To save energy and air, the test divers descended the shotline without undue motion, carried down by ten-pound hunks of scrap iron. They retarded their descent by holding the line. When a man reached the target depths, or the maximum distance he could stand, he signed in, jettisoned his weight, and took the line back to the surface. During the return the divers halted at depths of twenty and ten feet for short periods of stage decompression to avoid the bends.

I was in good physical condition for the trial, trained fine by an active spring in the sea, and with responsive ears. I entered the water holding the scrap iron in my left hand. I went down with great rapidity, with my right arm crooked around the shotline. I was oppressively conscious of the Diesel generator rumble of the idle *Élie Monnier* as I wedged my head into mounting pressure. It was high noon in July, but the light soon faded. I dropped through the twilight, alone with the white rope, which stretched before me in a monotonous perspective of blank white signposts.

At two hundred feet I tasted the metallic flavor of compressed nitrogen and was instantaneously and severely struck with rapture. I closed my hand on the rope and stopped. My mind was jammed with conceited thoughts and antic joy. I struggled to fix my brain on reality, to attempt to name the color of the sea about me. A contest took place between navy blue, aquamarine and Prussian blue. The debate would not resolve. The sole fact I could grasp was that there was no roof and no

floor in the blue room. The distant purr of the Diesel invaded my mind—it swelled to a giant beat, the rhythm of the world's heart.

I took the pencil and wrote on a board, "Nitrogen has a dirty taste." I had little impression of holding the pencil, childhood nightmares overruled my mind. I was ill in bed, terrorized with the realization that everything in the world was thick. My fingers were sausages. My tongue was a tennis ball. My lips swelled grotesquely on the mouth grip. The air was syrup. The water jelled around me as though I were smothered in aspic.

I hung witless on the rope. Standing aside was a smiling jaunty man, my second self, perfectly self-contained, grinning sardonically at the wretched diver. As the seconds passed the jaunty man installed himself in my command and ordered that I unloose the rope and go down.

I sank slowly through a period of intense visions.

Around the two hundred and sixty-four foot board the water was suffused with an unearthly glow. I was passing from night to an intimation of dawn. What I saw as sunrise was light reflected from the floor, which had passed unimpeded through the dark transparent strata above. I saw below me the weight at the end of the shotline, hanging twenty feet from the floor. I stopped at the penultimate board and looked down at the last board, five meters away, and marshaled all my

Dumas ascending a 120-foot rock chimney.

resources to evaluate the situation without deluding myself. Then I went to the last board, two hundred and ninety-seven feet down.

The floor was gloomy and barren, save for morbid shells and sea urchins. I was sufficiently in control to remember that in this pressure, ten times that of the surface, any untoward physical effort was extremely dangerous. I filled my lungs slowly and signed the board. I could not write what it felt like fifty fathoms down.

I was the deepest independent diver. In my bisected brain the satisfaction was balanced by satirical self-contempt.

I dropped the scrap iron and bounded like a coiled spring, clearing two boards in the first flight. There, at two hundred and sixty-four feet, the rapture vanished suddenly, inexplicably and entirely.

I was light and sharp, one man again, enjoying the lighter air expanding in my lungs. I rose through the twilight zone at high speed, and saw the surface pattern in a blaze of platinum bubbles and dancing prisms. It was impossible not to think of flying to heaven.

However, before heaven there was purgatory. I waited twenty feet down for five minutes of stage decompression, then hurried to ten feet where I spent ten shivering minutes. When they hauled in the shotline I found that some impostor had written my name on the last board.

For a half hour afterward I had a slight pain in the knees and shoulders. Philippe Tailliez went down to the last board, scribbled a silly message, and came up with a two-day headache. Dumas had to overcome dramas of heavy rapture in the fifty-

A diver pulls an octopus from a reef.

fathom zone. Our two tough sailors, Fargues and Morandiére, said they could have done short easy labor around the bottom. Quartermaster Georges visited the bottom board and was dizzy for an hour or so afterward. Jean Pinard felt out of condition at two hundred and twenty feet, signed in, and sensibly returned. None of us wrote a legible word on the deep board.

In the autumn we undertook another series of deep dives, with marker boards extending below fifty fathoms. We planned to venture beyond with lines tied to the waist, and a safety man stationed on deck, completely equipped to jump in and give aid in case of difficulty.

Diving master Maurice Fargues dived first. On deck we regularly received the reassuring conventional signal Fargues gave by tugging on the line, "*Tout va bien*" (All is well). Suddenly there was no signal. Anxiety struck us all at once. Jean Pinard, his safety man, went down immediately, and we hauled Fargues up toward one hundred and fifty feet, where they would meet. Pinard plunged toward an inert body, and beheld with horror that Fargues's mouthpiece was hanging on his chest.

We worked for twelve hours trying to revive Fargues, but he was dead. Rapture of the depths had stolen his air tube from his mouth and drowned him. When we brought up the shotline we found Maurice Fargues's name written on the three hundred and ninety-six-foot board. Fargues gave his life a hundred feet below our greatest penetrations, deeper than any helmet diver breathing unmixed air has ever gone in the sea.

Dumas in pursuit of a sting ray.

Adventure 18

Escape from the Ice

from Surface at the Pole, by James Calvert

TECHNOLOGY will never destroy adventure, only extend it. Modern ships and modern instruments make navigation safer, easier, and more assured in every ocean of the world, but it is in the nature of man to push technology to its limits and to risk new and unknown dangers to enlarge human knowledge and experience.

Until the present century there was one ocean of the world that was all but unexplored for lack of craft to venture into it. This was the Arctic, covered year round with thick blocks of shifting pack ice. In the summer there are a few small openings on its surface, created haphazardly in the wind-shifted ice; in the long winter even these become quickly frozen over. The few surface ships that have ever crossed it are those that have become frozen into the ice and carried helplessly with the drift of the pack.

The first craft able to penetrate this virtually unexplored ocean has been the atomic submarine, with its almost limitless independence of the surface. Able to cruise for months at depths where the weather of the surface is never felt, it can maneuver in any part of this great ice-locked ocean. The celebrated USS *Nautilus* was the first to traverse the Arctic under her own power, in the summer of 1958, but only two weeks later the USS *Skate* achieved an equally great triumph. Navigating carefully beneath the summer ice, her crew was able to find openings in the pack and to reach the surface in them, proving that submarines could not only navigate safely in the Arctic, but maintain periodic contact with the outside world as well.

The *Skate* topped even this triumph the following winter, cruising once more beneath the ice pack, and this time breaking through the frozen surface at places where recent shifts had left thin spots.

The risks were enormous. Collision with the heavy blocks of the ice pack was a constant danger; the possibility of mechanical breakdown below the surface an even greater one. And there was always the chance that the shifts that created the small gaps in the ice could suddenly close them again, crushing the ship once she was on the surface. It was a combination of these two last perils that brought the *Skate* close to destruction late in the second voyage. A leak had developed in a seal connecting an engine-room pump to the sea, and the need was urgent to find a place to surface and undertake repairs. What then befell the *Skate*, in thirty-below weather not far from the North Pole is described by her commander.

The submarine Skate surfaced near the North Pole.
A few minutes after this picture was taken by the author, the ship narrowly avoided being crushed
by a sudden shift in the ice floes around it.

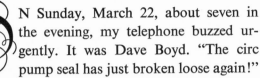

1959

"The ship fluttered and shook as the ice pressed around her"

ON Sunday, March 22, about seven in the evening, my telephone buzzed urgently. It was Dave Boyd. "The circ pump seal has just broken loose again!" he reported. "Much worse this time—spraying water all over the place. We'll have to get up and fix it as soon as we can," he said.

There was no need to go back and look. Dave's tone of voice was explicit enough. I went directly to the control center, where Guy Shaffer was on watch, and explained the emergency to him.

"This ice has been really heavy for hours," said Guy grimly. "No point in doubling back."

An air of tenseness and gloom settled over the control center, as the men on watch silently stared at the ice detector and the television. I thought to myself what a fool I had been not to make the pump repair that morning.

Two hours dragged by. Thirty-two miles of heavy, solid ice without a trace of a gap. Who knows how many openings we narrowly missed, going by them only a few yards to one side or the other?

Reluctantly, I went back to my room. I was not helping matters by standing out there staring at the ice machine and television. There were people on watch to do that, and my presence just made them uneasy.

And then, within an hour, the ship heeled to starboard and began a rapid turn. They'd found something! I immediately returned to the control center where Al Kelln had relieved Guy Shaffer.

"It's a big one!" exclaimed Kelln, with a smile from ear to ear.

I looked at the trace of the ice detector. Sure enough, we had passed under several hundred yards of thin ice. The river of light was strong enough to be clearly visible on the television.

We had practiced our maneuvers over and over to reduce the time required to perform them. Now time was all-important. We were soon under the skylight, ballooning slowly upward. Through the periscope, the now-familiar jade-green river was sharply outlined against the jet-black background of the pack.

At 10:13 P.M. we hit the ice with a heavy impact which brought butterflies to our stomachs. But on the television we could see the ice bow and then shatter. We were through.

The sun was just rising. As I climbed to the bridge I could see its faint glow on the horizon, obscured by clouds. A wind of about 10 knots swept across the ice. We had surfaced almost in the exact center of a long, straight lead, heavily hummocked on our port side. The ice in the lead was smooth and uniform, covered with a light coat of snow, and heavier than any we had yet broken. We came through without damage, but once up, were gripped fast.

The sky was gray and depressing; the temperature was 31 below, the coldest we had yet experienced. The tall pressure ridges to port were made of husky slabs 10 to 12 feet thick. Their green edges showed through the covering snow blanket like emeralds in cotton.

Dave Boyd immediately wanted to know if it was all right to go ahead with the pump repair.

"This looks like a good spot, Dave," I told him.

263

*Pressure ridges often tower several feet
above the surface of the floes.*

"Let's get on with it. How long do you think it will take?"

"I've just talked it over with Whitehead," he said. "We think about twelve hours."

We had never been on the surface that long at any time this winter, but I saw no reason why we couldn't manage it. After all, we'd been at Alfa the summer before more than twenty-four hours.

I decided to go out to have a look at the heavy ridges to port, and went below to put on my heaviest clothes and gather up my binoculars and camera.

The edges of the rafted ice blocks were sharp, showing that they had recently been broken. The ridge itself was about 15 feet high and stretched for hundreds of yards along the side of the lead. I climbed to the top of a hummock and looked back in the direction from which the *Skate* had come. Nothing but endless icefields stretched to the horizon.

I tried to take a few pictures, but had trouble in the biting cold. My fingers were still sore from

their nipping of a week before. They felt as though they had been burned on a hot piece of metal and were slowly healing. They were still painful enough to make buttoning a shirt or tying shoelaces difficult.

We had all been out on the ice enough to have keen respect for what the cold could do. We found no matter how carefully we dressed we had trouble keeping our hands and faces warm. Some of the men had taken to wrapping Turkish towels around the lower part of their faces for protection, but the towels were soon stiff and useless with the frozen condensation of their breath.

In the cold and wind, moreover, there was no way to prevent one's eyes and nose from watering. The water would run down cheeks, nose, and chin —and then freeze. As long as we could return frequently to the ship to thaw out we were all right, but attempting to pick or brush the ice off in the open resulted in removing a little skin with it. A raw place was created which itself froze in a short time.

I frankly do not know how men live in temperatures like these, day after day and week after week with no refuge or protection from the weather. Those who have done it have my heartfelt salute.

When I returned to the ship the engine room rang with the voices of men and the clatter of tools. The starboard condenser and its turbines had been shut down and isolated from the leaky seal. Chief Whitehead was in charge of a group of men who were removing the lockers, wires, and small pipes above the motor. Another group prepared a wire sling and block and tackle to hoist the motor.

In the design of the *Skate*, Admiral Rickover's engineers had spared no effort to ensure that every piece of machinery that might have to be repaired at sea could be reached and hoisted out. An elaborate model of the engine room had been built at the Electric Boat Division, in which every piece of machinery, every pipe, every wire, every fitting had been mocked up life-size in wood. Everything was

James Calvert

Surfacing an atomic submarine through the Arctic ice: the sail, or superstructure, breaks the first hole.

moved around like furniture in a new living room until Rickover's men and the Electric Boat engineers were sure that nothing was inaccessible. That effort was now paying off for us. To be sure, there were impediments around the motor—a submarine engine room must be too full of pipes and wires to avoid this—but they were all light and could be easily moved by the crew.

There was nothing I could contribute here; my presence just made it harder for them to work. I went forward to my room and tried to settle my nerves by reading.

Shortly after, my phone buzzer rang. "Captain," said Al Kelln in a tense voice, "I'd like to have you come up here."

I pulled myself into my warm clothes and climbed to the bridge. As I neared the top of the ladder I could hear a dull boom like distant thunder.

"What's up, Al?" I asked.

In his calm, deliberate manner he handed me his binoculars. "Look over to port," he said, "in the icefields beyond the hummocks."

In the distant icefields, moving with ponderous slowness, huge ice cakes rose up on end like giant green billboards, then slowly slipped back into the surrounding white. The dull thunderous boom grew louder. The ice was on the move.

I looked at my watch. It was 11:25 P.M. The engine-room job had been under way for about an

More of the sail emerges through the ice. This part of the ship is not watertight, and sea water drains out of it as the ship surfaces.

hour. Next to the ship there was still no sign of movement or pressure.

From close to the ship came a noise like the sharp report of a rifle. Startled, I spun around, but could see nothing. Kelln pointed to the bow, where a new crack ran diagonally forward.

Where was the pressure coming from? The wind, although brisk, didn't seem strong enough to cause all this commotion. I knew, however, that the closely packed ice floes, stretching to the horizon, could transmit pressure from far away. Somewhere, gigantic forces must have been at work to tumble 10-foot blocks of ice like a child's building blocks.

I looked at the fields to port. Now the rise and fall of the ice blocks gave the appearance of sluggish waves, all moving inexorably toward the *Skate*.

As the noise of the grinding, tortured ice grew louder, the ice in the lead started to creep slowly up the sides of the ship. Pieces of it caught on protruding parts of the superstructure, screeching like banshees as they forced their way past the protesting metal.

I could hardly believe what I saw. This was the fifteenth time we had surfaced in the Arctic Ocean and also the first we couldn't submerge easily and quickly.

"Is anyone out on the ice?" I asked.

"I got them down below before I called you," Al answered.

We were all on board and ready to leave this treacherous place—except that we were one hour into a twelve-hour repair job.

"Permission to come up?" It was Bill Layman and Walt Wittmann. I waved them up.

266

James Calvert

"This pressure is making an awful racket inside the ship," said Bill in a worried tone. "I wanted to see what it looked like."

By now the ice had been forced up over the deck far enough to cover most of the hull. With binoculars, Wittmann studied the ice beyond the steep hummocks to port. "That's mean-looking stuff," he commented. "Can you get out of here?"

I shook my head. "Not now, Walt. Do you think it will stop?"

"You just can't tell with this sort of thing," he said cautiously. "I sure don't see any signs of it stopping."

The pressure ridge that formed on our left was now at least 10 yards closer than when we had surfaced. The lead ice screamed as it was crushed between the moving field on one side and the still-unmoved ice on the other. The lead was closing, and when it did the *Skate* would be caught between the two heavy floes that formed its boundaries, like a walnut in a cracker.

The noise was terrifying. The heavy boom of the moving floes mingled with the high-pitched shriek of the ice in the lead to form an overpowering wall of noise. We all had to shout to make ourselves heard.

I asked Bill Layman to go below to get me a report on the pump repair. The ice of the lead was now being forced up over the deck from both sides, forming a tent-shaped canopy along its length.

From behind the ridge to port a huge blue-green slab of ice rose slowly on edge and hovered ominously as though poised to strike. It was not

Most of the sail is now above the surface of the ice.

Protruding portions of the hull begin to break through.

more than 30 yards away. The noises increased in intensity. Some sounded like the scream of a woman in agony, others like the low-pitched whistle of a night train.

Bill Layman came back to the bridge and told me that the men in the engine room were just ready to hoist the big circ pump motor. Everything was disconnected and nothing secured for motion. The time was 11:35.

"The noise is pretty bad inside the ship, Captain," said Layman. "I think you ought to go down and listen to it."

My mouth feeling dry as cotton, I went down

the ladder to the control center. I immediately discovered what Layman had meant. The noise of the ice scraping against the thin metal shell of the ship was immensely amplified, sounding as if we were in a steel barrel being dragged along a rock road. Even more disturbing than the noise was the vibration. The ship fluttered and shook as the ice pressed around her. She seemed to be protesting the agony she felt.

With a convulsive shudder, she suddenly took an alarming list to starboard. There was no more room for delay. We would have to dive. I was deeply worried about whether the ice might be pressed so tightly against the sides of the ship that she could not submerge. I ran to the engine room. With the noise and vibration of the ice pounding about them, men bare to the waist toiled with astounding haste.

I beckoned to Dave Boyd. "I've made up my mind," I told him. "We have to go down. Secure things as quickly as you can and let me know when you're ready."

Dave nodded taciturnly, and turned to his men to order them to undo what they had done. I started back to the bridge, but even as I walked forward into the control center, the noise of the ice against the hull diminished. By the time I mounted the ladder to the bridge it had almost stopped.

"It just stopped," Al Kelln said. "All of a sudden."

The narrow lead in which we lay was now about half its original width, and the ice that filled it was tumbled crazily in every direction; some of it spilled over into the icefield to starboard and much of it rafted like a collapsed house of cards.

"It's going to start again in a moment," Wittmann said, looking out to port with his binoculars. "The ice out there is still moving."

In a few minutes, building up like the climax of music composed in hell, the moaning and screeching reached an even higher level than before. The throbbing vibration could be felt through the deckplates of the bridge. The ice all around the *Skate* was in slow movement, all the more awesome in its deliberate ponderousness. The fragile rudder was buried under a pile of rafted ice and could not be seen.

Everything that I had read and heard about ships trapped in the ice went swiftly through my mind. The *Jeannette*, in these very waters; the *Karluk* of Stefansson, lost in the pressure near Wrangel Island; the *Endurance* of Ernest Shackleton, lost in the Antarctic—all of these had fought the ice and lost. The accounts by their captains of the ice which destroyed them had a striking similarity to what we were now seeing. We would not feel the real crush of the ice until the two heavy floes we rested between were forced together—but I dared not wait for that. The men of the *Jeannette*, *Karluk*, and *Endurance* had waited beside their crafts, stores and sledges and dogs already evacuated to the ice as the ships went through their death agonies. Their crews had, with great hardship in each case, made their way to land. But we could never do that—our safety lay only in the ship.

In a few minutes Dave Boyd stuck his head up through the hatch to report that the engine room was well enough secured to submerge. They had worked even faster than I had expected. We had only half our engineering plant; we would have to accept the risks and complications involved in operating under the ice this way.

Everyone but Al Kelln hurried below. I shouted to him to come down as soon as he had checked everything for diving.

A circle of gray, tense faces greeted me at the bottom of the ladder. I went to the periscope stand to wait for Kelln to shut the hatch and come down. Why was he taking so long?

The scraping and pounding on the sides of the ship had diminished again, but that did not interest me now. Having made the decision to go, I wanted to go.

The rudder punches a separate hole for itself.

"Captain, pick up the phone, please," grated the intercom from the bridge.

I snatched up the phone and said irritably: "What's the delay? Let's go!"

"There's not a sound up here. Not a sign of ice movement. Wish you'd come up and take a look," Al said quickly and a little apologetically.

Nothing is worse on a ship in danger than a captain who vacillates. A bad decision made and stuck to is usually better than indecision. Nevertheless, I put the phone down and went back to the bridge.

The silence was deep and complete. Not a sound could be heard. Was it a temporary respite? I looked at my watch: it was 11:55. It seemed that the pressure had started an eternity ago, but it had been only a little more than half an hour.

I decided to wait, unavoidably keeping one hundred men below in an agony of suspense. Ten minutes went by. I asked Wittmann to come to the bridge. He looked at the ice carefully and said nothing. Anxiously all three of us scanned the ice-fields beyond the pressure ridge for any sign of movement. None.

About 12:20, a sudden crash of noise nearby convinced me it was starting again, but this time it was the easing of pressure. We suddenly recovered from our list and floated naturally. A few inches of water were visible along the bow.

Now what to do? To hold up diving was one thing, but to begin the job in the engine room and have it again interrupted was another. I debated with myself silently for a few minutes, then leaned over and called down the hatch for Dave Boyd to come to the bridge.

When he arrived I told him to start the pump repair again. I frankly expected at least a mild argument in favor of waiting a bit longer. But all Dave said was a quick, "Aye, aye, sir," and he was on his way. This demonstration of trust and confidence bolstered me more than anything that happened during the whole nightmarish episode.

I resolved to stay on the bridge and watch the ice myself. Illogically, I felt that by my very presence I could prevent the ice from moving again. As the hours crept by with no further sign of ice movement, logic gradually got the better of superstition and I began to see the foolishness of what I was doing. It would be important for me to be fresh in the morning when many of my officers would be half-dead of exhaustion.

I went below to my room and, after taking off my heavy clothes, lay down on my bunk to rest. The nervous tension of the past few hours seemed to ebb away. I fell asleep before I could turn my light off.

I was awakened when Dave knocked on my door. It was six-thirty in the morning. Dave looked exhausted, his eyes bloodshot and his face haggard.

"Repair completed. Ready to submerge, sir."

The job had been done in less than seven hours.

The Skate, fully surfaced.

ACKNOWLEDGMENTS

If not otherwise noted, the text selections and illustrations come from sources in the Stillman Memorial Library, Mystic Historical Association, Inc.

Adventure I. *The Acts of the Apostles*, XXVII.
p. 2. Samuel Purchas, comp., *Purchas His Pilgrimes*, London, 1625, New York Public Library.
p. 3. II–III century relief, Ny Carlsberg Glyptotek.
p. 4. II–III century fresco, Vatican Museum, Anderson-Alinari photograph.
p. 5. After relief in Torlonia Collection, c. 193–211 A.D., in Victor Duruy, *A History of Rome and the Roman People*, Boston, 1890, New York Public Library.
pp. 6–7. *Bible Moralized*, first half XIII century, British Museum.
p. 8. Malta Tourist Board.

Adventure II. Jean de Joinville, *Histoire de St. Louis*, in *Memoirs of the Crusades*, translated by Frank Marzials, London: J. M. Dent & Co., and New York: E. P. Dutton & Co.
p. 10. Mamerot Sébastien, *Les Passages Faits Outremer par les Francais contre les Turcs et Autres Sarrasins et Maures Outremarins*, c. 1490, Bibliothèque Nationale.
p. 11. *Vie et Miracles de St. Louis*, XIV century, Bibliothèque Nationale.
p. 13. (above) The Limbourg brothers, *Belles Heures* of Jean, duke of Berry, c. 1410–1413, Metropolitan Museum of Art, Cloisters Collection, 1954. (below) *Statuts de l'Ordre du St. Esprit de Droit Désir*, 1352, Musée des Souverains au Louvre.
p. 14. *Vie de St. Louis*, XV century, Bibliothèque Nationale.
pp. 15, 20. Jean de Joinville, *Histoire de St. Louis*, c. 1320–1330, Bibliothèque Nationale.
p. 16. (left) Ms. Royal E 10 IV from the Priory of St. Bartholomew, c. 1330, British Museum. (right) Vegetius, *De Re Militari*, c. 1270, Fitzwilliam Museum, Cambridge.
p. 17. Relief from portal of Reims Cathedral, Caisse Nationale des Monuments Historiques.
pp. 18–19. Painting on parchment, first half XV century, Metropolitan Museum of Art, Gift of J. Pierpont Morgan, 1917.

Adventure III. Antonio Pigafetta, *Primo Viaggio intorno al Mondo*, c. 1525, in *The First Voyage Round the World, by Magellan*, edited and translated by Lord Stanley of Alderley, London: Hakluyt Society, 1874.
p. 22. Hans Holbein the Younger, *Das Schiff*, c. 1532, Städelsches Kunstinstitut, Frankfort.
p. 24. *Jan Huyghen van Linschoten, His Discours of Voyages*, London: 1598, New York Public Library.
pp. 25, 32. Antonio Pigafetta, *Primo Viaggio intorno al Mondo*, c. 1525, Biblioteca Ambrosiana, Milan.
pp. 26–27. Theodor, Johann Theodor, and Johann Israel de Bry, *Collectiones Peregrinationum in Indiam Orientalem et Occidentalem*, Frankfort, 1590–1634, Elkins Collection, Free Library of Philadelphia.
pp. 28–29. Globe gores, Nuremberg? 153?, New York Public Library.
p. 30. Adriaen Collaert, after Jan van der Straet (Joannes Stradanus), in *Speculum Diversarum Imaginum Speculativarum*, Antwerp, 1638, New York Public Library.
p. 31. Museo Naval, Madrid.

Adventure IV. John Hawkins, *A True Declaration of the Troublesome voyadge of M. John Hawkins to the parties of Guynea and the West Indies, in . . . 1567 and 1568*, London, 1569.
p. 34. The Anthony Roll, Pepys Library, Cambridge, photograph by Edward Leigh.
p. 36. Henry Holland, *Heroologia Anglica*, London 1620, Spencer Collection, New York Public Library.

p. 37. (above) Map tipped into copy of *Bucaniers of America*, London, 1684, New York Public Library. (below) After Pieter Bruegel the Elder, *Three Men of War before a Water Fortress*, Metropolitan Museum of Art, bequest of Alexandrine Sinsheimer, 1959.
p. 38. After Pieter Bruegel the Elder, *Man of War, Sailing to the Right*, Metropolitan Museum of Art, Rogers Fund, 1922.
p. 39. After Pieter Bruegel the Elder, *Man of War, Sailing to the Left*, New York Public Library.
pp. 40–41. Frans Hogenberg, *Events in the History of the Netherlands*, Metropolitan Museum of Art, Whittelsey Fund, 1959.
p. 41. Theodor de Bry, *America*, Frankfort, 1590, New York Public Library.
p. 42. Frans Huys, after Pieter Bruegel the Elder, *Three Vessels in a Tempest*, Metropolitan Museum of Art, Bequest of Alexandrine Sinsheimer, 1959.

Adventure V. Jens Munck, *Navigatio Septentrionalis*, Copenhagen, 1624, in *Danish Arctic Explorations*, edited and translated by C. C. A. Gosch, London: Hakluyt Society, 1897, New York Public Library.
pp. 44, 49. Gillis Joosten Saeghman, comp., *Verscheyde Oost-Indische Voyagien*, Amsterdam, (1663–1670?), New York Public Library.
pp. 46–47. (above) Henry Holland, *Heroologia Anglica*, London, 1620, Spencer Collection, New York Public Library. (below) George Best? *A True Discourse of the Late Voyages of Discoverie for finding of a passage to Cathaya by the North Weast, under the conduct of Martin Frobisher*, London, 1578, New York Public Library.
pp. 48, 57, 59. Jens Munck, *Navigatio Septentrionalis*, Copenhagen, 1624, John Carter Brown Library, Providence, R. I.
p. 52. Joseph Robson, *An Account of Six Years Residence in Hudson's-Bay*, London, 1752, New York Public Library.
p. 61. Thomas James, *The Strange and Dangerous Voyage of Captaine Thomas James . . .*, London, 1633, New York Public Library.

Adventure VI. William Bradford, *Of Plimoth Plantation*, published as *The History of Plymouth Plantation*, Boston: Massachusetts Historical Society, 1912.
p. 64. Standard Oil Company (New Jersey).
p. 66. Hugo Goltzius after Cornelius van Wieringen, *Marine*, Metropolitan Museum of Art, Dick Fund, 1927.
p. 67. Plimoth Plantation photograph.
p. 68. John Smith. Map of New England, first state, 1616, in *A Description of New England*, New York Public Library.
p. 69. Engraving, Bibliothèque Nationale, in *Histoire de France*, edited by Marcel Reinhard, Paris: Larousse, 1954.
p. 70. Thomas Blundeville, *M. Blundevile His Exercises*, London, 1613, New York Public Library.

Adventure VII. William Dick, *A brief account of Captain Sharp, and other his Companions . . .*, by William Dick, in *Bucaniers of America*, written and compiled by Alexandre-Olivier Exquemelin, London, 1684, (second edition), New York Public Library.
p. 72. Matthieu van Plattenberg, *Landscape*, Metropolitan Museum of Art, Dick Fund, 1945.
pp. 74, 77, 78, 79, 82. Alexandre-Olivier Exquemelin, *Bucaniers of America*, London, 1684, New York Public Library.
p. 76. Water color, British Museum.
pp. 80–81. Benjamin Robins, *Anson's Voyage Round the World*, London, 1749.
p. 82 (below). Charles Johnson, *A General History of the Lives and Adventures of the Most Famous Highwaymen . . .*, London, 1736, New York Public Library.
pp. 83, 86. Charles Johnson, *A General History of the Pyrates*, London, 1724, New York Public Library.
pp. 84–85. After W. Pocock, *Specter of the Cape*.

Adventure VIII. Jean Marteilhe, *Memoires d'un Protestant Condamné aux Galères de France pour cause de Religion*, published as *The Galley Slave*, edited by Kenneth Fenwick, London: Folio Society, 1957.
p. 88. J. P. Le Bas after Joseph Vernet, *Vue des Galères de Naples* (detail), 1750, Metropolitan Museum of Art, Dick Fund, 1946.
pp. 90–91, 105. Jean Rigaud, *Marines où sont representez divers suiets des Galères*. Metropolitan Museum of Art, Dick Fund, 1953.
pp. 92–93, 94–95, 96–97. Drawings showing the construction, armament, and sailing of a galley, Service Hydrographique de la Marine Française.
p. 94 (below) Stefano della Bella, *Port of Livorno* (detail), Metropolitan Museum of Art, Whittelsey Fund, 1949.
pp. 98–99. Claude Randon, engravings of galleys, Musée de la Marine.
p. 101. Stefano della Bella, *Divers Embarquements* (plate 69), Metropolitan Museum of Art, Gift of Harry Shaw Newman, 1935.
pp. 102–103. Stefano della Bella, *Scenes of Peace and War*, Metropolitan Museum of Art, Purchase, 1917, Joseph Pulitzer Bequest.
p. 106. Drawing, Musée de la Marine.

Adventure IX. George Robertson, *A Journal of the Second Voyage of H.M.S. Dolphin . . .* , edited by Hugh Carrington, London: Hakluyt Society, 1948.
pp. 108, 122–123, 129. James Cook, *Voyage toward the South Pole and round the World . . .* , London, 1777, New York Public Library.
pp. 110–111, 113, 117, 119, 121, 132, 136, 137, 139. John Hawkesworth, *An Account of the Voyages Undertaken . . . for making discoveries in the Southern Hemisphere . . .* , London, 1773, New York Public Library, The Library Company of Philadelphia.
p. 115. George Pinnock, *A View of Port Royal Bay at George's Island*, British Museum.
p. 125. Paul Gauguin, *Two Tahitian Women*, Metropolitan Museum of Art, Gift of William Church Osborn, 1949.

Adventure X. John R. Jewitt, *A Narrative of the Adventures and Sufferings of John R. Jewitt*, Middletown, Conn., 1815.
p. 142. George Vancouver, *A Voyage of Discovery to the North Pacific Ocean*, London, 1798, New York Public Library.
pp. 144–145. (José Espiñosa y Tello), *Relacion Del Viage Hecho por las Goletas Sutil y Mexicana . . .* , Madrid, 1802, New York Public Library.
p. 146. After Tomás de Suria, Museo Naval, Madrid.
p. 147. *A Narrative of the Adventures and Sufferings of John R. Jewitt*, New York, 1816, New York Public Library.
pp. 150, 151, 155. James Cook, *A Voyage to the Pacific Ocean*, London, 1785, New York Public Library.
p. 153. Tomás de Suria, *Danza Pagana de Mujeres de Nutka*, Museo Naval, Madrid.
pp. 160–161. Richard Alsop, *The Captive of Nootka*, New York, 1835, New York Public Library.
p. 162. Jean François de Galaup La Pérouse, *Voyage . . . autour du Monde*, Paris, 1797.

Adventure XI. William Beatty, *Authentic Narrative of the Death of Lord Nelson*, London, 1807, New York Public Library.
pp. 164–165. John Cousen after Clarkson Stanfield, *The Battle of Trafalgar*, Metropolitan Museum of Art, Dick Fund, 1947.
p. 166. Robert Dodd, *The Victory*, 1807, National Maritime Museum, Greenwich.
p. 167. William Barnard after Lemuel F. Abbott, *Lord Nelson*, 1799, National Maritime Museum, Greenwich.

p. 168. John Godby after William M. Craig, *Lord Nelson . . . explaining the Plan of Attack*, 1806, National Maritime Museum, Greenwich.
p. 169. Thomas Sutherland after Thomas Whitcombe, 1816–1817, *Trafalgar: Beginning of the Battle*, National Maritime Museum, Greenwich.
pp. 170–171. Denis Dighton, *Nelson Falling*, National Maritime Museum, Greenwich.
p. 173. James Walker after John A. Atkinson, *Nelson Is Carried Below*, 1806, National Maritime Museum, Greenwich.
p. 175. Arthur W. Devis, *The Death of Nelson* (detail), National Maritime Museum, Greenwich.
p. 176. Thomas Rowlandson, *Delineations of Nautical Characters*, 1799, Metropolitan Museum of Art, Whittelsey Fund, 1959.
p. 177. William Beatty, *Authentic Narrative of the Death of Lord Nelson*, New York Public Library.

Adventure XII. Nelson Cole Haley, *Whale Hunt*, edited by Carl P. Cutler and Sumner Putnam, New York: copyright 1948 Ives Washburn.
pp. 182–183. Konrad von Gesner, *Historiae Animalium*, Zürich, 1551–1587, New York Public Library.
p. 184. L. Le Breton, *Baleinier Americain*.
pp. 185–191. Drawings by Robert Weir, 1856–1858.
pp. 192–193. Frédéric Martens after Louis Garneray, *Cachalot Fishery, Whale Fishery*, c. 1840–1850. The Old Print Shop.
pp. 194–195. Benjamin Russell, *Sperm Whaling with Its Varieties*, 1870, The Old Print Shop.

Adventure XIII. Elisha Kent Kane, *Arctic Explorations*, Philadelphia, 1856, New York Public Library.
All illustrations come from the book.

Adventure XIV. Joshua Slocum, *Sailing Alone Around the World*, *The Century Illustrated Monthly Magazine*, September 1899 to March 1900.
pp. 218–223, 226–229. Thomas Fogarty and George Varian, in *Sailing Alone Around the World*.
pp. 224–225. James Imray, *Strait of Magalhaens*, London, 1858.
p. 230. Pan American Union.

Adventure XV. William Beebe, *Half Mile Down*, New York: Duell, Sloan & Pearce, copyright 1934, 1951 William Beebe.
pp. 232, 238. New York Zoological Society.
pp. 234, 236, 237, 239, 240. Else Bostelmann, Helen Tee-Van, watercolor drawings, New York Zoological Society.
p. 235. Pseudo-Callisthenes, *Adventures of Alexander*, XIII century, Bibliothèque Royale de Belgique.

Adventure XVI. William H. Venables, *The Torpedoing of the Assyrian*, in *Touching the Adventures . . . of Merchantmen in the Second World War*, edited by J. Lennox Kerr, London: copyright 1953 George G. Harrap & Co. Ltd.
pp. 242, 247, 249, 250. Acme.
p. 244. The New York *Daily News*.

Adventure XVII. Jacques-Yves Cousteau, *The Silent World*, New York: Harper & Brothers, copyright 1950 Time, Inc., copyright 1953 Harper & Brothers.
All photographs from the book.

Adventure XVIII. James Calvert, *Surface at the Pole*, New York: McGraw-Hill Book Co., copyright © 1960 James Calvert.
All photographs by the author.

Composition and Reproduction Proofs by Westcott & Thomson, Philadelphia
Printed by Offset Lithography by Edward Stern & Company, Philadelphia
Bound by The Haddon Bindery, Camden, New Jersey

A NEW MAP of the TE

to the latest Discoveries and most general

NORTHERN unknown CONTINENT.

GROEN LAND

Arctick Circle

NORTHERN OCEAN.

New found land

AMERICA

C.Raze

C.Sable

C.Charles

PARTS as yet UNDISCOVERED.

THE WESTERN or NEW CONTINENT

ATLANTICK

I.California

NORTH

Caribbe I.

PACIFICK OCEAN

Tropick of Cancer

largely taken, which from its situation between the East and West INDIES may also not improperly be stiled the GREAT

C.Corientes

called also

150 160 170 180 170 160 150 140 130 120 110 100 90 80 70 60 50

1 80

Æquinoctial Line

C.S.Maria

Gallapagos I. 90

INDIAN OCEAN.

AMERICA and t

WEST INDIES.

Tropick of Capricorn

first found out by Columbus a Genorese about the Year 1490

I.of Iohn Fernando

SOUTH

Amazo

NEW ZELAND supposed to be part of ye SOUTHERN unknown CONTINENT.

SOUTHERN

Rio de la Plata

Straits of Magellan

Terra del Fuogo

C.Blanco

I.of Sibble de Wards

Maires Straits

C.Horn

OCEAN

Antarctick Circle

PARTS as yet UNDISCOVERED.

90 80 70 60 50

Delin.M.Burghers sculpt.Univ.Oxon.